Finders *and* Keepers

Helping New Teachers Survive and Thrive in Our Schools

JOSSEY-BASS
A Wiley Imprint
www.josseybass.com

Published by Jossey-Bass
A Wiley Imprint
989 Market Street, San Francisco, CA 94103-1741   www.josseybass.com

Jossey-Bass books and products are available through most bookstores. To contact Jossey-Bass directly call our Customer Care Department within the U.S. at 800-956-7739, outside the U.S. at 317-572-3986, or fax 317-572-4002.

Jossey-Bass also publishes its books in a variety of electronic formats. Some content that appears in print may not be available in electronic books.

Library of Congress Cataloging-in-Publication Data

Johnson, Susan Moore.
    Finders *and* keepers : helping new teachers survive and thrive in our schools / Susan Moore Johnson and the Project on the Next Generation of Teachers.— 1st ed.
         p. cm. — (The Jossey-Bass education series)
    Includes bibliographical references and index.
    ISBN-13 978-0-7879-6925-7 (alk. paper)
    ISBN-10 0-7879-6925-7 (alk. paper)
    ISBN-13 978-0-7879-8764-0 (paperback)
    ISBN-10 0-7879-8764-6 (paperback)
    1. Project on the Next Generation of Teachers.   2. First year teachers—Massachusetts—Longitudinal studies.   3. Teachers—In-service training—Massachusetts—Longitudinal studies.   4. Teaching—Vocational guidance—Massachusetts—Longitudinal studies.   I. Project on the Next Generation of Teachers.   II. Title.   III. Series.
    LB2844.1.N4J65 2004
    371.1'009744—dc22   2004000148

Printed in the United States of America
FIRST EDITION
HB Printing   10 9 8 7 6 5 4 3
PB Printing   10 9 8 7 6 5 4 3 2 1

Susan Moore Johnson
and
The Project on the Next Generation
of Teachers
Sarah E. Birkeland
Morgaen L. Donaldson
Susan M. Kardos
David Kauffman
Edward Liu
Heather G. Peske

The Jossey-Bass Education Series

This book honors some of the teachers who have inspired us:

Mr. William Dykins, twelfth grade English teacher and speech coach,
Boardman, Ohio
Ms. Ilona Mellor, eleventh grade English teacher,
Fair Lawn, New Jersey
Ms. Carol Bierbaum, eleventh grade English teacher,
Gillette, Wyoming
Mr. Howell Kiser, tenth grade literature teacher and tennis coach,
Atlanta, Georgia
Mr. Robert Roddy, eleventh grade English teacher,
Erie, Pennsylvania
Ms. Marie Stanislaw, seventh grade social studies teacher,
Seattle, Washington
Ms. Joyce Whitmore, tenth, eleventh, and twelfth grade
social studies teacher, Ellsworth, Maine

Contents

Tables, Figures, and Exhibits

Preface

When we began this study in 1998, the issue of teacher quality had not yet made headlines. Education reformers across the United States were feverishly pitching policies to improve schools, but they paid scant attention to the teachers needed to implement their ideas. They seemed to assume a steady supply of skilled and committed individuals standing ready to staff the nation's classrooms and take on the difficult challenge of improving them. At the time, we thought that this assumption was unfounded, as half the teaching force was projected to retire between 2000 and 2010, and there was evidence that these veteran teachers would not easily be replaced. They had been hired several decades earlier, when most other professions were off-limits to women and to men of color. Many had become teachers by default.

In today's labor market, however, all fields are open to prospective teachers. Often recruiters from such careers as finance, law, or engineering actively pursue the very types of individuals who were once excluded. Many fields other than teaching provide far better pay, working conditions, and opportunities for advancement. For the first time in history, public schools must compete for new talent and work hard to retain the teachers they hire.

We started our research with questions about who was entering teaching, what these novices expected, what they found, and how long they planned to stay. We discovered that the fifty teachers we studied were very different as a group from the veterans they were replacing. Few expected to have a lifelong career in the classroom. Many—especially those entering teaching at midcareer from other fields—were stunned by the shortcomings of their schools. They experienced haphazard hiring, lacked sufficient curriculum and supplies, and encountered distant, if polite, colleagues. Most knew that if teaching failed to satisfy them, they could move to a different career. After four years, one-third of the teachers we studied had left public school teaching, a rate consistent with findings in recent national research.

But attrition is only part of this worrisome story, for another one-third of the teachers we studied changed schools or districts by their fourth year. At first this might not seem problematic, as these individuals remained in teaching. However, from the perspective of a school, when a teacher leaves it matters little if she moves to another school across town or returns to a career in software development. Her skills and accumulated knowledge are lost, and the school must invest scarce resources to hire and initiate a replacement. Losing two-thirds of new teachers to other careers, other schools, or other school districts carries steep financial costs. A district not only forfeits its initial investment in hiring, induction, and professional development but also must then pay those costs for each replacement. And those figures do not include the organizational losses that accompany turnover.

Reformers who overlooked the importance of teachers in 1998 today voice urgent concern about the quality of teachers' training and performance. Researchers not only have concluded convincingly that teachers are the most important school-level factor in students' learning but also have demonstrated that differences in the quality of teachers' work have far-reaching consequences for their students. An effective teacher can ensure a student's ongoing development, whereas a series of ineffective teachers can severely compromise that student's chance of success. If public schools are truly to ensure that all students are well educated, there must be an effective teacher in every classroom.

This recent and growing concern about teacher quality is apparent in the No Child Left Behind Act of 2001, which required that all public school teachers be "highly qualified" by June 2006, a deadline that no states met, despite a relatively low standard. However, the problem is not only the overall lack of qualified teachers in each subject but also the uneven distribution of teachers who are employed. Schools and districts serving low-income communities (with many students of color and English language learners) are far more likely to be staffed with teachers who are less prepared and less experienced than those in middle-income or high-income communities (where most students are white and English speaking). This unfair distribution of teachers occurs not only because some districts and schools fail to attract qualified and experienced teachers but also because they fail to retain them.

Research shows that teachers leave low-income schools at higher rates than other schools. Some abandon teaching entirely; others take jobs in different districts or transfer to higher-income schools within the same district. As a result, low-income schools often have many new and enthusiastic teachers, but few effective senior teachers to establish a positive school culture, set high standards for instruction, and provide support for less experienced colleagues. When these new recruits are left to cope on their own, they often find the demands of their work overwhelming. Experiencing little success, they leave the school or the profession after a short time.

Most policymakers and analysts who address the problem of hard-to-staff schools focus on the teachers themselves—their preparation, teaching experience, and school assignment—rather than the context in which those teachers work. Some reformers propose to right inequities by ensuring that administrators have the authority to assign teachers to the schools that most need them, thus prohibiting their transfer from low-income to higher-income schools. Others recommend strategies for redistributing talent that are less regulatory, such as offering financial incentives to experienced teachers for working in hard-to-staff schools and districts. Although both approaches have some merit, neither will succeed unless the schools become settings that support teaching and learning. For, ultimately, any teacher can choose to leave the profession or move to another district. Our research shows that when schools fail to support new teachers today, they are inclined to exit quickly, without looking back.

Those seeking to ensure a fair distribution of teachers often assume that teachers prefer not to work with poor and minority students, that when they transfer to higher-income schools and districts, they do so in search of whiter, wealthier students. Our research shows something different. Often schools that enroll low-income and minority students have decrepit facilities, inadequate resources, unfriendly school cultures, and ineffective principals. When teachers leave such schools, it is the environments, not the students, they abandon. We found that schools serving low-income students were far less likely to hire teachers carefully, to offer them opportunities for sustained work with experienced colleagues, to provide the curriculum and resources needed to teach well, or to ensure an orderly environment for teaching and learning. Notably, however, some new teachers we studied taught in low-income schools that did provide what they needed, and those schools were not hard to staff. In fact, they readily attracted and retained teachers to work with their students. Reformers who understand the importance of teacher quality and seek to ensure that each child has an effective teacher will thus find in this book crucial lessons and strategies for achieving that goal.

For the long term, however, it is not enough to make all schools places for good teaching and learning, for the career of teaching must be redesigned as well. Increasingly, we hear of successful teachers leaving the classroom after three to five years. Although they have developed competence and confidence, have achieved tenure, and have been told that they are valued, they see little future in teaching. They are discouraged by the static and uniform role of the classroom teacher, which requires them to do the same thing year after year as workers on an educational assembly line. We found that today's early-career teachers, unlike their predecessors, expect to have varied responsibilities and expanded influence over time. Pay, which they once thought was adequate, no longer is, and there is no way to be rewarded for better skills or performance. Those outside education look down on them, often praising their dedication and sacrifice, but seldom granting them the status they deserve.

Changes in the career are needed not only to retain the most promising teachers but also to increase the instructional capacity of schools. Accomplished teachers are needed to support new entrants as they learn to teach, ensuring that even those planning to stay only a few years will do their best work. Skilled teachers can exercise much-needed leadership in schools as curriculum specialists, induction coordinators, peer reviewers, instructional coaches, data analysts, and team leaders or department heads. Such roles serve as career goals for new teachers and afford expert teachers wider influence, while at the same time earning them higher pay and recognition. Unless teaching adopts a new, differentiated career structure, schools will be staffed like summer camps, annually hiring and then exhausting a new supply of recruits. Covering classes will be the goal. Expertise will be discounted. And teaching will become temporary work, marked by early exit and rapid turnover. Surely our students and our society deserve better.

September 3, 2006

Susan Moore Johnson
Newton Highlands, Massachusetts

Acknowledgments

In 1999, I was stepping down from six years as academic dean and planning my return to the faculty. I wanted to create a new venture that would integrate my efforts as a researcher, advisor, and teacher. Susan Kardos, David Kauffman, Ed Liu, and Heather Peske—all former teachers and current doctoral students studying administration and policy—expressed an interest in working together on a project about teachers. We had no idea what our joint venture—eventually called the Project on the Next Generation of Teachers—would become, but we certainly had great hopes. Sarah Birkeland and Morgaen Donaldson, both former teachers and current doctoral students, joined the project in 2001 and 2002, respectively. It is a true privilege to work with this extraordinary group of individuals. They hold high standards, work hard, and take good care of each other. They are talented, inquisitive, skilled, imaginative, generous, and witty. Together, we have collaboratively designed studies, collected and analyzed data, prepared and presented conference papers, published journal articles, issued press releases, and now, written a book. I can always count on each of them to deliver on commitments, to see what else should be done, and then to do it. In times of personal loss, they have supported me with a magical web of sympathy, caring, and practical help. Like other mentors who are blessed with promising and appreciative apprentices, I have learned as much as I have taught, received far more than I have given. My greatest acknowledgment of thanks, then, goes to these project researchers, my coauthors on this book.

We are deeply indebted to the fifty teachers who allowed us to interview them in 1999. At the time, we did not anticipate that we would eventually ask to follow their careers for four years. They have been generous in responding to our requests for subsequent interviews and periodic updates. As new teachers, they agreed to talk, despite being frantically busy and, sometimes, very discouraged. Although this book features only ten of our respondents, we are deeply grateful to all fifty, whose rich and candid stories are at the heart of this book. We wish that we could offer all of them the public recognition they deserve for their contribution to this study, but we must keep their names confidential.

We also were fortunate to visit and document three exemplary school-based induction programs and are indebted to the sponsors and coordinators of these programs: Gayle Davis and Margaret Metzger at Brookline High School, Laura Cooper at Evanston Township High School, and Mary Russo at Murphy Elementary School in Boston. These enterprising and expert educators recognized early on the new teacher's need for school-based induction, and they have developed and refined programs that now serve as models for others. We are grateful for their welcome and help as we explored their programs, and we appreciate the many teachers and administrators at their schools who also took time to talk with us.

This research has been supported by grants from the Spencer Foundation and the Russell Sage Foundation. A grant from Russell Sage supported our research on hiring. An early Spencer Mentor Grant supported the doctoral students as we got the project under way. Subsequent funding from Spencer has carried us through. Each of the team members has also received individual support from Spencer, through a Research Training Grant to Harvard or a Dissertation Grant. I am especially indebted to Patricia Albjerg Graham, who, as president of the Spencer Foundation in 1998, encouraged me to pursue this work. I also appreciate the ongoing support of others at Spencer including President Ellen Condliffe Lagemann (now my dean), and Program Officers John Rury, Mark Rigdon, Jay Braatz, Lauren Young, and Catherine Lacey. Each has helped us along the way. Although these foundations' investment in our project has been substantial, they bear no responsibility for the findings of this research.

We have benefited greatly from the backing of various administrators and staff at the Harvard Graduate School of Education. Former Dean Jerry Murphy and current Dean Ellen Condliffe Lagemann have lent their support to our endeavor. We are indebted to Robert Peterkin, Norma Diala, Carol Kentner, and Wendy Angus, who have generously provided space, assistance, and good will. We are especially grateful to Dottie Engler, Christine Sanni, and Margaret Haas from the School's Department of External Relations for their enthusiastic endorsement and hard work on our behalf.

Various people have generously contributed to our research along the way. Jill Harrison Berg and Will Marinell, participants in the Project's Doctoral Research Practicum, conducted interviews with us at Brookline High School and Murphy Elementary School and assisted us in analyzing data. Will Marinell was enormously helpful during the final weeks by reading and responding to our manuscript. Cheryl Kirkpatrick also generously found time on short notice to provide thoughtful feedback on the draft. Betsy Baglio, Megin Charner-Laird, and Lilly Siu provided helpful advice as participants in the Project's Doctoral Research Practicum. Laurie Kardos and Abby Reisman kindly participated in pilot interviews. Dan Green generously volunteered for several months analyzing hiring data. Tate Gould taught us about the South, helped us in countless ways, and always kept us entertained.

We are indebted to our many student and faculty colleagues at the Harvard Graduate School of Education. They have encouraged us, listened to us, advised us, assisted us, and baked us cookies. We are indeed fortunate to work among so many good, dedicated, and interesting people. Although we could never list all of them or the many contributions that they have made to our work, we want to offer special thanks to John Willett, who has provided generous advice on the quantitative parts of our research.

My daughter, Erika Johnson, deserves special thanks for her part in this research. For me, she has been my muse. Her decision to join Teach For America first focused my attention on the theme of generational differences that runs throughout this work. Early on, as we tried to understand what was worth studying, she became our Favorite Data Point (FDP) with first-person accounts of a new teacher's day-to-day life in the classroom.

Our families and friends have encouraged and supported us, patiently enduring our absence during intense periods of work, which claimed precious time. We are especially grateful to Daniel, Natalia, and Sylvia Hernández Kauffman, who have become honorary members of the team. My son, Krister Johnson, who is intently pursuing a career outside the family business, has entertained me and reminded me about the important things in life, such as the fate of the Boston Red Sox.

Finally, I am grateful to Glenn, my companion in life, for supporting me in the many ways that he always does. I count on his love, insight, advice, knowledge of word derivations, can-do spirit, and sense of excitement about new endeavors. I am grateful that he, too, has genuinely welcomed and enjoyed knowing members of the project team.

S.M.J.

The Authors

Susan Moore Johnson is the Carl H. Pforzheimer, Jr. Professor of Teaching and Learning at the Harvard Graduate School of Education, where she served as the academic dean from 1993 to 1999. She received her A.B. degree (1967) in English literature from Mount Holyoke College and her M.A.T. degree (1969) in English and her Ed.D. degree (1982) in Administration, Planning, and Social Policy from the Harvard Graduate School of Education. A former high school teacher and administrator, Johnson studies and teaches about teacher policy, school organization, educational leadership, and school improvement in schools and school systems. Johnson is a member of the board of directors of the National Academy of Education and recipient of a Senior Scholar Grant from the Spencer Foundation. She is the author of *Teacher Unions in Schools* (1983), *Teachers at Work* (1990), *Leading to Change: The Challenge of the New Superintendency* (1996), and many published articles. Johnson is the director of the Project on the Next Generation of Teachers.

Sarah E. Birkeland is an advanced doctoral student in Administration, Planning, and Social Policy at the Harvard Graduate School of Education. She holds a B.A. (1994) in English from Stanford University and an M.A. (1999) in education psychology from the University of Colorado at Denver. She taught high school English in Jakarta, Indonesia, and elementary and middle school in Denver, Colorado. Birkeland coauthored "Pursuing a Sense of Success: New Teachers Explain Their Career Decisions" in the *American Education Research Journal* (2004), and has coauthored several articles about new teachers' experiences in schools at the Project on the Next Generation of Teachers. She is a recipient of the Spencer Research Training Grant.

Morgaen L. Donaldson taught in a Thai university and in American urban and suburban high schools and is a founding teacher of the Boston Arts Academy, Boston's public high school for the arts. As a researcher, she studies collegial exchange within diverse K-12 faculties, new teachers' experiences, and current changes in rural schools. She is a proud Mainer and a product of Downeast Maine's public schools, Princeton University (A.B., 1994), and the Harvard Graduate School of Education (Ed.M., 1997), where she is currently an advanced doctoral student. Donaldson co-edited and contributed to *Reflections of First-Year Teachers on School Culture: Questions, Hopes, and Challenges* (Jossey-Bass, 1999). She is a recipient of the Spencer Research Training Grant.

Susan M. Kardos taught middle school in New York and New Jersey before moving to Massachusetts. She received her A.B. from Brown University (1989), her Ed.M. from Harvard University (1992), and expects her doctorate in Administration, Planning, and Social Policy from Harvard University in 2004. She has worked in teacher education, consulted to Boston schools, taught in Ghana, and directed a service learning project for teenagers on the Blackfeet Indian Reservation in Montana. Her primary research interests include education policy, professional culture, new teacher induction, school leadership, and teacher unions. In addition to coauthoring several articles on new teachers, Kardos is first author of "Counting on Colleagues: New Teachers Encounter the Professional Cultures of Their Schools," published in *Educational Administration Quarterly*. Kardos is also author of "Clandestine Schooling and Resistance in the Warsaw Ghetto During the Holocaust," published in the *Harvard Educational Review*. She is a recipient of a Research Training Grant and a Dissertation Fellowship from the Spencer Foundation.

David Kauffman received an A.B. (1991) in International Relations from Stanford University and an Ed.M. (1998) from the Harvard University Graduate School of Education, from which he expects an Ed.D. in Administration, Planning, and Social Policy in

2004. Kauffman taught sixth grade in Houston, Texas, for six years and has worked with several Boston public schools. His primary research interests are curriculum materials, teachers' professional development, and school leadership. He is first author of "'Lost at Sea': New Teachers' Experiences with Curriculum and Assessment," published in *Teachers College Record*. Kauffman is a two-time recipient of a Research Apprenticeship Grant from the Spencer Foundation.

Edward Liu received his B.A. (1992) in history from Yale University, his M.B.A. (1997) from the Stanford Graduate School of Business, and his A.M. (1997) from the Stanford University School of Education. He expects to earn his doctorate in Administration, Planning, and Social Policy from Harvard University in 2004. A former high school history teacher and a founding co-director of the nonprofit Summerbridge Portland Program, Liu studies teacher hiring, school reform, educational policy, and the nonprofit sector. He is also a former co-chair of the *Harvard Educational Review* Editorial Board. Liu is a native of Seattle, Washington, and has lived in Oregon, California, Connecticut, and Massachusetts. He is a recipient of the Spencer Research Training Grant.

Heather G. Peske taught elementary school in East Baton Rouge Parish, Louisiana, and worked as a summer school director for Teach For America. She is currently an advanced doctoral student in Administration, Planning, and Social Policy at the Harvard Graduate School of Education, and expects to earn her Ed.D. in 2004. She received her B.A. (1992) in religion from Kenyon College and her Ed.M. degree (1998) from the Harvard Graduate School of Education. Peske is the lead author of "The Next Generation of Teachers: Changing Conceptions of a Career in Teaching," published in *Phi Delta Kappan*. She is a former editorial board member of the *Harvard Educational Review*, for which she served as solicitations editor. Peske studies alternative certification programs for teachers, educational policy, teacher leadership, and teacher recruitment and retention.

For more information about the Project on the Next Generation of Teachers, visit the Web site [www.gse.harvard.edu/~ngt].

Chapter One

Greater Expectations, Higher Demands

Coauthor: Morgaen L. Donaldson

Esther Crane spent nine years as an engineer designing flight sim-ulators for Navy pilots before she considered teaching.[1] She loved her job for its intellectual challenge, the collegial nature of her workplace, and the variety of tasks and responsibilities it offered. But she resigned when her first child was born because she did not think the demands of the job were compatible with raising a fam-ily. Her substantial salary had allowed Esther and her husband to build savings that would support them for several years on a single wage. However, after six years, their savings were low, prompting Esther to decide to work part-time as a substitute teacher in her children's school where she already served as a volunteer.

Gradually, Esther began to think about becoming a teacher. People had always said that she was good at explaining things, and she had enjoyed her work as a substitute. Also, teaching would make it possible for her to be home with her children after school and during vacations. But the decision was not easy. Teach-ing was at least one step down in status from engineering. Her father, a mechanic, was proud that Esther was an engineer and, at first, felt disappointed that she might give it up to become a teacher. He believed, she said, "Those that can, do. Those that can't, teach." Moreover, a beginning teacher's salary would be at least $30,000 less than she could earn if she returned to work as an engineer.

Nonetheless, Esther began to investigate education programs that would lead to a teaching license. Then, in spring 1999, the

Massachusetts Department of Education announced the Massachusetts Signing Bonus Program (MSBP), which offered outstanding candidates $20,000 to participate in an intensive summer training institute and then teach in the state's public schools for at least four years. Not only did the state anticipate a substantial teacher shortage, but there was also convincing evidence that teaching was not attracting strong candidates. One indication was that 59 percent of prospective teachers in Massachusetts had failed the state's new teacher test (Zernike, 1998). Massachusetts legislators intended the program to recruit talented individuals who traditionally would not have considered teaching, particularly in high-need subject areas, such as math, science, or special education, and in schools serving low-income populations (Fowler, 2001, 2003).

Esther found the bonus and its selectivity appealing, but she was most attracted by the fast-track alternative preparation program that state officials created to move bonus recipients quickly into the classroom. A seven-week institute, which included student teaching in a summer school, would enable Esther to have her own classroom of students by September. Given the length and expense of traditional teacher education programs, she found this very attractive and applied. She recalled, "It got me in at least a full year, if not more, earlier than I would have [entered]."

Soon after Esther learned that she had received the bonus, she was encouraged to apply for a job working on the space shuttle, a job she would have pursued if a suitable job had been available for her husband nearby. But this did not work out, so Esther completed the summer institute for Signing Bonus Program teachers, and accepted a position teaching ninth grade math in an urban, vocational high school. Given the shortage of mathematics and science teachers, particularly in urban areas, Esther was just the sort of skilled, unconventional candidate Massachusetts reformers had hoped to recruit. With idealism and enthusiasm, she hoped to draw on her experience as an engineer to help her students enjoy learning math.

The Demand for Teachers Grows

Esther is one of fifty new teachers we interviewed in 1999 and again in 2000 in an effort to understand the perspectives and experiences of new teachers today. As Esther and her counterparts began teaching in 1999, public educators and policymakers across the country were preparing in earnest for a predicted teacher shortage. At the start of the new century, more than 30 percent—approximately one million—of the nation's nearly three million public school teachers were over fifty years old (Young, 2003). This cohort of retiring teachers had entered the profession in the late 1960s and early 1970s, the last period of wholesale hiring by U.S. public schools. Their impending retirement meant that nearly one-half of the current teaching force would leave the classroom by 2010 (Kantrowitz & Wingert, 2000).

At the same time, increasing birth and immigration rates were rapidly expanding student enrollments, particularly in the southwestern United States. During the 1990s, Nevada's student population grew by 69 percent and Arizona's enrollments increased 37 percent (Young, 2003). In response to burgeoning student numbers, districts hastily built new schools and filled parking lots with "temporary" classroom trailers. Each time a new classroom opened to educate this growing student population, a new teacher had to be found to teach there.

In some states, class-size reductions further expanded the need for new teachers. In 1996, California passed legislation providing funds to reduce the size of primary classes (kindergarten through third grade) to twenty students or fewer. Since many primary classes across the state had forty pupils, this policy created an immediate demand for new teachers. According to state-appointed evaluators of this policy, the total number of teachers employed in California surged 38 percent within just two years (Stecher, Bohrnstedt, Kirst, McRobbie, & Williams, 2001).

Experts projected that with these demographic and policy changes an unprecedented need for new teachers would arise nationwide. The country's public schools would have to hire 2.2 million teachers during the first decade of the new century (Hussar, 1999). The magnitude of the demand quickly became the subject of public concern. On its cover, *Newsweek* confronted readers with the provocative challenge: "Who will teach our kids?" (Kantrowitz & Wingert, 2000). There had long been shortages of qualified teachers in particular fields (math, science, and special education) and certain types of settings (the inner-city and remote, rural areas). The shortage of special education teachers, particularly in urban and rural districts, had become especially severe. In 2000, for instance, 97.5 percent of districts in the council of the Great City Schools reported an "immediate need" for special education teachers (Fideler, Foster, & Schwartz, 2000). The projected size of the new demand would mean that even wealthier districts, which usually had their pick of candidates from an abundance of applicants, would be searching for teachers in all subjects and grades.

As news spread about the growing shortage of skilled teachers, states offered a range of inducements to lure new teachers to their schools. Maryland offered new recruits mortgage subsidies and Mississippi promised to forgive student loans. Texas education officials aggressively poached Oklahoma's teachers with offers of higher salaries and better working conditions, while simultaneously recruiting teachers in Mexico (Blair, 2000; Bradley, 2000; Kantrowitz & Wingert, 2000; Stutz, 2001). Despite this flurry of activity, schools in most parts of the country were unprepared to meet the challenge presented by the shortage. A large proportion of the retiring cohort had made teaching a lifelong career for the first time in United States history (Grant & Murray, 1999; Rury, 1989; Spencer, 2001) and, thus, decades had passed since most schools had mounted an intensive campaign to recruit and hire teachers.

The Changing Profile of the Teaching Force

The career longevity of the cohort of teachers hired in the late 1960s and early 1970s, along with reduced demand for teachers in the 1980s due to declining student enrollments, has had a significant effect on the distribution of teachers. As a group, the retiring cohort has moved like a bubble through the teacher workforce. From 1971 to 1983, the largest proportion of the teaching force was under the age of thirty-five. This same cohort of teachers still constituted the largest group, at ages thirty-five to forty-four, between 1983 and 1991, and again, at age forty-five and older, after 1991 (Wirt, 2000). This fact, coupled with the recent increase in new hires, causes the profile of the national teaching force today to be increasingly U-shaped, as shown in Figure 1.1, with one peak of educators about to retire, another peak beginning to teach, and a valley in between. Today's U-shaped distribution stands in direct contrast to the distribution of the teaching force in 1986 (see Figure 1.2) and in 1971 (see Figure 1.3).

In practical terms, the valley between the two peaks in this U-shaped distribution has come to be a generation gap. For many years, the teachers who now approach retirement have had no formal responsibility for the induction of new colleagues, because so few entered and those who did usually received little attention. As a group, therefore, these veteran teachers have become accustomed to working alone and have tacitly endorsed the isolation and prized the autonomy that have typified classroom teaching for at least

Figure 1.1. Distribution of Teachers by Years of Experience, 2001

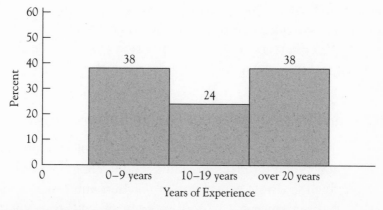

Source: National Education Association, *Status of the American Public School Teacher, 2000–2001*, Table 6, "Years of Full-time Teaching Experience, 1961–2001."

Figure 1.2. Distribution of Teachers by Years of Experience, 1986

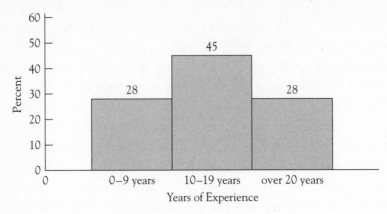

Source: National Education Association, *Status of the American Public School Teacher*, *2000–2001*, Table 6, "Years of Full-time Teaching Experience, 1961–2001."

twenty-five years (Johnson, 1990; Lortie, 1975). They have com-mitted their adult working life to helping students succeed in school and to preparing them for a prosperous future. Overall, they have proved to be a conservative group on the job, focusing within their classroom on their teaching and their students, and quietly but intently resisting reforms that were intended to engage them in joint work (Evans, 1996; Little, 1990b). In the name of equity, they generally have withstood the efforts of administrators or policy-makers to make distinctions among them, such as recognizing and rewarding individuals' special skills, strengths, or contributions. As new teachers enter schools today on the other side of the genera-tion gap, they often encounter the opposition of veteran teachers who resist reforms that would change the way veterans work.

Finders and Keepers: New Teachers and Their Schools

This inevitable, steady shift in the proportions of veteran and novice teachers and its effect on public schools creates a need for research about the next generation of teachers entering schools today. Who are they and how do they compare with the experi-

Figure 1.3 Distribution of Teachers by Years of Experience, 1971

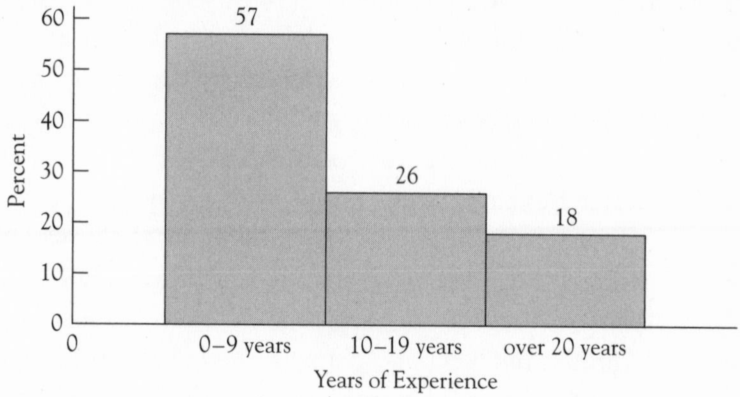

Source: National Education Association, *Status of the American Public School Teacher,* 2000–2001, Table 6, "Years of Full-time Teaching Experience, 1961–2001."

enced teachers they are replacing? What do they seek in teaching? How have they prepared to teach? What do they expect from their schools, and what do they find when they enter the classroom? Most important, what will it take to support and sustain them so that they and their students can succeed?

As we discuss in this book, although the next generation of teachers is more homogeneous in race and gender than the retiring generation, it is more diverse in terms of age, prior experience, preparation, expectations regarding the workplace, and conceptions of career. These new teachers are entering teaching in a context very different from the previous generation's. Individuals who consider teaching today have many more career options than members of the retiring generation. In addition, today's new teachers are encountering unprecedented demands on schools and teachers. The public now expects schools to teach all students so that they achieve high standards—rich and poor, immigrant and native-born, white and minority, special needs and mainstream—and to take on new functions beyond the traditional scope of schools' responsibility. Teachers bear the burden of society's newer, higher expectations for schools (Hargreaves, 2003).

As Esther Crane and her counterparts in the new generation of teachers enter the profession, they find most schools, as they are currently organized, ill-prepared to help them succeed in their work. School structures and practices forged in a bygone era are no longer adequate to support either teachers' development or students' learning. They perpetuate private practice, fail to acknowledge the unique developmental needs of new teachers, and, in many cases, leave new teachers to sink or swim on their own. Yet some new teachers have the good fortune to work at schools that deliberately and thoughtfully attract and retain them. These schools are "finders *and* keepers." They provide appropriate supports for novice teachers and promise varied growth opportunities in the future as these novices gain expertise. Unfortunately, such schools are all too rare. In order to attract and retain the next generation of teachers, school leaders must first understand who the next generation of teachers are. With better insight into their early experiences and subsequent career decisions, public policymakers, education officials, and school leaders can act to support them so that they not only survive but also thrive in their schools.

Is Teaching a Less Attractive Career?

First, however, schools must convince promising candidates to enter the classroom. Indeed, as schools gear up to recruit, hire, and induct a vast cohort of novices to replace many retiring—often expert—teachers, researchers report that the quality and diversity of new teachers has declined over time. Assuming that teaching quality depends on intelligence, researchers have demonstrated that the IQ scores of teachers have fallen since the early 1970s, and teaching candidates have lower SAT scores than their counterparts preparing for other professions (Henke, Choy, Geis, & Broughman, 1996; Murnane, Singer, Willett, Kemple, & Olsen, 1991). If these trends continue and if test scores are appropriate measures of intelligence, any success achieved in recruiting a new teaching force through traditional routes will be tempered by the fact that these entrants, as a group, may be less capable than the veterans they replace. Although there is considerable debate over the use of SAT and IQ scores as measures of teacher quality and competence (Goldhaber, 2002), these findings arouse alarm. Why does teaching as a career today fail to attract large numbers of candidates whose caliber is beyond dispute?

School leaders are also troubled by the shortage of teachers of color. In 2003, nearly 40 percent of United States public school children were members of minority groups, compared to less than 10 percent of teachers (Snyder & Hoffman, 2003). This problem has intensified over the last decade, as the proportion of teachers of color has declined in relation to the total number of teachers. While the nation's student population becomes more and more racially diverse, the teaching force is moving in the opposite direction, becoming more racially homogeneous (Henke, Chen, & Geis, 2000; Snyder & Hoffman, 2003).

Addressing the Shortage

It is important to understand that states and districts face a far greater challenge in staffing their schools than simply addressing a shortfall of newly prepared teachers. If the teacher shortage were simply a straightforward problem of recruitment, states could expand, subsidize, and promote their teacher education programs for a few years until there were enough strong recruits to cover all classrooms. Or, like Massachusetts, they could relax entry requirements and quickly license able candidates through alternative routes. However, the problem with today's teacher supply runs much deeper than that. For although teaching is worthwhile and compelling work, potential recruits today find it far less attractive than their counterparts did thirty years ago. They are put off by teaching's low pay and low status, the relentless demands of the job, and the conditions of the school as a workplace. Many people who might become fine teachers never seriously consider the profession; others who earn a license never enter the classroom; and increasing numbers who begin to teach leave after only a few years. In fact, if all of those who have prepared to teach did so, the projected shortage would never materialize.

Until the mid-1960s, teaching was the primary career option for large numbers of well-educated women and people of color, for whom other professions were formally or informally off limits. That is no longer true. Comparable candidates today also are actively recruited for other careers, many of them more attractive than teaching. The earnings gap between teachers and others who hold a bachelor's degree is even larger than many people realize and it widened in the late 1990s (Nelson & Drown, 2003). In 1998, teachers between the ages of twenty-two and twenty-eight earned $7,894 less than similarly aged graduates with bachelor's degrees; this gap was three times larger for teachers aged forty-four to fifty (Wilson, 2000). Moreover, low pay in this country is linked to low status. Although individual teachers may be revered and remembered fondly by their students, the U.S. public continues to have little respect for teaching as a profession.

Working conditions further detract from the appeal of teaching (Johnson, 1990). Critics often belittle teachers for their secure salaries, short workdays, and long summer vacations, but anyone familiar with schools knows that stories about the easy job of teaching are sheer fiction. Good teaching is demanding and exhausting work, even in the best of workplaces. A teacher is virtually always "on," hour after hour, day after day, week after week. A typical school day reliably brings constant, though often unpredictable, demands from students, administrators, and parents. Even the most experienced teacher simply cannot rely on acquired expertise or dare to teach on automatic pilot, because each group of students presents unique instructional dilemmas and opportunities. The best lesson plan still requires continuous adjustment and improvisation. The school day rarely ends at 3:00 for a teacher, who must grade papers, plan the next day's classes, and gather resources to ensure that lessons go smoothly. And that is under the best of conditions.

In the worst of conditions, school facilities are dilapidated and outmoded, with leaky roofs, broken blackboards, and substandard wiring. Teachers often lack the basic equipment needed to teach their subjects well. Science teachers have no Bunsen burners or microscopes. History teachers struggle with decades-old textbooks and lack current maps. Elementary school teachers have but one computer for over thirty students. With budget cuts, there are recurrent shortages of basic supplies—paper, crayons, pencils, paper clips, and rulers—which teachers discover they must purchase with their own money if they want their teaching to go well. On average, a first-year elementary school teacher spends $701 of her own money on classroom materials (Quality Education Data, 2002). The school's photocopy machine is routinely broken. Few classrooms have working phones, and clocks throughout the building, if they run at all, seldom show the same time. With these conditions and the media's repeated stories about unmotivated and rude students, dangerous corridors, and unreasonable administrators, it is no wonder that a career in teaching seems unattractive, particularly to candidates who could as easily choose another line of work.

Teacher Attrition: The Undertow

Recently, it has become clear that the attrition of teachers in the early years of their career severely exacerbates the challenge of staffing schools today. Anticipating the demand for new teachers, states and districts initially focused their money and efforts on recruitment, operating on the assumption that once hired, teachers would stay for a lifetime. Given the retention rates of teachers hired in the 1960s and 1970s, this was a reasonable assumption (Huberman, 1993). However, as John Merrow pointed out in 1999, such expectations were unfounded: "The teaching pool keeps losing water because no one is paying attention to the leak. That is, we're misdiagnosing the problem as 'recruitment' when it's really retention" (1999, p. 64).

The increasing rate of attrition among novice teachers today constitutes a steady undertow in any progress that states, districts, and schools make in dealing with their staffing demands. With every new report, the statistics on teacher attrition are more alarming.

Nationally, approximately 30 percent of new teachers leave teaching within three years, and 40 to 50 percent leave within five years (Ingersoll, 2002; Ingersoll & Smith, 2003).

However, it is not enough to monitor the numbers of teachers who leave the profession. For as educational researcher Richard Ingersoll has documented, there are also large numbers of teachers each year who are dissatisfied with their school and transfer to another. Ingersoll and fellow researcher Thomas Smith report that nationally 15 percent of new teachers leave the field within the first year while another 15 percent change schools. A typical school annually would lose 30 percent of its newly hired staff, thus creating continuous disruption and discontinuity (Smith & Ingersoll, 2003). From the perspective of the individual school, it matters little whether a teacher leaves teaching altogether or transfers out, since the school still loses that teacher's knowledge of the students, curriculum, and community.

This is especially important, given compelling evidence that attrition and transfer most severely affect schools located in low-income urban and rural communities, where students arguably deserve the best teachers and the most continuity in their schooling. A considerable number of low-performing, low-income schools lose a high proportion of their first-year teachers each year and, as a result, they perpetually must recruit and hire. Given the cost of turnover, which is estimated to be 20 percent of the leaving teacher's salary (Benner, 2000), the schools that can least afford such expense are paying the highest price in the rush to keep up with the "revolving door" of attrition—hiring new, and possibly the least qualified, teachers in August only to lose them again by June (Ingersoll, 2001).

Inequities in the Competition for Qualified Teachers

In the competition for qualified teachers, some schools and districts get more than their share, while others go wanting. When the school year opens, most unfilled positions are in rural and urban schools serving low-income students. However, since children cannot be left untended, administrators eventually find an adult to cover every classroom, although there is often no assurance that this adult will be a competent or caring teacher. Large disparities in teacher qualifications already exist among urban, rural, and suburban schools and between schools serving low-income and high-income students (Boyd, Lankford, Loeb, & Wyckoff, 2002; Darling-Hammond, 2001; Haycock, 2000; Olson, 2003). As schools and districts compete for able new teachers, there is the danger that these disparities will become even greater.

A Preview of the Teacher Shortage

California provides the rest of the nation with a preview of how inequitably a shortage might play out. In the early years of the state's class-size reduction initiative, the percentage of primary grade teachers working without full credentials increased from 1.8 percent in 1995–1996 to 12.5 percent in 1997–1998. Simultaneously, a teacher credential gap opened between schools serving low-income and high-income student populations. In 1995–1996, such schools had similar proportions—under 4 percent—of uncredentialed teachers. By 1998–1999, 21.2 percent of the teachers at schools with a high concentration (more than 30 percent) of low-income students lacked full credentials, compared to only 4.3 percent of teachers in schools serving few low-income children (less than 7.5 percent). This gap persisted through at least 2001 (Bohrnstedt & Stecher, 2002). In 2002, voters in Florida—where student enrollments rose 31 percent in the 1990s (Young, 2003)—approved a mandatory reduction in class size (Johnston, 2002), which, if fully implemented, will almost certainly lead to similar shortages and dysfunction.

The No Child Left Behind Act of 2001

In an effort to address disparities in teacher quality such as those experienced in California, the federal government passed the No Child Left Behind Act of 2001 (NCLB), requiring that all teachers employed by local school districts be "highly qualified" by 2005–2006. Before the law, districts that could not find fully licensed teachers routinely granted emergency credentials to adults willing to staff classrooms on a temporary basis and, thus, hard-to-staff schools could cope with growing demand. However, over time, many such emergency placements achieved *de facto* permanence. Moreover, as the California example shows, these unlicensed teachers were concentrated in high-poverty schools and districts, once again subjecting low-income students to unprepared teachers (Olson, 2000). For a time, it seemed that traditionally prepared and certified teachers would be in great demand when districts began to comply with the law. However, controversy about the definition of "highly qualified" ensued and, in April 2003, federal education officials urged state education agencies to adopt the loosest interpretation of the law, making it possible in some states for prospective teachers to enter the classroom with no preservice training (Finn, 2003).

It is impossible to predict whether a relaxed definition of "highly qualified" will attract strong, new candidates to teaching, as some argue. It seems clear, however, that if the law is enforced it will prevent public schools from hiring teachers on emergency credentials, who are often the least able or least prepared candidates. It is important to recognize, however, that excluding this group of teachers will both restrict a supply of teachers that many schools have relied on and create an even greater demand for new teachers as positions previously held by emergency credentialed teachers open up.

Conditions for a Perfect Storm

There is a convergence, then, of several factors that increase the demand for new teachers—massive retirements by veteran teachers, enrollment growth, class-size reductions, the requirements of NCLB, potential teachers' decisions not to pursue a career in teaching, and the attrition and transfer of many new recruits. Together, they create the conditions for a "perfect storm" in education, a storm in which valuable teaching expertise is lost and never replaced, schools suffer repeated disruption as new teachers come and go, and low-income schools are further undermined by their inability to attract and retain strong teachers. Such a storm might severely weaken the quality of our nation's schools and compromise the future of our nation's students. Its impact cannot be precisely predicted and, in fact, it might change course or seem to dissipate in the wake of state budget cuts or amended licensing regulations. Its effects will differ from state to state and across regions of the country.[2] However, if this turbulence proceeds on course without careful monitoring and response by those in policy and practice, it could well have enormous costs for students and enduring consequences for society. When it subsides there will be a changed teaching force in its wake. Who will teach, how long they will teach, and how well they will teach depend on choices made today.

Research Methods

In an effort to understand the motivations, priorities, and experiences of the new generation of teachers today, we began a study in 1999 of fifty first- and second-year Massachusetts teachers who had entered teaching via various paths. Based on the recommendations of teacher education program directors, we selected new teachers who had participated in traditional teacher education programs at either undergraduate or graduate levels in public and private institutions. We also selected individuals from the first group of participants in the Massachusetts Signing Bonus Program, which provided recipients with a fast-track alternative certification program sponsored by the state. Finally, we solicited the participation of new teachers in charter schools, who at that time were not required to hold state licenses. As we selected participants, we sought to ensure that our sample would include variation by race, gender, ethnicity, and career stage.

We interviewed these teachers twice, once during the 1999–2000 school year and again after the 2000–2001 school year. In the summers of 2002 and 2003, we sent them a brief survey to track their career decisions year to year. In our interviews, we sought to understand why they had chosen to teach, how they prepared, what their early experiences were, and what their career plans were. We have explored these teachers' experiences from an organizational perspective, first trying to understand their needs and what they encountered and then drawing implications for how best to organize schools so that teachers such as these can succeed and thrive in their work. The methodology for this study and for additional, supporting studies that we draw upon here is explained more fully in Appendices A and B.

The Plan of This Book

The following chapters examine the experiences of ten new teachers, and through this subgroup, the experiences of the larger group of fifty in our study. Chapter Two introduces these featured teachers and explores the characteristics of the next generation of teachers, a cohort that is far more diverse in experience, preparation, and career plans than the retiring generation. This diversity has implications for schools and the support they can offer new teachers. Chapter Three considers the role of pay and incentives in individuals' decisions to enter and stay in teaching. It examines the costs of teaching and reveals why some teachers cannot afford to teach. It explains how individuals who are initially attracted by the intrinsic rewards of teaching may become dissatisfied with pay when they do not succeed in the classroom. Chapter Four looks at the role that students play in teachers' efforts to succeed in their work. It is students who simultaneously provide the primary motivation for teachers' work and introduce the greatest source of uncertainty. This chapter considers the challenge teachers face when their students' lives are very different from their own. It explains how well-organized and supportive schools enable teachers to succeed with a wide range of students. However, as Chapter Five shows, traditional school organizations promote isolated rather than interdependent work among teachers and thus compromise teachers' chance of success with their students. This chapter explains how schools and school leaders can provide the infrastructure and integrated work experience that new teachers need.

In the next two chapters, we closely examine two crucial aspects of teachers' experience in their schools—the curriculum and their work with colleagues. Chapter Six explains how curriculum has taken on new importance in this age of standards and assessment. It reveals how only a few teachers reported having adequate guidance about what to teach and how to teach. Many novice teachers reported being uncertain and anxious, spending long hours translating state curriculum frameworks into lessons and creating teaching materials from scratch. Chapter Seven considers the professional culture that new teachers encounter in their school— the mix of norms, values, and patterns of practice among their colleagues. It shows how new teachers who have rich and ongoing interactions with teachers of all experience levels report greater success and satisfaction with their work.

The next three chapters look toward new and promising practices of hiring, induction, and career development, all approaches that can improve recruitment and retention. Chapter Eight examines the process of hiring, both what it is and what it might be. It explains how the hiring experiences of most of our new teachers gave them little information or insight into the school where they would teach, and it highlights certain schools where hiring provided for a rich exchange of information, leading to a good match between prospective teachers and their school. Chapter Nine focuses on the process of teacher induction. Because our study began in 1999, before most schools began to offer formal induction programs, few teachers in our study experienced a deliberate and sustained system of induction. However, we have documented the induction programs of three additional schools, each of which goes well beyond one-on-one mentoring and helps new teachers establish themselves at their new school. Chapter Ten discusses the professional growth that teachers sought and found, as well as the opportunities they envisioned for their future as teachers. Traditionally, teachers have confined their vision of professional growth to a continuous refinement of classroom practice. Our research shows, however, that the next generation of teachers seeks a range of roles, both within the classroom and outside, by which to exercise broad influence. Finally, Chapter Eleven discusses the implications of this research for policymakers and practitioners, including new teachers themselves.

Chapter Two

The Next Generation of Teachers

Coauthor: Heather G. Peske

The next generation of teachers makes career decisions in a labor context that is strikingly different from what it was thirty years ago, and the interests and options of today's prospective teachers are unlike those of any teachers who have preceded them. In the late 1960s and early 1970s, public service was respectable, even admired work. In those years, prospective teachers could hear echoes of President Kennedy urging citizens to ask what they could do for their country. In addition, access to other professions was restricted for women and people of color, teaching's traditional labor pool. It has been said that this cohort of retiring teachers, who as a group were well-educated, provided a "hidden subsidy" for public education. Because of discrimination, both deliberate and unintentional, these teachers' talents, knowledge, and time came at a discount, much to the advantage of the public schools (Troen & Boles, 2003). Even when unions began to bargain collectively on teachers' behalf in the mid-1960s, these teachers were not well-paid compared with professionals in other lines of work that required similar training.

Those who consider teaching today have an array of alternative career options, many offering greater social status, providing more comfortable work environments, and offering far higher pay than teaching. Moreover, alternative work settings, such as law offices, engineering firms, technology companies, and consulting firms, are far better equipped to support successful work than are most public schools, which often suffer from the lack of basic equipment and supplies. Finally, the pay gap between teachers and others who hold a bachelor's degree grew substantially in the 1990s and continues to widen (Nelson & Drown, 2003). Those who teach today do so realizing that they could have higher status, work more comfortably, and earn substantially higher salaries in other settings.

Whereas U.S. workers once stayed with a career for a lifetime, serial careers are common today. It is not unusual for individuals to have pursued two or three different lines of work in the first decade after college. According to one recent study, the average American has worked for nine firms by the time he or she turns thirty-two years old (Editors, 2000). Although such a job history would have been seen as a liability thirty years ago, it now may serve a candidate well, signaling versatility and vitality. New teachers today begin the profession much more tentatively than their predecessors did. Further, unlike new teachers in past decades, many of today's new teachers enter teaching as a second or third "career" and may not complete many years in the classroom. A decision to teach today is not easy, inevitable, or immutable.

The career preparation and plans of the next generation of teachers—those beginning their work in classrooms today—look notably different from those of the retiring generation. As we will see in the chapters that follow, these generational differences have important implications for the organization of schools and the induction of new teachers. In particular, the next generation of teachers differs from the retiring generation in three significant ways: stage of entry, the routes they took to the classroom, and their expectations for a career in teaching (Peske, Liu, Johnson, Kauffman, & Kardos, 2001).

Entering Teaching at Different Career Stages

Although the current teaching force looks homogeneous in terms of gender (female) and race (white), that similarity masks unprecedented variety in these teachers' career experiences and professional plans (Snyder & Hoffman, 2003). As in the past, many new teachers today are still first-career entrants, but far more than ever before are entering teaching at midcareer, most having worked for a substantial period of time in another field.

In our purposive sample of fifty Massachusetts teachers, 52 percent (twenty-six) entered teaching as a first career, at an average age of twenty-four, whereas 48 percent (twenty-four) entered at midcareer at an average age of thirty-six. Although this is a high percentage of midcareer entrants, we had deliberately included a substantial number of what we thought were "atypical" teachers in our sample and thus had anticipated a high percentage of midcareer entrants. However, subsequent random samples of first- and second-year teachers in seven states, including Massachusetts, which were drawn after the start of the qualitative study reported here, revealed that our purposive sample was actually quite representative (Kardos, 2001, 2003; Kauffman, 2004; Liu, 2001, 2003). The random sample survey of Massachusetts teachers, conducted in 2001–2002, included 54 percent first-career entrants and 46 percent midcareer entrants—very much like the deliberate, qualitative sample of teachers we report on in this book (see Table 2.1). Other states we studied show a range of midcareer entrants (from 28 percent in Michigan to 47 percent in California).

The increasing proportion of midcareer entrants is important for several reasons. First, these new teachers begin teaching with work experience in a variety of settings, many of which offer far more resources than public schools typically do. The retiring generation of teachers, who for the most part entered the classroom right out of college, had little previous work experience in settings outside of education and, therefore, may have had more modest expectations about what their new workplace could be or would provide. Entering teachers who today move to the classroom from other fields such as finance, technology, law, or management are accustomed to working in well-equipped facilities that support their work. They are often dismayed when they find that their new workplaces are dreary or dilapidated, that they have scant access to

Table 2.1. First- and Midcareer Entrants and Average Age of New Teachers in Seven States

	MA 50 Purposive Sample 1999– 2000 n =50	MA Random Sample 2001– 2002 n = 144	CA Random Sample 2001– 2002 n = 112	FL Random Sample 2001– 2002 n = 113	MI Random Sample 2001– 2002 n = 117	NC[a] Random Sample 2002– 2003 n = 99	NJ Random Sample 2000– 2001 n = 110	WA[a] Random Sample 2002– 2003 n = 131
First-career	52%	54%	53%	68%	72%	67%	54%	65%
Average age	24	25	26	25	25	26	26	26
Midcareer	48%	46%	47%	32%	28%	33%	46%	35%
Average age	35	38	38	35	36	35	35	35

[a]Includes only second-year teachers, not first- and second-year teachers, as the other samples do.

telephones or the time to use them, that basic resources such as paper may be in short supply, and that they must use precious time to do routine, clerical tasks.

Second, experience working in other settings has provided midcareer entrants with a reservoir of organizational insight to draw upon when they and their colleagues are stymied about how to improve schooling. For them, the traditional structure of schools is not something they take for granted, and they may be surprised to find the isolation and lack of interdependence among the teaching staff that this established structure fosters.

Third, because midcareer entrants are older and often have children of their own, they potentially have greater first-hand understanding of children's development and a larger repertoire of strategies than first-career entrants as they interact with and try to motivate their students. They may also be better equipped to manage the possible tensions between forming relationships with students and maintaining authority (Kegan, 1994). One midcareer entrant in our study said: "It is my first year, and judging from everything I've heard from people over the years, I'm having a heck of a lot easier time of it than others, both because of my age, organizational skills, and I've raised kids. So I have a certain background to draw on and ability to put things in perspective and not take things too seriously when they don't need to be taken too seriously." By contrast, first-career entrants, who have just left their college classrooms when they take charge of their school classrooms, often feel closely identified with the youth they teach and may find it hard to cope with their new authority (Kegan, 1983; Lortie, 1975).

The ten teachers featured in this book include five who began teaching as their first career and five who entered at midcareer after a substantial period of time in another line of work. These individuals' experiences and views reflect themes that arose in the full sample of fifty teachers, and illuminate the differences between the rising and retiring generation.

First-Career Entrants

Many of the first-career entrants approach teaching in ways that are similar to the retiring generation. They have wanted to teach for many years and remained undeterred on their paths to the classroom, never seriously considering any other careers. Several said that they had always wanted to teach: "I feel like I always just knew," explained one. "It sounds corny, but I was born wanting to teach," echoed another. They believed that teaching would be socially valuable and personally rewarding work, yet recognized that the work was neither high-paying nor high-status. Many solidified their commitment to teaching during high school and college, working as coaches, counselors, or tutors in settings akin to schools: camps, tutoring programs, community sports, and after-school programs. To them, teaching was meaningful work that matched their talents and interests.

Midcareer Entrants

Unlike their first-career counterparts who moved from their own seventeen or eighteen years of schooling directly to the front of a classroom, the twenty-four midcareer entrants in our study had spent substantial time in an array of other work settings. In general, they viewed teaching as an opportunity to do more meaningful work than their previous employment offered. Some were unsatisfied with the substance of their work and came to teaching in response to what they thought was a true calling. Others, who were unhappy with their jobs and workplaces, explored a variety of alternative careers and eventually chose teaching. Sometimes they realized that they most enjoyed the aspects of their prior job that resembled teaching, such as counseling clients or training colleagues. Some midcareer entrants left their prior job because of child-rearing responsibilities and chose teaching because they imagined the schedule would be family-friendly.[1]

As a group, these midcareer entrants brought with them a familiarity with large and small organizations, for-profit and nonprofit enterprises, entrepreneurial and bureaucratic settings. Some had worked for multiple supervisors, whereas others had been supervisors themselves. They worked freelance or led teams. Some experienced well-defined, progressive on-the-job training, and some devised such training for other employees. Thus, midcareer entrants often entered their new school expecting a workplace that was better equipped, more flexible, and more committed to their success than the one they found.

Routes to the Classroom: Preparation and Licensing

Given the increasing variation in new teachers' ages and career stages, it is not surprising that they seek routes to the classroom that were rarely available when their veteran colleagues entered the profession. The new teachers in our sample varied in the paths they took to the classroom and in their preparation for teaching. Some entered teaching by traditional routes, pursuing undergraduate and graduate programs that included extensive pre-service coursework, student teaching, and ultimately certification. Others prepared by participating in an alternative route to certification—in this case, the Massachusetts Signing Bonus Program (MSBP). And there were those who began teaching with no formal preparation, securing jobs at charter schools, which at that time did not require that teachers be licensed—an option that the state has since eliminated.[2]

Traditionally Prepared Teachers

Over two-thirds (thirty-six) of our respondents completed traditional teacher education programs, which required at least one academic year of coursework and a substantial period of full-time, supervised student teaching (six weeks to ten months) during the school year.[3] A few traditionally prepared teachers in our study participated as teaching interns in professional development schools—schools sponsored in partnerships between the university and a local school district. Although these thirty-six teachers chose different types of programs, they all invested time and money to earn certification through a traditional preparation program. In general, this group of traditional entrants appreciated that the programs they attended offered them valuable information about pedagogy and opportunities to practice their craft during the school year and under the supervision of an experienced veteran.

Alternative Certification

While some entrants prepared through traditional routes, others took advantage of state policy changes that created alternate routes to the classroom, including the Massachusetts Signing Bonus Program and charter schools. The MSBP participants were employed as classroom teachers after completing a seven-week, summer preparation program operated by the state, including a short stint of student teaching in summer school. Through that program, these teachers earned a provisional license with advanced standing, the same license held by graduates of traditional teacher education programs.

Massachusetts is not alone in offering these new paths to teaching. In response to forecasts of a teacher shortage, many states have changed requirements for licensing teachers and have authorized a range of agents—local districts, private vendors, and intermediate education agencies—to create alternative training and certification programs. Some of these programs offer abbreviated preservice preparation with on-the-job support; others provide job-embedded training for teachers who lack preservice preparation and work on emergency licenses. Some states, including Massachusetts, also grant licenses to secondary school teachers who pass subject matter tests for a field in which they hold an undergraduate major.

The regulations for the No Child Left Behind Act, which grant the states discretion in determining what a "highly qualified" teacher will be, continue to expand the entry options of prospective teachers. The movement toward alternative certification, which has accelerated greatly in recent years, is also fueled by critics of traditional teacher education programs who argue that these programs include useless coursework in pedagogy. These alternative pathways are proving particularly attractive to nontraditional teaching candidates, such as midcareer entrants and minority teachers (Shen, 1997). As of 2003, forty-six states and numerous districts offered alternative certification programs, and an increasing number of candidates see them as viable routes to the classroom (Feistritzer & Chester, 2003).

Alternatively Prepared Teachers

Eighteen teachers in our study entered through an alternate route—thirteen of them participating in the MSBP. Nine of these thirteen had entered the MSBP with no preparation in teacher education, three others had completed certification requirements in traditional master's programs before joining the program, and one had completed all but the student teaching requirement in an undergraduate teacher preparation program. Five other teachers who had not completed any teacher preparation program—traditional or alternative—went to work in charter schools, where they were hired without licenses.

In general, this group of nontraditional entrants counted more on the value of innate teaching ability and professional experience than on the content of education courses or a student teaching experience—features that a traditional program would offer. Charter school teachers without previous preparation expected that they could learn what they needed on the job. Many said they had chosen an alternate route in order to move quickly into a teaching position, avoiding the time and expense of a year of courses and student teaching. The alternative route was particularly appealing for the midcareer entrants who otherwise would have had to forego a year's pay while completing a traditional program.

Career Expectations

Until the 1950s, teaching was largely short-term, itinerant work. In the nineteenth century, men taught for a few years on the way to other professions, such as law or the ministry. In the first half of the twentieth century, women taught until their district required that they resign when they married or had children. During the 1960s, teaching began to become long-term employment (Rury, 1989). The number of teachers in our study who plan to stay in teaching for the short term, or for only part of their careers, suggests that teaching as a career may revert to being short-term, itinerant work once again.

In contrast to their colleagues who are about to retire from a lifelong career in the classroom, many new teachers in our sample—including those who completed traditional teacher preparation programs and some who did not—approached teaching tentatively, conditionally, or as one of several in a series of careers they expect to have. Although some expected to make education a long-term career, there were surprisingly few who envisioned a long-term commitment to classroom teaching.

Long-Term Expectations

Although many of the first-career entrants entered teaching like their predecessors—deciding early and investing in preparation—they differ dramatically from the retiring generation in their conception of a career in teaching. The first-career entrants in our sample, who thirty years ago would probably have approached teaching as a long-term endeavor, were surprisingly tentative about a career in teaching. In fact, only four of the twenty-six first-career entrants said that they planned to remain classroom teachers until they retire. Eleven first-career entrants made a commitment to the field of education but did not think they would remain in the classroom for the duration of their career. It is important to observe that although many of the first-career entrants said that they plan to remain in education, the schools will still experience a loss if they leave the classroom. The departure of a teacher means that a school will lose the benefit of that teacher's acquired knowledge and experience and will be left with one more position for the school to fill.[4]

The midcareer teachers, whose career trajectory already differed from that of the retiring generation of teachers, were also hesitant to commit long term. Only six of the twenty-four midcareer teachers intended to stay in the classroom full time for the rest of their careers, and five more had made a commitment to education in general but did not plan to stay long-term in the classroom.

Short-Term Expectations

In contrast to those who envisioned committing to education long-term, the remainder of the teachers in our study—eleven first-careers and thirteen midcareers—stated explicitly that they had not entered teaching intending to stay for the rest of their careers. Those who were unsure of their commitment described two orientations to teaching: an exploring orientation and a contributing orientation. These "explorers" viewed teaching as a short-term way of sizing up the work of teaching, which might lead them to a longer commitment if they liked it. One respondent, a former software developer, explained, "I'm a career changer. I figured, Why not explore a new field?"

Although the "explorers" were uncertain about whether they would stay, they felt open to the possibility that teaching would become a longer-term endeavor. Others, however, viewed teaching as a short-term opportunity to contribute to society for part of their career. These "contributors" included those with plans to teach for a few years before moving on to other professions, or those who entered teaching as the capstone to another career. One recent college graduate planned to enroll in medical school after teaching for two years. He said, "I knew I wanted to go to medical school. I knew I did not want to go right after college, and so I decided, What can I do that won't pay too badly and that will make me feel like I'm doing something interesting and important?" Though these explorers and contributors made only a short-term commitment to teaching, they were not at all casual about what they hoped to achieve in the classroom during that time. Rather, they intended to pour themselves into the job, giving it all they had, but only for a few years.

Ten Featured Teachers

This book features ten new teachers, a subset of the fifty teachers we interviewed in 1999–2000 and 2000–2001. Although the accounts of all fifty teachers were rich and informative, we narrow our focus here so the reader may become well-acquainted with these ten individuals' interests and experiences. As a group, the teachers we selected reflect the diversity of our larger, purposive sample. They include women and men who differ by race and ethnicity; first-career and midcareer entrants who prepared in traditional and alternative programs; teachers in conventional and charter schools in the cities and suburbs; and professionals working alone or with others in self-contained, departmentalized, and interdisciplinary programs. In choosing these ten teachers, we also considered their career decisions over time; some in our sample left teaching, others changed schools, and others stayed in their original schools for the full four years of this study. Summary information about each of the ten featured teachers is presented in Tables 2.2 and 2.3. Their stories illuminate the challenges and hopes for recruiting and retaining the next generation of teachers.

First-Career Entrants

The following descriptions introduce the five first-career entrants featured in the book.

Derek Lewis. Derek Lewis, a twenty-six-year-old, African American man, chose a career in education because he wanted to work for social justice. Like many of the fifty teachers we studied,

Table 2.2. 1999–2000 Participant Information for Ten Featured Teachers

Name	Gender	Race	Age	Entry Stage	Route to License
Fred Chambers	M	White	24	First-career	Traditional
Esther Crane	F	White	38	Midcareer	Alternative
Amy Day	F	White	23	First-career	Traditional
Mary Donahue	F	White	36	Midcareer	Traditional
Bernie Fallon	M	White	32	Midcareer	Alternative
Carolyn Harrington	F	White	22	First-career	Alternative
Brenda Keppler	F	White	31	Midcareer	Traditional
Derek Lewis	M	African American	26	First-career	Traditional
Victoria Tran	F	Asian American	30	First-career	Traditional
Keisha Williams	F	African American	29	Midcareer	Traditional

he had family members in teaching; his mother and father were both career teachers. He explained that he decided to teach as the "logical" way to reform society and to work with the children he sought to serve: "I always wanted to make a difference in my community . . . I just wanted to be in a position somewhere where I was doing direct service. I've always wanted to get into teaching. I always have known that I was going to get into teaching. . . . And I just knew that I wanted to be working with young people in communities like the communities that I grew up in."

Derek had spent much time working with adolescents even before pursuing formal credentials. During and after college, he worked with gang-affiliated youth in two large cities. At his private, liberal arts college, he pursued his interest in teaching by enrolling

Table 2.3. 1999–2000 Participants' School and District Information for Ten Featured Teachers

Name	School Type	District Size[a]	School Size[a]	Location of School	Students on Free and Reduced-Price Lunch at the School	Grade Level Taught	Subject(s)
Fred Chambers	Professional development school	26,000	100	Large city	76%	7–9	Social studies
Esther Crane	Conventional	26,000	1,000	Large city	53%	10	Math
Amy Day	Conventional	60,000	850	Large city	80%	2	All
Mary Donahue	Charter	60,000	200	Large city	79%	7	Humanities
Bernie Fallon	Conventional	5,000	1,100	Small city	25%	9	History
Carolyn Harrington	Conventional	60,000	700	Large city	70%	5	All
Brenda Keppler	Conventional	7,000	450	Small city	52%	6,7,8	Spanish
Derek Lewis	Charter	60,000	200	Large city	64%	10	Humanities
Victoria Tran	Conventional	6,000	675	Inner ring suburb	11%	3	All
Keisha Williams	Conventional	60,000	500	Large city	92%	2	All

[a]The numbers of students in the districts and schools are close approximations based on 2002–2003 enrollment.

in the undergraduate education studies program before budget cuts forced it to close. On the advice of his professors, he applied for a fellowship that would pay his graduate school tuition.

After a brief stint working as a youth development worker for a nonprofit organization, Derek used the fellowship to attend a graduate-level teacher education program in exchange for teaching in a high-need school. He earned a master's degree and certification in secondary social studies. He explained that after completing the graduate program in education, he did not consider any other career choices: "[I]t just didn't make any sense to do anything else. I mean I had my certification, and I was going to at least teach for maybe two or three years and see what happens after that."

Having done his student teaching in a large, conventional urban high school, Derek took his first job teaching humanities, an integrated curriculum of social studies and English, to tenth graders in a small, urban charter high school. He chose this as the place to make a difference, citing the "tremendous amount of opportunity" he believed the school would offer him to use his talents and background in developing curricula and working with a diverse group of students in an environment that also promoted teacher collaboration.

Derek said he was "extremely, extremely proud" of his four-year-old charter school, which he called "unique." He described his fellow teachers as "like no other group of people I've ever worked with, period, in my working experience." In 1999, the school served under two hundred students, all from urban neighborhoods. The majority of the students at the school are African American, with a substantial percentage of Latino students.

When we first interviewed him, Derek was halfway through his second year. He reported that he felt great pride both in his accomplishments and those of the school, though he was unsure about his future as a classroom teacher. He had entered teaching certain that he would teach for at least several years and then evaluate his circumstances. After teaching almost two years, he found that although he loved his students, he was frustrated by the low status of teaching, the low pay, and some elements of his charter school. He was dismayed that teaching would not offer enough income to support the lifestyle he hoped to live, and he was angry about the public's disdain for teachers, which was signaled by low levels of education funding. These factors—status and pay—were foremost in his mind as he considered his commitment to his students and social justice and struggled to decide whether to remain in the classroom.

Fred Chambers. Fred Chambers, a white, twenty-four-year-old man, is a traditional, first-career entrant. Like Derek, he was influenced by family involvement in education; his mother was a preschool teacher. He decided he wanted to teach while he was attending a parochial high school, having found that he enjoyed the coaching and tutoring experiences he had there. He thought about other lines of work but dismissed them in favor of teaching: "I considered being a physician at one point. I considered being a law enforcement officer. But teaching was always kind of on the forefront. It's always what I wanted to do." Fred was also attracted by the social power of teaching: "I suddenly realized that teachers have a greater impact than any other profession in the world." He recalled "teachers that were influential in my life. And you think to yourself, this one person can affect so many lives, have a positive effect on so many lives, that's what I wanted to do."

Fred attended a private university, where he earned a double certification for history and social studies, grades five through twelve. During his first two years as an undergraduate, the university launched a fifth-year master's degree program for teaching candidates. A new professional development school (Holmes Group, 1990; Teitel, 2003) was to be cosponsored by his university and a local urban school district. During the school's first year, Fred worked as a full-time intern teacher, co-teaching with an expert teacher, and completed traditional graduate studies in the evenings.

Fred was so pleased with this small, neighborhood school, which he described as "extremely unique," that he signed on for a full-time job teaching middle and high school social studies. Though he came from "a primarily middle class suburban school system," he was happy to be teaching in an urban setting with a diverse population of students and colleagues that he respected. During his first year, the school enrolled approximately a hundred students in grades seven through nine, though it would gradually expand to include grades ten through twelve. The school had one clear and over-arching goal: to send all of the students to college. Fred, like Derek, described his school as a place where the teachers "wear a lot of hats . . . because it's a small faculty."

Fred said he hoped to remain at his school "forever." Although he entered expecting to have a long-term career in education, it was his appreciation for his school that reinforced his commitment: "I plan on making it a career. So twenty, thirty years." Despite days that were difficult, he concluded that "teaching is a good fit" for him, though he did speculate that he might someday become an administrator.

Victoria Tran. Victoria Tran, a thirty-year-old, Asian American woman, explained that her decision to teach had solidified over time: "I think pretty much since college, even in high school, I wanted to work with kids. I knew I didn't want to go into business. I didn't want to go into a field where I'm sitting on my bottom for eight hours a day . . . I knew I wanted to work with kids. So I thought teaching would be good because, you know, I thought I would be a good teacher."

Like Fred, Victoria was inspired by having "lots of good teachers. So that's kind of made me want to become a teacher as well, because I know I can . . . in a way . . . be as good as my teachers were to me. . . . So, I'm thinking, 'You know, if I was a kid sitting in that class, I would want someone good to teach me.'" Asked what other career options she had considered, Victoria said, "Actually, really not much. I really didn't go off the path hardly at all." Her parents, who never completed high school, had moved the family from Vietnam to ensure greater opportunities for their children. They were surprised when Victoria decided to teach. "[T]hey actually thought [I could have become] a doctor, or a lawyer, you know, to do anything. . . . They thought that I could have done something more high-powered, because of my background."

Victoria acknowledged that at times she thought, "I want to do something more exciting, more glamorous, more whatever it is—do traveling, do all that. I played with it, but still, when I came down to it, I didn't pursue any of it." She observed that some people think teachers choose to teach "because it's an easy profession, or it's a profession that people go into because you're not smart enough to do anything else. I know that's not the reason why I went into teaching, because I could have done anything, really, because I got good grades all through college. . . . But I always wanted, I think, to be a teacher."

Victoria received an undergraduate degree in family studies, with a concentration in elementary education, but the program did not include student teaching or certification. During college, she had worked with children in a preschool, then taught there for a year after graduating. In preparing to be a teacher, Victoria chose a master's degree program that offered a full-time, paid internship co-teaching with an experienced, expert teacher, much like the program Fred completed. Subsequently, she took a job teaching third grade at an elementary school in the same suburban district where she had completed her internship. The school, which included kindergarten through eighth grade, served approximately 675 students whose families came from many countries.

Victoria planned to stay in teaching "for a while," but thought that she might later work with children in another capacity, one in which she might exercise leadership. In the early stages of her career, she said that she loved "the teaching part of it," but had ambitions and goals that might lead her out of the classroom: "I'm not going to stay in teaching for the rest of my life, because I want to do things related, as well. . . . I'm not saying that being a teacher the whole time is bad, but to further my mind, to get higher goals, or different goals for myself, to do other things besides just being in the classroom as a teacher."

Amy Day. Amy Day, a twenty-three-year-old white woman, also chose her career at a young age: "I think I always have loved working with children, and I had babysat since I was ten, even before that." She worked in an after-school and summer program for nine years, from the time she was fourteen until she finished college. As a teenager, Amy thought briefly about becoming a veterinarian, but that, she said, was "just a phase."

As a student, Amy was not happy in school. She dropped out of the private, Catholic high school her parents insisted she attend and pursued a GED, but she said this never deterred her from her plan to teach: "I knew even when I dropped out of school, I knew that I wanted to teach. . . . I didn't want to go to that high school anymore, and my parents weren't willing to let me have another alternative. So, I said, 'Let me drop out. Let me get my GED and just start college.'" Amy chose to attend a local two-year community college, in part because she could continue working in the after-school program nearby. She went on to complete her bachelor's degree with a major in psychology and a minor in elementary education at a state university campus near her home, earning her certification in elementary education.

Amy's first job as a second grade teacher was located at a school in the same urban district where she had done her student teaching. She obtained the position by pursuing principals in the district where she wanted to teach. She chose her school over another where she had an offer because it was easily accessible by public transportation and she knew the school had a good reputation. She explained, "So it was . . . this school is supposed to be great. I really want to work there!"

Amy's school, which serves approximately 850 students, is one of the largest elementary schools in the district, located in a neighborhood with many immigrants. Although the architectural plan of the school incorporates an open model with few walls or doors separating the classrooms, Amy felt fortunate to have a closed classroom where she would not be on display as a new teacher, and her students would not be distracted by others.

Amy said she intends to teach "for the rest of my life," until retirement, and she thought she might be interested in roles as a lead teacher. She explained that teaching offers her a good fit as a career:

"I have worked with kids for so long. I know that this is what I want to do. I love kids, and I like teaching a lot."

Carolyn Harrington. Carolyn Harrington, a white, twenty-two-year-old woman, majored in English literature at a private Midwestern university. Although she worked with children, she was far less certain than Amy that she wanted to teach. She explained: "I came into teaching because I enjoy working with kids, but I also wanted to work with educational policy more." Carolyn's parents both work with children—her father as a child psychiatrist and her mother as a psychologist in a nonprofit foundation serving young children. Carolyn became interested in teaching during high school, seeing it as a way to effect change. As an adolescent, she was troubled by the "disparity that existed in public schools. . . . I went to public schools my whole life, but I came from more of an affluent town."

While in high school and college, Carolyn tutored urban students in cities nearby, an experience that intensified her concern about inequities in children's access to educational opportunity: "I didn't do anything to deserve [anything] over any other kid. . . . There should not be so much disparity among public schools. So, that's kind of my philosophy and kind of my passion, I guess." Carolyn had long-term plans to work in education policy, but she wanted to teach first, she explained, "to just gain some credibility . . . I wanted to get my own ideas, my own opinions before I went out there and just listened to others. So that's really what brought me here." Like Victoria's parents, Carolyn's father was somewhat disappointed that she wanted to enter teaching; he felt that she was wasting her talents, a sentiment echoed by some of her friends at college.

Carolyn had originally hoped to participate in Teach For America, a fast-track program that places recent college graduates in high-need urban and rural public schools. However, when she discovered that the organization had no sites in Massachusetts, where she wanted to live, Carolyn applied for, and was accepted by, the Massachusetts Signing Bonus Program (MSBP), which at the time offered training for prospective elementary school teachers.

After an intense summer program of courses and student teaching, Carolyn began work as a fifth grade teacher in a large, urban elementary school. She had investigated the school on the recommendation of her aunt. Carolyn was attracted by the principal's promises of support and the professional relationships she hoped to establish with her colleagues. Like Amy, she had kept in touch with the principal for several months, hoping that a position might open. Carolyn explained that the school has "all types of kids"—with about seven hundred students, including bilingual students and a large population of students with special needs. In September, she began teaching the twenty-one students in her fifth grade class.

Carolyn was a short-termer from the start: "In my mind I was thinking, OK, I'll teach for two or three years and then go into more policy, nonprofit work." Whether she would stay longer would depend on how satisfied she was.

Midcareer Entrants

The following descriptions introduce the five midcareer entrants featured in this book.

Esther Crane. Esther Crane, a thirty-eight-year-old white woman whose story opened this book, entered teaching as a midcareer professional, having worked as an engineer. She had been happy in her previous work but resigned her job in order to care for her children. She began to consider teaching full-time while working as a substitute: "I've always liked explaining to the kids, to my own kids, how things work and doing things with them, and I can do this with other kids. And I liked the subbing." She was also interested in teaching because she perceived the schedule to be compatible with raising a family.

Like some other midcareer entrants in our sample, Esther joined the MSBP with no preparation in teacher education. She hoped teaching "would be a good fit between something that I thought would be a good lifestyle and something that I was interested in and could make use of what I knew." After completing the program, Esther took a job teaching tenth grade mathematics at a large urban vocational high school. She was assigned to teach five different classes, with approximately a hundred students total.

Esther remained ambivalent about her career decision; often she thought about returning to engineering in the midst of her teaching: "I think I might go back to engineering at some point . . . if I just can't take [teaching]. It's a lot of work for a fairly small amount of money." Like other short-termers, she envisioned herself working in a series of careers: "I consider this my third career, my first being engineering . . . my second one being a full-time mom—which is a continuing career. . . . And this is my third. I still think there's a fourth one in there somewhere."

Bernie Fallon.   Bernie Fallon, a thirty-two-year-old white man, became interested in teaching after six years as a lawyer. Whereas Esther Wright loved her job as an engineer in the space industry, Bernie became disenchanted with both his work and his workplace. He entered law school intending "to use [his] intellectual skills to help people, and also make a decent living doing it." He excelled academically and achieved rapid success as a corporate lawyer. After six years of practicing law, he "found that the only thing I was getting out of it was a paycheck—a good one. But I was working a lot of hours, and I was driving myself crazy with a lot of work." He wanted to spend more time with his wife and young son: "I was paying lip service to the fact that, you know, the family was the number one priority. . . ." Disturbed by the demands of practicing law, he also began to acknowledge that he didn't like the work itself: "The content— it's very adversarial. Even if you're not doing litigation, it can be adversarial dealing with your client. There were just incidents where, you know, your integrity was sometimes called into play."

Bernie began systematically to explore alternatives, visiting a career counselor and taking interest inventory tests. Teaching kept appearing as a career that matched his interests. He recalled, "So I became intrigued by that. I have people in my family that are teachers." Once he had decided that he should teach, he planned a gradual transition from the law office to the classroom. He recalled thinking, "Well, maybe long range, maybe ten years from now. And in the meantime, I'd make as much money as I can, and I'd pick away at the classes here and there."

One day he heard an advertisement for the Massachusetts Signing Bonus Program on the radio and it seemed to be a "perfect match, absolutely" for him. Given his financial obligations, he was attracted by what he called "the bypass" of traditional teacher education courses, which he did not feel were necessary and would require him to give up his job and salary. He recalled a time of rapid transition: "I had a ninety million dollar bond deal and, in the meantime . . . I'm cramming for the teacher's test."

With the summer program behind him, Bernie was hired "at the last minute" to teach ninth grade history in the large, racially diverse, comprehensive high school of a small city. He was assigned to teach five classes of students with a range of ability levels.

In discussing his career expectations, Bernie was not sure whether he would continue teaching, and he worried regularly about meeting his family's expenses on a teacher's salary: "I can't tell you for sure that I'm going to do this for four years, or I'm going to do it for five years, or ten years." He said, "You know, I'm a work in progress. I can't tell you exactly what I'm going to do." He went on to say that the demands of the job left him feeling ambivalent about the duration of his commitment—"I'm not sure that to do the job right there's anybody that has these superhuman powers to give it their all for a career"—but he pledged to evaluate his options carefully.

Keisha Williams. Keisha Williams, a twenty-nine-year-old African American woman, was also a midcareer entrant. Prior to teaching, she had earned a master's degree in higher education administration and had been an administrator for five years in several settings—a private college, a public university, and a community college. Her desire to teach arose from her concern about the weak literacy skills of students she encountered. She said she was "really appalled" that "so many of the students arrived at college so ill-prepared. On a college level, when you cannot string sentences together, it's painful. It was painful for me to watch. They spent so much of their time in remedial courses. . . . It was wasting their money."

Keisha knew from tutoring middle school students that this problem of limited skills had early origins. She explained her decision to teach and her focus on the elementary-school level: "I knew I needed to teach, because I needed to correct that problem. I realized that problem started from day one. It starts from day one because at the elementary school is when you learn all of your foundations. After that, it's more and more and more and more. It just kind of builds on it."

Keisha chose a traditional master's in education program when she decided to move from higher education administration to elementary school teaching. She did her student teaching in a highly acclaimed urban elementary school. After completing extensive preparation, she applied for the Massachusetts Signing Bonus, both for the money it promised and for the additional preparation it offered. Keisha wanted a job teaching primary grade students in an urban district, and she took the first such job she was offered —(a second grade position at an urban elementary school)—even though she knew "nothing" about the school.

Keisha, who said, "I'm just kind of day-by-daying it," did not see herself as a long-term classroom teacher, even though she felt "comfortable in the classroom" and "enjoy[ed] teaching kids." Though she had planned to spend just a few years in the classroom, she expected that she would remain in the field of education for the long term: "I know that I wouldn't be teaching forever, or anywhere close to what a forever-career would look like. I think that education is for me forever, but I'm not sure if teaching is for me forever." When Keisha spoke about whether teaching was a good fit for her as a career, she said, "I haven't decided that yet. I am still trying, literally—maybe I'll make a decision this summer—but I am not sure yet. I am not sure if this is where I want to be for the long haul, or half of the long haul. I don't know." As a midcareer entrant with short-term plans to stay in teaching, Keisha was still uncertain about her future in the profession.

Mary Donahue. Mary Donahue, a thirty-six-year-old white woman, decided to become a teacher for reasons similar to those of Keisha. In her previous job, she had done crisis work with adults for six years and, like Keisha, Mary decided that "more prevention needed to occur." When she decided to make a career shift from working with adults in crisis to teaching adolescents, it was because she realized "that by the time that I was involved in working with these women, it was sort of too late. They had already not been educated, and already had certain roles, in terms of gender relationships."

Although Mary considered other careers, such as social work, "law, as a way to be an advocate for people," and faith-based social services work, she chose teaching because she had enjoyed the teaching responsibilities in her prior work of supervising college students and law students who were learning to do crisis work: "I began to sort of like the role of teaching people, and helping them develop in some way—that sort of mentoring type of relationship. . . . I think that's probably like the core of what was really appealing to me about teaching—having the kind of relationship with a person where you would help them develop."

Mary prepared to teach in a middle school. She thought that if she worked with students at this age, she "would have more of a role in prevention. Not only prevention in terms of creating school climates where . . . girls would achieve, but also just having skills, so that, when you're twenty, twenty-two years old, you can really take care of yourself." Mary reasoned, "I would rather be in an area where I'd feel like I could make a difference."

When Mary decided to make a career shift, she chose a master's degree program at a private university that would license her to teach middle school. Whereas Esther and Bernie both prepared to teach through the MSBP, Mary, like Keisha, attended a traditional teacher education program. She thought that enrolling in a traditional program was "the way you do it." She was less concerned with the particulars of the program or the subject matter she would focus on: "It wasn't as important to me—and especially with this age group, there are so many subjects, that you have to sort of intertwine [them]."

After completing the program, Mary found a job teaching humanities—history and language arts—to seventh graders at a charter school. She described her school: "It's very small. A two hundred–student middle school. It is a new school. It's a [charter]. It's based on project-oriented learning. So [we do] long-term learning projects." She said that the school is "different than a typical large city school" though it is situated in an urban neighborhood. The school had about 250 students, most of whom were African American. Mary viewed her colleagues as "really committed to the children."

When we asked Mary during her first interview how long she would stay in teaching, she responded with ambivalence: "I don't know. I don't know what to do. I really—I'm not sure." She could not imagine herself as a life-long teacher: "I definitely don't anticipate working as a full-time teacher for a very long period of time. You know, for like ten years even [I see as] a long time. I don't see teaching full-time even for ten years."

Brenda Keppler. Brenda Keppler, a thirty-one-year-old white woman, considered a move to teaching after discovering that she liked the aspects of her work that were most similar to teaching. After graduating from college, she began doing public health research and, over time, found the experiences of training interviewers rewarding: "I just found that I enjoyed the teaching part, and being able to work with people and explain things. I found that was a strength I had." In addition, she had always been concerned about children: "I really like kids. . . . Their well-being is just very important to me." She considered work in education, though not necessarily as a teacher. However, teaching was something that she had been "thinking about. It was always a big possibility." Brenda grew up in South America, so she anticipated that she would teach Spanish: "[S]peaking other languages has always been a part of my life."

Brenda began a master's program in education at a private university, but decided not to enroll in the teacher education program. Though her master's program did not license her to teach, she was convinced that she would find a teaching job, either in a charter school, an after-school program, or as a language teacher in a conventional school: "I was certainly thinking I was going to teach. . . . I was thinking somehow it would . . . work out. And I knew that . . . especially for language teachers, there's really a shortage. I know that sometimes public schools even hire people that aren't certified and then work with them. So I thought somehow I would end up teaching."

Brenda was consulting the State Department of Education's Website to learn about alternate routes to the classroom when she discovered an announcement for the Massachusetts Signing Bonus Program. Like Bernie and Esther, Brenda was relieved to find a path to teaching that didn't require "having to go somewhere and do very specific things in order to be able to get certified." She was accepted to the MSBP and completed the summer program.

As she expected, finding a job as a Spanish teacher was not hard. She chose to teach in an urban middle school where she had volunteered as a graduate student and knew the principal through a "mentoring program." She discovered that the previous Spanish teacher, with whom she had volunteered while in graduate school, was leaving: "[T]his teacher found out he was leaving and he called me and he said, 'You know, we really want to have you at this school.'" The K-8 school included about 450 students. Many of the students in the upper grades had attended the school from the early grades, which Brenda thought contributed to the "nice sense of community" there. The school, which housed a magnet program as well as the standard program of study, served a racially diverse group of students.

When we asked her how long she expected to stay in teaching, Brenda answered frankly: "I don't know. I have no idea." She said that much would depend upon whether she found teaching to be a career that offered personal fulfillment: "I think personally I'm just going to need to decide whether it's something I can do, and whether it's—whether it can be a positive experience for me."

Where Were the Ten Featured Teachers After Year Two of the Study?

We conducted initial interviews of the ten featured teachers in 1999–2000 and interviewed them for a second time in 2000–2001. At the time of the second interview, two of the ten had left teaching altogether—one for another field, and one for an administrative position in education. Three had moved to different schools. Five had stayed in their original schools for a second year.

Those Who Left.   Derek left teaching to take an administrative position at the same charter school where he had begun his teaching career. In the fall of her second year of teaching, Brenda left her school for a part-time position teaching Spanish at two K-8 schools in a suburban district. After finishing her second year, she decided to leave teaching altogether and returned to work in the nonprofit sector.

Those Who Moved.   Esther changed schools after completing her first year, moving from her urban vocational school to a suburban high school. After her first year, Keisha moved from one urban school to another. Mary also went to a new school, from an urban charter school to a suburban middle school, after her second year.

Those Who Stayed.   Fred stayed at his original school. Amy was still teaching at the school where she began and had started to assume new responsibilities. After their second years of teaching,

Bernie, Carolyn, and Victoria were still teaching in their original schools.

Where Were the Fifty Teachers After Year Two of the Study?

Two academic years after this study began, eleven of the fifty teachers had left public education altogether. There were eleven participants who had changed schools. Eight of them moved voluntarily; three moved involuntarily due to budget cuts or termination. Of the fifty teachers in the study, twenty-eight were still teaching in their original schools after the second year of the study (2000–2001).

There are many complex reasons for the new teachers' career decisions. One of the considerations in their decisions about career is pay, the subject of the next chapter.

Chapter Three

What Teaching Pays, What Teaching Costs

Coauthor: Edward Liu

Derek entered teaching out of a commitment to social justice and a desire to make a difference in his community. The son of teachers, he knew that the pay would be modest compared to other professions, but he accepted this in exchange for meaningful work. By his second year, however, Derek was already planning to leave teaching. Among other things, low pay and the public's lack of respect for teachers were driving him out of the classroom. He explained, "I need to make money. . . . If this profession offered more money, I'd stay here forever, but it doesn't. And I'd like to have a family, and you know, live a little better than I live now. So, I'm going to have to leave."

Scholars and policy analysts have long debated the role of pay in teachers' work. Some place great importance on pay and argue that substantially increasing salaries is essential to solving the teacher shortage and teacher quality problems (Brewer, 1996; Ferris & Winkler, 1986; Murnane, Singer, Willett, et al., 1991; Termin, 2003). Others dismiss the importance of pay, contending that money matters little to teachers who really care about their work (Public Agenda, 2000) or that eliminating licensing requirements would have a bigger impact than raising pay on increasing the supply and quality of teachers (Ballou & Podgursky, 1997). Although various studies have been designed to measure whether and to what extent pay is a key factor in staffing schools, little is known about *how* money matters to teachers.

Our research suggests that pay plays a complicated role in new teachers' decisions to enter or leave the classroom. Very few choose to teach because of the pay, since there are easier ways to make comparable income. Many of the new teachers we interviewed agreed with the twenty-six-year-old middle school teacher who said: "Well, teaching is the reward itself. I didn't go into teaching because I wanted to be a millionaire, you know." Everyone knows, they suggested, that teachers do not make good money; they teach because it is good work that brings personal rewards, not financial ones. However, it would be a mistake to conclude that money is unimportant to teachers, even those who are deeply committed to their work. These teachers' accounts suggest that although money surely is not the main incentive for entering teaching—intrinsic rewards are—pay can become a disincentive or barrier for those who otherwise might be attracted to teaching. The costs of entering and remaining in teaching are quite high and often discouraging, especially given the modest long-term pay potential. Once in teaching, pay can take on heightened importance as individuals contemplate their future financial needs or encounter working conditions that make it difficult to gain the personal rewards for which they entered teaching. Ultimately, many respondents worried about whether they could afford to teach over time and were uncertain, therefore, if they would stay in the profession long term.

The teachers' inclination to downplay the role of pay in their career decisions was predictable, not only because there is not much money to be made in teaching, but also because social norms call for it. As sociologist Dan Lortie (1975) observed over twenty-five years ago, "many people both inside and outside teaching believe that teachers are not supposed to consider money, prestige, and security as major inducements" (p. 30). A forty-one-year-old midcareer entrant's comments reflected these norms: "I'm not here for the compensation. . . . I'm OK with it. I don't really care one way or the other. I guess, philosophically, I think you need to have people in this field that are intrinsically motivated to be in it." Despite such deliberate efforts to discount its importance, concerns about pay emerged repeatedly in teachers' comments.

For instance, one of the fifty teachers in our study had walked out of her accounting job one day, never to return. After a year in the classroom, she explained that she liked what she was getting from teaching: "I need to enjoy what I'm doing. I need to feel useful. It seems to fulfill all of my needs, and I hope I'm doing the same for the kids." At the same time, she was candid in describing her ambivalence: "I love the kids, don't get me wrong, [but] every day in the back of my head, even when I'm showering or cleaning my oven, I'm thinking, 'What can I get into? What profession could I get into that's just as rewarding, but I don't have to put up with the . . . salary and [not being] treated as a professional?'"

The new teachers we interviewed had multiple career options. Many had considered a number of professions before choosing teaching, and almost half had switched to teaching from other work. The opportunity costs of their decisions loomed large in respondents' thoughts about whether to stay in teaching. First-career entrants saw their peers in other careers making more than they while apparently working no harder. Midcareer entrants missed the higher income from their previous jobs and calculated what they might have been making had they stayed on. Many teachers wondered aloud whether their choice of teaching was worth it.

Are Teachers Underpaid?

Analysts bring different assumptions to different sets of data and, therefore, reach different conclusions about whether teachers' pay is substantially lower than that of comparably trained employees in other fields. An analysis conducted by *Education Week* showed that the 1994 salary gap between teachers with bachelor's degrees and nonteachers with bachelor's degrees was $11,035 (in 1998 dollars). Just four years later, in 1998, this gap had risen 61 percent to $18,006. For master's degree recipients, the analogous salary gap between teachers and nonteachers almost doubled between 1994 to 1998, rising from $12,918 to $24,648 (Olson, 2000). A recent report from the National Center for Education Statistics provides more evidence that teachers have lost financial ground to their peers. Among bachelor's degree recipients who graduated in 1993 and were working full-time five years later, teachers "earned among the lowest annual salaries of their college cohort" (Henke et al., 2000).

Economist Richard Vedder, however, used data from the National Compensation Survey of the Bureau of Labor Statistics to compare hourly wages of teachers and nonteachers, and reached a different conclusion. Counting the hours that teachers are required to be present in schools (and excluding any additional time they might spend preparing to teach), Vedder concluded that "teachers earned more per hour than architects, civil engineers, mechanical engineers, statisticians, biological and life scientists, atmospheric and space scientists, registered nurses, physical therapists, university-level foreign language teachers, librarians, technical writers, musicians, artists, editors, and reporters" (Vedder, 2003, p. 16). His analysis, however, makes the questionable assumption that it is possible for teachers to complete all of their work within the hours of the contracted school day.

Whether teachers are paid well or paid poorly depends, in some ways, on how one views teaching and on one's choice of comparison group. If teaching is seen as a job with short workdays and summers off and the proper comparison groups are seen to be journalists, nurses, and laboratory technicians (all occupations that require a college education but pay moderate salaries), then perhaps teachers are paid relatively well (Podgursky, 2003; Vedder, 2003). However, if one views teaching as work requiring extensive time beyond the school day and views the proper comparison groups to be engineers, accountants, and lawyers, then teachers are paid relatively poorly.

Over the past two decades, changing societal conditions and expectations and new federal mandates have increased the demands placed on teachers and the skills required to teach well. If we are to have a teaching force that can teach all children to high standards and that will truly leave no child behind, the teaching profession must be able to attract highly skilled individuals. What is important in staffing the schools, particularly as they face shortages, is the effect that pay has on strong candidates' decisions to consider, enter, and stay in teaching. Our teachers' responses suggest that pay—both the level and structure of their salary—serves as a serious disincentive for new teachers as they make decisions about whether or not to stay in teaching.

Low Pay and the High Costs of Choosing to Teach

In various ways, the new teachers in our study talked about the high opportunity costs of choosing teaching over other higher paying occupations. They also cited the additional costs—both opportunity and out-of-pocket—of teacher preparation and subsequent licensing requirements.

Modest Salaries

Participants were well aware that in choosing teaching they were committing their skills and efforts to a profession that would pay them less than other careers they might have pursued. The first- and second-year teachers who participated in this study reported full-time teaching salaries between $15,000 and $45,000 in 1999.[1] At the low end of the salary range was one teacher who had his own class as a full-time substitute and made $85 per day (about $15,000 for the year). At the high end were teachers who had master's degrees, teachers with law degrees who were given credit on the salary scale for having doctorates, and one teacher who was credited for experience teaching in another country. Excluding the full-time substitute, the median for the entire group was $34,000. Although this was considerably higher than the national average of $27,989 for beginning teachers in 1999–2000 (American Federation of Teachers, 2000, p. 8), these new teachers lived in a region with one of the nation's highest costs of living. Table 3.1 summarizes the range of salaries, by degree held.

Some new teachers in our study were satisfied with their paychecks. Overall, however, most believed that they could have made more in another field, that they were underpaid for what they did, and that low pay for teachers reflected the public's lack of regard for

Table 3.1. Self-Reported Salaries of the Fifty Participating First-and Second-Year Teachers, by Degree Held, in 1999

	Low	Median	High
Bachelor's	$15,000[a]	$32,000	$45,000[b]
Master's	$27,800	$34,500	$41,000
Doctorate	$33,000	$38,000	$40,000

[a]Full-time substitute who was paid $15,000. The second lowest salary in this group was $26,000.

[b]This teacher was credited for her experience teaching in another country. Excluding this individual, the highest salary among bachelor's degree holders was $38,000.

teachers and for their work. Most first-career entrants could only estimate what they might have made in other fields, but midcareer entrants, such as Esther and Bernie, compared their teaching salaries with what they had actually earned before switching careers. Esther, who said her salary could easily be $60,000 if she returned to engineering, noted, "I'm making less than I did when I started working [as an engineer] in '83."

Bernie had taken a $40,000 annual pay cut when he left his position as a corporate lawyer to enter the classroom. Despite his conviction that teaching is meaningful work, he was burdened with doubts about his decision, doubts that were driven primarily by finances. Saying that he is "not a man that's driven by money," Bernie worried that he and his wife, who worked as an accountant, could not maintain their relatively comfortable lifestyle in the years ahead as their young family grows. For him, as for other teachers, the prospect of meeting mortgage and car payments while saving for his children's education was daunting. Bernie's concern about pay was exacerbated by the challenge of his new work—its long hours and mediocre working conditions. He was unsettled by the disparity between how hard he worked and how much he was paid.

Seven midcareer entrants (less than one-third of that group) did not take pay cuts when they entered teaching; three of these said that, as teachers, they earned about the same, and four reported earning somewhat more. However, members of this group also judged their pay relative to the demands of teaching. One mid-career entrant who was making more than she had in the past still characterized her teaching salary as a "pittance," considering the increased workload and responsibilities she now had.

Living on a Teacher's Salary

For first-career teachers, being able to live on a teacher's salary meant being able to pay for food and rent, cover their student loan payments, buy holiday gifts, and have something left over to "put into savings" or "for emergencies." For midcareer teachers (and first-career teachers looking ahead), managing to live on a teacher's salary also meant being able to make mortgage and car payments, pay for children's education, and set aside savings for retirement.

First-career entrants, many of whom were single, had fewer financial obligations than their midcareer counterparts. Yet they, too, told of their financial struggles. Six respondents lived at home with their parents to save on rent. One, who taught elementary science in an urban district, said that he "get[s] by barely" on what he makes. "Every now and then, I have to ask my dad to borrow a hundred bucks, and it shouldn't be that way." Another first-career teacher raised a similar concern: "You're out of school; you want to be an adult. I can pay my rent; I can buy food; I can pay my loans, mostly, and my bills. But what if an emergency came up? You know, the car needs repairs. You need to send money to your family. My brother needs books. And it's like I'm living check to check. There's no opportunity for saving, or for growth in that. It makes it difficult."

In response, many deliberately lowered their standard of living or took on additional work. Fred, who was trying to save for a house, was living simply and supplementing his income by working weekends as a part-time patrolman and emergency medical technician. First-career entrant Victoria's comments illustrate how respondents typically weighed their options: "Where I live . . . right now, my rent's OK. But if I decide to move to another place where the rent's higher, then it's tough. I go from paycheck to paycheck. Let's put it that way. But it's all in how you look at it, too, where you come from. I wish we were paid . . . better. But I don't think I would leave this to go to a higher paying job. Because if I wanted to, I could have done it."

Being Subsidized by a Partner

Many teachers in our study, both first-career and midcareer entrants, said they could get by on teachers' wages because they were subsidized by their partner's salary. Keisha called her husband her "additional salary," and said, "because of my husband, I'm fine." Amy thought that her starting salary of $34,600 was "a huge amount of money to get for 180 days work." Yet she said she still could not have managed to buy a house, had her fiancé not earned a higher salary. Another midcareer entrant said bluntly, "If I wasn't married, [teaching] wouldn't be an option."

Although the new teachers appreciated this crucial support, being the subsidized partner was not always easy. A midcareer entrant who took a 50 percent pay cut called it "hard. It's just hard. My husband is still skeptical about the change." Only partly joking, she said that her salary "pays for the groceries." Another midcareer entrant told a compelling story about going to a lawyer's office to discuss initiating a divorce only to realize the financial implications of going ahead with it. Sitting in that office, she began to think: "You know what, I can't even leave. You know, [my husband] pays the mortgage. I almost felt like, 'Jeez, I've got no right to even ask for half this house, because I don't contribute anything.' My entire salary just covers my debt from school, my car loan, insurance, that kind of thing. And what's left over for disposable [income]? I don't think I had any disposable. You know, just like from when you're a student, and it's tough. It was tough for me." For her, teaching did not offer financial independence.

Repaying College Loans

Unlike their counterparts in the retiring generation of teachers, these new entrants often carried substantial debt from undergraduate and graduate loans, sometimes exceeding what they could earn in a full year of teaching. Derek, who was deeply dissatisfied with his pay, said, "The bottom line is the money is not there. I owe more in loans than I make in salary. You just can't do it."

Over the past twenty years, college tuition has grown much faster than inflation, while median family income has stayed almost flat.[2] As a result, student borrowing has risen dramatically. In 1995–1996, half of all bachelor's and master's degree recipients graduated with some federal student loans (American Council on Education Division of Government and Public Affairs, 1997). On average, bachelor's degree recipients had borrowed $12,000 from public institutions and $14,300 from private institutions. Master's degree recipients graduated with, on average, $15,100 in loan debt from public institutions and $21,400 in debt from private institutions. Today's cohort of entering teachers routinely carry such debt and must consider what it will mean to pay off loans on the salaries they will earn.

Looking Ahead at Finances

Teachers were not only concerned about their current financial situation. The money worries of their veteran colleagues and the district's salary scale, which usually put a low ceiling on teachers' wages, confirmed their fears that the long-term financial prospects for teachers were not good either. Where their friends in business, engineering, or law might reasonably expect to double their income in a decade, teachers could expect to work thirty years or more before that occurred. One first-career teacher's comments about what might keep her in teaching illustrate our respondents' concerns about long-term pay: "Money, definitely more money, no doubt. Not even starting off a lot, but the idea of knowing that, OK, if I stay in this for two or three years, I will get paid ten grand more or fifteen grand more, which is not the case. It's like three grand more, if you are lucky."

Many younger, single teachers speculated about whether they could manage once they married and had families. Despite living "paycheck to paycheck," Victoria said that she was "managing. I'm not struggling to pay my bills right now, because I'm single. I have no other responsibilities but to myself. And I'm sure someone else that has a family and kids may feel different." Carolyn echoed: "[R]ight now, the salary is fine. I'm single. I'm not sure what my family situation, what my [future] husband's salary might be or not [be]." She wondered what role pay eventually would play in her career decisions: "So, it might be because of salary that I might [leave teaching]." As Mary said, "People don't expect to be paid like investment bankers. Money is not why you go into teaching. But you should be able to live on a teaching salary." These new teachers never expected to get rich, but they did not expect to struggle financially.

Who Never Answered the Call?

In our study, we did not identify and interview prospective teachers who chose *not* to teach. It seems likely, though, that many individuals may have been attracted by the prospect of intrinsic rewards but chose other work because of the higher pay. Working in technology or sales may have paid more without requiring further training. Tuition for law school or business school might be higher, but so too would eventual take-home pay. The likelihood that many strong candidates never explore teaching is supported by a Public Agenda survey (2000) that identified a sizeable group of college graduates under the age of thirty who held jobs outside of teaching but who expressed considerable interest in the profession. These individuals, whom Public Agenda called "leaners," reported that they would seriously consider teaching if pay, working conditions, and support for teachers were improved (p. 14). Public Agenda's interpretation, however, downplayed the role that money might play in attracting these individuals to the teaching profession. Instead, the report suggested that policymakers ought to focus on improving working conditions. Our study shows that pay continues to be important as well.

The Costs of Preparing to Teach and Maintaining a License

For first-career entrants, the expense of preparing to teach is no greater—sometimes much less—than the expense of preparing for careers in fields such as social work, engineering, business, law, medicine, or architecture. For the participants in this study, however, the issue was not so much how costly teacher preparation would be relative to training for other fields, but whether their eventual salaries would warrant the initial investment and whether they would be better off spending their money on law school or business school, which would lead to higher-paying careers.

However, for the large number of midcareer entrants—many of whom had already spent time and money earning a degree in another field—the costs of preparing to teach in a traditional university-based program presented significant barriers. Bernie had become increasingly dissatisfied with his work as a corporate lawyer, and career counselors had led him to seriously consider teaching. However, he did not think that he could leave his high-paying job for a year to become licensed. He had "started to think, 'Well, maybe long-range, maybe ten years from now.' And in the meantime, I'd make as much money as I can, and I'd pick away at the classes here and there. I wasn't in the situation where I could take the time off to do a student teaching gig."

Midcareer entrants who had decided that they wanted to teach—particularly those earning high salaries or having significant family obligations—were initially deterred from teaching primarily by the costs of teacher preparation. Most were leaving a career that had failed to provide personal fulfillment, and for the time being, these individuals were reconciled to the reality of a teacher's paycheck. However, a year of preparation would have cost a year of foregone salary ($40,000 to $80,000) plus tuition. Some of our respondents, such as Mary and Keisha, accepted that expense, both because they saw no alternative and because they believed that formal preparation was essential to their success as teachers. Keisha was able to limit the expense by studying part-time while employed as an administrator in higher education.

Even when individuals have completed their teacher preparation, they may not be able to afford to teach immediately because of accumulated debt. One first-career entrant said that her loans made her hesitate to take a teaching job right after college. She recalled thinking: "No, no, no, I'm not going to be a teacher. . . . I can't be a teacher. . . [because] I have thousands of dollars in loans and I'm not going to be able to pay off my loans." Another first-career entrant said that he had a huge debt load because he "came from very poor family and I had to pay for everything, basically. I got a lot of financial aid, but still, there was $40,000 that was not covered by financial aid. . . ." He chose to first work in industry—"[I] made a lot of money and had fun, but I never felt great about what I was doing." Eventually, he paid his debts, quit his job, and switched to teaching.

Massachusetts' requirement that new teachers complete a master's degree within five years in order to maintain a permanent license added yet another professional expense to be met on a modest salary. One respondent said that she was "just kind of surviving for awhile" on her $28,000 salary, from which she had to pay off undergraduate student loans and cover basic living expenses. Although she hoped to remain in teaching for some time, she was already worried about how to pay for her required master's degree: "I mean, with the salary that I have, I can't imagine—well, I don't want to go back on financial aid, but I can't see being able to pay for classes that I need to take to remain a teacher."

The Massachusetts Signing Bonus Program (MSBP)

The impact of the costs of teacher preparation (opportunity costs and tuition) in new entrants' decisions to teach came sharply into focus when we interviewed recipients of the $20,000 Massachusetts Signing Bonus. Its legislated goal was "to encourage high achieving candidates to enter the profession who would otherwise not consider a career in teaching" (Massachusetts State Legislature, 1998). To further this goal, the law called upon the state Department of Education to select "the best and brightest teaching prospects" and provide them with "a $20,000 signing bonus over at least three years with at least $8,000 distributed in the first year of the bonus." As Massachusetts Senate President Thomas F. Birmingham explained at the time, "This is an effort to level the playing field a little bit so teaching will not be the profession of last resort. . . ." (Ferdinand, 1998).

In order to receive each year's bonus payment ($8,000 for the first year and $4,000 for each of the three subsequent years), recipients had to be certified to teach and have a job in a Massachusetts public school. In enacting the Signing Bonus legislation, the Department of Education created a free summer training institute to provide the fifty-nine bonus recipients with an accelerated route to certification. Of the fifty teachers participating in our study, thirteen were members of the state's first group of Signing Bonus recipients. We had included them, in part, so that we could better understand how the bonus worked as an incentive and to learn about their experience teaching after having participated in a fast-track alternative certification program.

We were surprised to find that the bonus—which was widely believed to be a large financial incentive—was of modest importance to these new teachers. Recipients of the Signing Bonus who participated in our study repeatedly said that the primary incentive was the accelerated route to certification that the MSBP provided, rather than the $20,000. Indeed, in various ways, many recipients, such as Bernie, Esther, and Keisha, were already on their way to teaching and probably would have entered on their own, although it might have taken them some years to do so. The Signing Bonus Program simply "galvanized [their] resolve," as one teacher put it, by reducing the costs. Although it did not make teaching any more financially desirable, it did make quick entry feasible. It was not the prospect of the bonus, itself, that attracted them but the option of sidestepping the requirements (and costs) of preparation and licensing, which had posed powerful disincentives.

In describing the Signing Bonus Program, Esther remarked: "Oh, I think the Signing Bonus is excellent. It's a quick and dirty way to get into the classroom. I mean it's *fast*." Asked whether she was more attracted to the program by having quick access than by receiving the bonus, she responded quickly: "Oh, yes. Ask anybody who's in the program, I mean, they're not doing this for the money." Bernie, the former lawyer, had a similar response: "Oh, it wasn't the money, you know (*Laughs*). I mean, the twenty thousand over four years, I'm taking that fives times over in terms of a pay cut. . . . So it wasn't the money, it was the fast—it was the bypass of what I didn't think was necessary." The Signing Bonus Program as a whole facilitated Bernie's entry into the profession and spurred him to act on his existing interest in teaching. Before, it seemed, the costs of switching to teaching were prohibitive. Indeed, Bernie said that if he had been offered only the accelerated route to teaching without the $20,000 Signing Bonus, he "would have given it some serious consideration." However, the first year's installment of $8,000 had been useful in helping to cover his living expenses during the summer, when he had to quit his job to attend the summer institute.

A research scientist who received a Signing Bonus also spoke of the disincentive that certification requirements pose to potential career switchers. She pursued the Signing Bonus Program, "simply because of the fact [that] it's an easier process than certification. If I had to do it by myself, I would have to take so many classes and it's a thousand steps before you get to the first level [of certification]." She said that without the Signing Bonus she would not have entered teaching. However, when asked whether she would have become a teacher if she could have taken the quick route without the $20,000 bonus, she replied, "that still would have been good."

Recipients of the Signing Bonus who completed the summer training and submitted an acceptable teaching portfolio six months later received a provisional license with advanced standing, the same license awarded to individuals who successfully completed traditional teacher education programs offered by colleges and universities. Although these respondents had avoided the costs of entry, they would face the additional expense of completing a master's degree to maintain their license in the future.

In reflecting on her decision to enter teaching through an accelerated route, Esther observed that the Signing Bonus Program "got me in quick, but it also got me in low [on the salary scale]." Had she completed a master's degree while preparing to teach, her starting salary would have been higher. In support of the Signing Bonus Program, the university site where Esther completed her summer training offered participants a free master's degree if they chose to pursue it. Esther found this attractive: "Four thousand dollars [the size of annual installments], honestly, is not much money. I mean, it's a nice little chunk. But if you spread it out over a year, and after you take a third of it for taxes, you know, you would really have to look at what it was. More of my incentive is that I have a free master's at [the university]. That is more of my incentive." For Esther, the Signing Bonus Program's accelerated route to certification decreased the cost of entering the profession, and the free master's degree offered by the university helped reduce the cost of maintaining her teaching license.

Skeptics might well question whether these respondents were entirely candid in downplaying the importance of the Signing Bonus in their decisions. However, subsequent career decisions made by these individuals suggest that this financial award did not "level the field" as legislative proponents had hoped. Only five of the thirteen remained in Massachusetts public schools long enough to receive the full bonus; the others left primarily because they were not able to find the success and satisfaction in teaching they had hoped for. Other research on the program also reports high attrition rates. Education researcher Clarke Fowler (2003) completed an analysis of the recruitment, preparation, placement, and attrition of the first cohort of Signing Bonus recipients and found that in the first year of the MSBP 20 percent of the Signing Bonus recipients left teaching.

Working Conditions and Low Status: Two Aggravating Factors

There are surely many people who might become teachers, but who reject the career because of low pay. The teachers in our study, however, had chosen to teach, aware—though perhaps not fully cognizant of the implications—that their salaries would be less than what they might earn elsewhere. They had already traded— at least for the time being—the opportunity to earn high pay for the chance to do meaningful work. For this group, pay never stood alone as the reason to leave. However, when they were hampered in their work by poor working conditions and lack of public support for schooling, they often reconsidered the terms of the bargain they had struck. As former lawyer Bernie's case illustrates, low wages became a greater irritant when his job took long hours but yielded only modest success. Having no classroom or file cabinet, coping with an unrealistic quota on photocopy paper, and lacking a mentor, Bernie thought more and more about whether his move to teaching had been wise. "You know the financial payout versus the amount of time, and effort, and energy that you can put into a job, notwithstanding the time off that you have. It was very close in my mind as to whether or not it was worth it."

Midcareer entrant Mary concurred and described working in "a very critical environment," which provided little support for teachers. "So you put those things together, and people aren't going to stay with it. You know, this is an emotionally demanding job with little reward. You know, there's a lot of other things you could do with your skills, which pay better and are less emotionally demanding, and where you can still make a difference."

The teachers in our study who left teaching within three years because of low pay had never planned to stay long-term. In some cases, however, other factors that interfered with their work hastened their departure. Day to day, their dissatisfaction with pay was aggravated by other annoyances and disappointments. For example, Derek had invested in a master's program in teacher education at a private university, yet he had already decided to leave teaching after his second year at a charter school. In addition to the low pay, Derek was frustrated by the public's lack of respect for teachers and by society's failure to fund the supports needed to help children grow up healthy and ready to learn:

> One of the reasons I'm leaving the teaching profession is I don't like the shit that teachers get. . . . The way in which people outside of the profession view the profession makes me sick. . . . When they [fail to] take care of their jobs and responsibilities, and making sure that our communities are the communities in which kids can come totally prepared for school and ready to learn, then they really can't, you know, in my opinion, talk about what is wrong with our schools. . . . And that's not to say there aren't terrible teachers. . . . But to single out a group of people . . . and say that this is the reason why Massachusetts lags behind in terms of education [is unfair].

The lack of support made it difficult for Derek to achieve the personal rewards that originally drew him into teaching, and he was also disappointed by some of the dysfunctions at his school. After his third year, Derek moved into administration, where he could earn more and potentially exert greater influence on schooling.

Differentiated Pay

Respondents were also troubled by the fact that there was little they as individuals could do, beyond taking more courses, to increase their pay in the short-term or the long-term. Their salaries were based solely on their years of teaching experience and the amount of education they had completed. Esther said this was "very discouraging." For many, completing the master's degree required by the state for a long-term license would add no more than $1,000 or $2,000 to their annual salaries.

Further, the new teachers were dismayed that, day to day, the quality of their work would have no effect on their paycheck. Respondents, such as Bernie, who had come to teaching from the private sector, found this particularly galling:

> I think it should be run like a business. I think it's absolutely ludicrous that personnel decisions be based sheerly on the number of years that you've been able to survive in some place. . . . If you want the best, you need to have some level of incentive based on performance. I'm working like a dog outside of the classroom. I don't know how long I'm going to be able to maintain that type of attitude if, over the long run, really, all you can be hopeful for is to be given the same pay as somebody else who is not doing half the work that you are.

Esther, who was struggling to teach math in her urban vocational school, said: "I could have these kids doing calculus tomorrow—it's a miracle! And I would still get my step [fixed salary increase] next year. I think that's pathetic. I think that's like a major thing wrong with the entire teaching profession."

The Possibility of Performance-Based Pay

The new teachers expressed general support—some of it enthusiastic—for proposals to base some part of a teacher's pay on performance. But as they went on to discuss this option, they reiterated the many concerns that have long made merit pay difficult to implement—the threat of administrative favoritism, the difficulty of documenting performance, the problem of teachers' gaming the system. Amy conveyed the views of many when she said, "I think [performance-based pay] is a good idea . . . [but] I don't know how they would judge it."

Some teachers said that they would like their pay to reflect the amount of work they did, particularly when compared with some colleagues who seemed to do so little. However, they had no idea how a teacher's level of effort could be measured and some wondered whether effort, in itself, warranted extra pay. Others, such as Amy, suggested that student performance could be used as a measure: "I guess they could judge it kind of what we were doing with the baseline in September, seeing how much the kids are improved." But others, such as Mary, doubted that teachers deserved to be fully credited or fully blamed for students' performance on standardized tests. She was "uncomfortable with that idea because I feel there are so many other factors that have to do with learning besides teaching." Some said that test scores could never begin to measure all their accomplishments. Victoria wondered whether looking at "how well you test, and how well you perform" makes sense: "Is that a good measure? I don't know if it is." She said she was "all for getting us better pay, but I think it has to be a way where all those who deserve it should get it." Others worried that pay based on test scores would encourage teachers to work only with students likely to show the greatest gains. Despite his dissatisfaction with pay, Derek thought that basing a teacher's salary on student performance was "just a bad idea." He worried that it would reward teachers "who can't teach or who can't do anything, [but who] work in homogenous classrooms with A-plus kids," while others (like himself) who work with students "who really need specific help" would "get nothing. . . . You know, somebody will be judged harshly because of something not in their control."

Some respondents saw promise in a career ladder that would allow teachers to advance to higher levels and more pay as they demonstrated increasing competence and assumed greater levels of responsibility. But for these teachers, who with very few exceptions worked in schools that offered only fixed roles and pay, a career ladder was no more than an idea. They would base their decisions about whether to remain in teaching on the limited options currently available to them.

Taking Pay Seriously

The teachers in our study had decided to teach in the context of a strong economy, which probably had heightened their attention to what they might have been paid in other lines of work. Also, recently published reports suggested that the opportunity costs of choosing to teach had increased dramatically for prospective teachers (Henke, Chen & Geis, 2000; Olson, 2000). However, as the economy weakened after September 2001 and their peers in other careers lost jobs, they may have become less critical of their pay and more appreciative of the job security that teaching has historically provided. Still, pay will surely remain an ongoing concern, one that may intensify as the supports for good teaching are eroded further by budget cuts.

The individuals in our study chose teaching for its intrinsic rewards and hoped that they could afford to do the work that would yield these personal rewards. However, when the public assails teachers' intellect and effort, the legislature severely cuts school funding, and teachers encounter working conditions that increase the difficulty of teaching, the fact that they are barely breaking even takes on greater weight. Some leave teaching. Others contemplate it.

The next generation of teachers has career options that the retiring generation never had. Although our interviews show that money alone—even a substantial signing bonus of $20,000—will not keep teachers in teaching, it is also clear that personal rewards, in themselves, are not enough. They do not pay the bills or reassure teachers that the public values their work. If schools are to attract the strongest possible pool of candidates, teachers' pay must be competitive with careers that also vie for their talent and skills. Therefore, it makes good sense to raise teachers' pay and devise new ways to reward initiative and achievement. Yet such changes must also be matched with improved conditions of teaching. Otherwise, able teachers will find a way to do good work elsewhere.

Chapter Four

Seeking Success with Students

Coauthor: Sarah E. Birkeland

Most teachers enter the profession in search of meaningful work, with the hope of influencing the lives of children and making a difference in the larger community. As Fred put it, "it's the kids that we're here for." Teaching students effectively is both complex and uncertain work. The goals of successful teaching have long been ambiguous, and recent changes in the context of public education have added new pressures as well as new uncertainties. Students, too, serve as a source of uncertainty for teachers, as successful teaching ultimately relies on students' engagement and transformation. Teachers' prospects for forging productive relationships with their students are far from assured; however, achieving success with students—something the new teachers in our sample described as both relational and academic—is key to teachers' interest in staying in their schools and in the profession.

The Intrinsic Rewards of Teaching

For many teachers, spending each day with children is, in itself, a source of joy. Carolyn, whose first position entailed teaching all subjects to twenty-one fifth graders, did not like everything about the job, but she did enjoy the students: "I came into teaching because I enjoy working with kids. . . . Since I've been here, I've really loved it, and I love being with kids and just having the opportunity to really touch their lives." Second grade teacher Amy, who only half-heartedly considered other careers before settling on teaching, said it was the opportunity to spend her days among children that drew her: "I had always loved working with children."

Many, like Keisha, came to teaching in hopes of giving children the academic tools they will need to succeed as adults. As a second grade teacher, Keisha found an opportunity to help children learn to read and write competently while they were still young. She saw an urgency to her work that had been missing before: "To me it is a life or death situation. If the kids don't get the proper education, they are dead in society." Others want to share a subject they love, like the teacher in our sample who said he chose the profession because, "I get to interact with kids [and] I get to talk about history, which I like doing."

Mary, who left a career in social services to teach, was less focused on academics than on helping children develop into healthy adults. For her, teaching provided an opportunity to build relationships that would aid students in their personal and social development. She explained, "The core of what was really appealing to me about teaching was having the kind of relationship with a person where you would help them develop. . . . And I think in terms of the subject matter, it really wasn't as important to me." She enjoyed the opportunity to be part of her students' larger community, interacting with them in the grocery store and at the movies as well as in the classroom.

Pride in doing socially responsible work motivated several of the people in our sample to teach. A third grade teacher explained that this was integral to his decision to teach:

> First of all it would just be simply the enjoyment of being around children, and kind of the energy that comes from that. . . . And then if you take it to the step of thinking about careers, it's really the sense of social service, that it's a good thing to do. . . . And so it satisfies my own kind of morals or grounding, whatever you want to call it. Sense of feeling good about what I am spending my time doing. . . . And there is just a certain level of pride that comes

along with that. Of course it's a real challenge, too. But I think it's worth it.

For some, teaching was about giving back to society. Carolyn said she knew she wanted to teach "underprivileged" children who did not have access to the same opportunities she had as a child; another teacher in our sample was certain from the outset that she wanted to work with "city kids." The feeling that she was helping children sustained her. She explained, "If anything, I am completely, pleasantly surprised by how good this job makes me feel. I said to someone once, 'People say being a teacher is so selfless. It's such a generous job.' But I leave here sometimes feeling completely selfish, because [the] kids just feed you."

The Ambiguous Goals of Teaching

For all of its potential rewards, teaching is uncertain work. In some professions goals are clear and explicit, and success is easily measurable. Increasing the profit margin of a business, transporting a busload of people safely from here to there, or building a set of cabinets to fit a particular space each offers a straightforward outcome; success in those cases can be seen and measured. As sociologist Dan Lortie pointed out in his influential 1975 book, *Schoolteacher*, teaching does not have such straightforward outcomes. This is because the purposes of schooling extend well beyond the intellectual; schools are also charged with the social, emotional, and moral development of children. Given the various purposes of education, teaching's goals are hard to define, in turn making their attainment hard to measure.

Teachers receive multiple, sometimes conflicting, messages about their roles. They are supposed to build skills while nurturing creativity and a love for learning, foster development of the "whole child" while closing the achievement gap, and respond to the individual needs of students while managing the group. These goals are overarching; one of the "givens" of being a teacher is knowing you will not be able to do all that society asks of you.

The Changed Context of Teaching

Since the retiring generation began teaching in the late 1960s, the work of the classroom teacher has changed dramatically. Federal involvement in education policy has generated increased funding for meeting the needs of all students through legislation such as Title I and the Individuals with Disabilities Education Act. It has also generated more regulations, paper work, and accountability mechanisms for teachers. As we better understand learning disabilities, differences in learning style, and conditions such as attention deficit hyperactivity disorder, teachers must learn to address them effectively. Students who were once pulled out of classrooms for individual instruction are now mainstreamed. Students whose cognitive and physical disabilities once precluded them from participating in school are now guaranteed education. Public schools take on a growing commitment to meeting all students' needs, every day, with little additional support or training for the teachers who are charged with that task.

Schools also have taken on extensive custodial functions, such as serving breakfast, sponsoring after-school programs, and providing medical and psychological services on site. Teachers now are asked to conduct classes on sexuality or drugs and alcohol; they are required to report suspected physical abuse or suspicious activity to local authorities; and they are called upon to "bully-proof" schools and instill a sense of safety.

It has become increasingly apparent that traditional schooling has failed to academically prepare many students, particularly students of color living in low-income communities. Experts have shown that the skill levels of high school graduates are declining, yet the skills required to hold today's middle-class jobs are more complex than they were three decades ago (Murnane & Levy, 1996). Responding both to the public's demand for accountability and to the requirements of *No Child Left Behind*, all states now have instituted standardized tests to monitor students' academic progress. Some of these assessments carry "high stakes" because they determine which students will be promoted to the next grade or graduate from high school. Schools that fall below the established performance standards can be taken over by state officials or closed down altogether, and parents have the right to remove their children from low-performing schools. Faced with exams that carry such far-reaching consequences, teachers experience increased pressure to deliver high test scores for the sake of their students, their schools, and themselves.

Students Introduce Uncertainty

Students are at the center of a teacher's world. They are the reason teachers go to work each day, the focus of planning and preparation, and teachers' daily companions in the classroom. Teachers loom large in students' experiences, as well. Recent research by William Sanders at the University of Tennessee demonstrates that the teacher is the single most important factor in student achievement—more important than the curriculum, students' socioeconomic status, or the other students in the room. One good teacher can have lasting positive impact, but the negative effect of one bad teacher can also stick with a child for years (Sanders & Rivers, 1998).

Yet new teachers are often deeply unsure about whether they will be able to teach their students effectively and build productive relationships with them. Will the students do what I ask them to do? Will they know what I expect them to know, and have the skills they need to do my assignments? Will they learn what I try to teach them? Students "co-produce results" with teachers, and successful learning depends on the will, cooperation, and skill of both (Cohen, 1988, p. 55). As Carolyn explained, "this is just a profession where you could have everything perfectly planned and organized and thought of, and one kid can come in in an angry mood and change the whole day."

Uncertainty About What to Expect from Students

New teachers bring to their work various degrees of past experience with children, and that experience often mediates their expectations of what students will be like. Many of the teachers in our study had worked with children as tutors or camp counselors before they decided to teach. Amy, for example, had nine years of experience working in an after-school program. When her students entered the classroom on her first day as a second grade teacher, she already knew what it might be like to spend the day surrounded by seven-year-olds. Derek and Keisha, both of whom are African American and both of whom chose to teach in schools serving predominately African American students, also described feeling at ease with their students' communities. As Keisha put it, "The kids are not a surprise to me, that I would have to say. The types of kids that are in the class—inner city. I'm used to it. I grew up in New York. I get that. That was probably the most normal part."

However, the students—their behavior, their skills, and their needs—can be the most surprising part of teaching for new teachers. This is particularly true for those who have been out of school themselves for a long time, or who are teaching in schools outside of the communities most familiar to them. Having imagined teaching as joyous and heroic work, new teachers often are surprised by the realities of students' lives and unprepared for the difficulties of day-to-day classroom management. The first year of teaching can be a period of adjustment and rapid learning—adjusting to the group of students in the class and learning how to reach them.

Uncertainty About Student Engagement and Discipline

Willard Waller's classic 1932 study of teaching emphasized the importance to new teachers of gaining and keeping authority; indeed, the struggle to maintain student discipline has long been a theme in new teachers' discussions of their work. However, a second, sometimes conflicting theme arises as well: the importance of forming bonds with students in order to engage and motivate them (Feiman-Nemser & Floden, 1986). The tension between these goals creates ambiguity, especially for new teachers. Brenda described the struggle to allow her middle school Spanish students the voice they wanted, while also maintaining order:

> It seems like the kids' attitude is one of, that anything that you present them is up for debate, or anything as far as classroom procedures or just systems that are in place can be debated and changed if they want to. There's very much a feeling [among students] like 'We're the ones that should be able to say what we want in here.' And that's difficult. . . . I am definitely one that thinks, you know, you should listen to kids, what they want, their voices. But the way they talk to each other and to adults, I'm just blown away. . . . It's definitely made me have to tap into strength that I didn't know I had. It's hard. It's hard not to come away some days feeling like my ego has just been completely, completely deflated.

When she left her job in public health research to become a teacher, Brenda was prepared for long hours and difficult work. She knew she had a lot to learn about how to plan and conduct lessons, and how to organize her time and materials. However, she was not prepared to struggle every day to maintain authority in her classroom.

Other teachers reported being surprised at how hard it was to win students' attention and keep them engaged. A high school history teacher who had hoped students would love the topic as much as he did wryly remarked, "Well, maybe there's one kid in the class who's excited about the Middle Ages." He relied on tight, well-articulated classroom routines to keep his students on task. A former research scientist in her first year teaching at a predominately white, middle-class high school lamented, "out of the ninety to ninety-five kids I have, probably like maybe two kids are actually interested in science. . . . It is a required class so they have to pass. They're there because of that." She was surprised at how little the students—"even the good ones"—seemed to care about her class and struggled mightily with classroom management: "I dreaded those ninety minute classes."

Student disengagement, and the negative behavior often associated with it, is common in schools all over the country: based on a large survey study of American teenagers, Laurence Steinberg, a psychologist who studies adolescents, reported that fewer than 20 percent of high school students say that their friends think getting good grades is important, and one in three students say they get through the day by "goofing off with friends" (1996, p. 18).

There were a few teachers in our study of Massachusetts new teachers who reported having an easy time managing and engaging their students. Victoria, one of the few, commented that even in the first few months of her first year of teaching third grade she felt comfortable leaving her students alone in the room and confident that they would behave appropriately: "The students are fine when I leave the room. And they'll work when I leave if I need to ask a teacher something or if I need to go run down to make copies." She chose this well-resourced, high-achieving school in part for its reputation as one in which students behaved well. She said, "I wanted to teach in [a] setting where I actually feel like I am teaching the content instead of having to handle or deal with a lot of the other issues."

Uncertainty About Students' Skill and Preparedness

Also surprising to many new teachers is the low level of skill and knowledge many students possess. Even Keisha, who came to her school expecting to address what she saw as a growing literacy problem among African American children, was amazed by what she found in the classroom. "I'm just appalled at the amount of kids that can't read or can't read on grade level." She knew that her school had an unusually high concentration of students reading below grade level—83 percent—but reading levels in the rest of the district were similarly discouraging. According to the Massachusetts Department of Education, 65 percent of the third graders in Keisha's district were reading below grade level in 2002, as were 33 percent of the third graders in the state (www.profiles.doe.mass.edu).

Students' low skill levels can be discouraging for teachers as well as students. Brenda wondered whether studying for her Spanish classes was a good use of her students' time, given their lack of skill in math and literacy: "In the eighth grade, they're functioning at a fourth grade reading and math level. And I just ask myself, like, yes, they should have the opportunity to learn a foreign language. But they don't want to, you know. That's the last thing they want to do. And I feel like, in some ways, it's almost unfair to be expecting them to be learning grammar in another language when . . . they're struggling so much just in their first language."

Uncertainty About the Limits of Teacher Responsibility

Teachers struggle to define and limit their responsibilities for the children they teach. They are responsible for teaching academics, but many children need much more than academic support. Teaching can be isolating work, and it is easy for a teacher to feel as though she is the only person in a position to help a given child. Sometimes figuring out how best to help that child is a challenge. Amy shared one such example: "There is one child in my classroom that I am really concerned about. Last year he had three deaths in his family . . . all three by gang violence. One was his brother, one was his uncle, one was his cousin. So he has been up and down all year, a very big behavior problem, even before these incidents happened. So that just made it even worse." Amy wondered how best to support this child emotionally and academically, given the recent events in his life. She described the school social worker as "pretty helpful" in general, but "very busy," leaving Amy on her own to provide support for her student while also attending to the needs of the group.

Mary was surprised by the level of personal responsibility she felt toward her students and by the challenge of determining her role in helping them cope with the day-to-day issues of teenage life:

"They are fourteen-year-olds. I mean, half of them, the parents are split up, and they have a lot of needs." Halfway through her first year of teaching she said,

> It's a little different than what I expected. I think what's different about it is sort of the sense of responsibility. I mean, I expected, of course, there would be a sense of responsibility in terms of the work. But [I did not expect] the sense of responsibility with children who belong to other people. And the values, and culture, and different family issues that the children bring with them to school. And how do you—what is your role and responsibility with these kids, wherever they're coming from? And that's a part for me that is much more complex than I thought it would be.

For some, like Keisha, being able to see students' many needs but not being able to meet them was overwhelming and disheartening. When she described the students in her first school she said, "They are on so many different reading levels. How do you attend to all of these different needs? It's just me. I was feeling unbelievable guilt. There is no way I can do this." Striving to reach all of the students by herself, while she was also learning how to plan and teach lessons, exhausted her.

Crossing Borders

As the new teachers we interviewed discussed their struggles to build productive working relationships with students, they often raised issues of race and social class. Some observed disparities in the achievement levels of white and minority students in their schools and tried to understand why they existed and what they, as teachers, could do about them. For example, Brenda noticed disturbing trends in her large urban middle school. She described the lower-level classes as "mostly Latino students, African American students and white—very much working class students." The honors classes in her school included "white students, more privileged, a few African American students, and one or two Latino students. It very much feels broken up by race, by class." She did not know what she could do as an individual to address the inequities. "It just feels bad. . . . I just go in there and I'm faced with all these issues . . . even more than what I expected."

Achievement test scores in Massachusetts vary dramatically by race, and tracked classes often break down along racial lines as well. In 2002, white third graders were more than twice as likely to be reading at or above grade level than African American or Hispanic third graders; a similar pattern held in tenth grade (www.profiles. mass.doe.edu). Laurence Steinberg also reports differences by race in student engagement in school—defined by concentration, effort, participation, and care (1996, p. 15). In his survey of American teenagers, Asian American and white students reported the highest levels of engagement and African American and Latino students the least (1996, p. 87). Asian American and white students also reported feeling more control over their school achievement than African American and Latino students.

Racial patterns in student achievement and engagement surely have complex causes, but student-teacher relationships form some part of the equation. Teachers report that building positive, productive relationships with children is more difficult when they do not share characteristics such as social expectations, race, ethnicity, and first language with their students, and many teachers lack the skills and knowledge to form successful bonds across such differences (Dilworth & Brown, 2001).

Understanding the difficulties that so many teachers experience in teaching across race and class is not easy. Several scholars argue that significant cultural differences exist among different racial and ethnic groups in the United States; teachers may attribute unfamiliar classroom behavior to students' problems or deficits when they are, in fact, the result of cultural differences (Delpit, 1988; Irvine, 1990). Gloria Ladson-Billings, who writes about successful teachers of African-American children, argues that teachers are more likely to succeed with students when they see themselves as members of the students' larger communities (1994).

While the proportion of teachers of color in this country is declining and the proportion of students of color is growing steadily (Snyder & Hoffman, 2003), the question of how to ensure that no child is left behind remains unanswered. Some people believe that recruiting more minority teachers is the best option, though the diversity of student populations within individual schools means that teachers will always encounter students who are different from themselves. Others advocate more extensive teacher preparation designed to train candidates to effectively teach across race, class, and cultural differences. Whatever the approaches, today's teachers must find ways to reach the students who come to their classes, and they must do so in a profession structured with the assumption that teaching is the same work no matter the context. It is difficult for any teacher— and particularly a new one—to do this without support.

The Importance of Efficacy in New Teachers' Career Decisions

New teachers' perceptions of whether or not they were meeting the needs of the students in their classrooms—their sense of efficacy— infused their accounts of job satisfaction and career plans. Given the low pay and low status associated with teaching, this attention to achieving intrinsic rewards is not surprising. However, these teachers described images of successful teaching that were both personal and measured; no one expected to teach flawlessly from day one. For example, one midcareer entrant explained what it would take to keep him in teaching: "I'll need a sense of success, not unqualified constant success, because I know that's completely unrealistic. But, overall, you know, on average, that I'm making more of a difference for kids and that they're learning from me." That sense of success is not easy to come by, but when teachers achieved it, they felt encouraged to remain in their schools and in teaching.

When the new teachers we interviewed reflected on what they were most proud of in their work, they nearly always spoke about their relationships with students. Derek, despite a tough first year in the chaotic environment of a new charter school, remarked, "I'm proud of my connection with my students. I have a really good connection with my students. But I question whether or not I'm really making a difference in their experiences. So that kind of tempers the pride I feel in terms of my connection." He was not sure whether he was making enough academic progress with them. If all of the students went on to college, he explained, "that would be a real indicator of progress."

Fred, a white teacher in a low-income, high-minority school, said that given his middle-class, private school upbringing, "getting used to urban kids" was one of the most difficult parts of teaching. However, the relationships he formed with students were his greatest source of pride: "I think the fact that the kids can come to me with anything, that I'm more than a teacher, that I'm a mentor to them. That makes me proud that I can have that effect on the kids. And that's why I became a teacher." He elaborated, "I sometimes put so much work into my career that it gets frustrating when you don't think the kids appreciate it . . . [but] most of my frustration comes from things that happen outside of school and my classroom."

Keisha, too, was buoyed by her success with students during an otherwise difficult first year. "I have already begun to move some kids along, which is great." Victoria also described her teaching job as "great," because "I feel like I'm influencing their lives, and what they think, and how they learn. . . . And it's going well so far. I'm very satisfied, happy." She had found a sense of success with students, at least for the short-term.

As new teachers looked ahead and considered their career plans, their feelings of success with students again surfaced as paramount. One teacher in the sample explained, "This is a really, really hard job, and you don't get a lot back. I mean, the things that you get back, if you're looking for feedback, I guess you get it in success with your students. . . . You don't get it back in terms of how well you're paid, or what your benefits are, or any of those sorts of things."

Esther and Bernie: Learning to Work with Students

Esther and Bernie both came to teaching in their mid-thirties after working for a number of years in higher-paying, more prestigious fields. Both grew up in working-class households, enjoyed school, and thought of themselves as high achievers. When they decided to become teachers, both chose the Massachusetts Signing Bonus Program, which offered abbreviated training and immediate access to classroom teaching jobs. Esther and Bernie, both white, accepted jobs in large, diverse public high schools. About two-thirds of the students in Bernie's high school were white, and about a fifth qualified for subsidized lunch; Esther's vocational high school was fairly evenly split between whites and minorities, with nearly half of the students receiving subsidized lunches.

Although these two teachers' initial responses to the students were similar, the results for Esther and Bernie were different. Bernie remained at his school and sought to improve in his teaching there, while Esther left to teach in a more homogenous, affluent school. The difference in their experiences hinged on two related factors: the support they received from their colleagues and administrators, and the level of success they achieved with their students.

Difficulty with Classroom Management

During the first two weeks of teaching math at her vocational high school, Esther thought about quitting every day. She could not figure out how to get her students to listen to her. In December of that first year, she reported, "They won't sit still; their rudeness; their total disrespect for each other; for the teacher; their language; everything. They can't speak to you; they only yell . . . I have never seen anything like it. It has gotten a little bit better, but they still have no respect for a teacher at all, for an adult, you know, nothing. And it's really hard . . . there's nothing I could do that would make a difference." She had expected her teenaged students to be more mature, disciplined, and ready to learn. "It's like, 'you're in high school, guys.' Coming prepared is such a problem. But they're just kind of rude and obnoxious. And everybody always needs something and of course [it's] the most important thing in the world. They're teenagers, and they're undisciplined."

Bernie left corporate law for teaching in part because he so valued his own education; he had assumed that students would participate willingly, if not gratefully, in the quest for knowledge: "I expected there to be classroom management issues. I expected it to be, though, where I would get in with a group of kids and treat them like people. And they'd gel together and buy into my plan, you know? Bring all their materials, be prepared, their pencils." Students did not buy into Bernie's plan as readily as he thought they would. Their seeming lack of interest in learning surprised him: "It's been a lot more challenging [than I expected], in terms of having a handle on the classroom management piece . . . I'm still trying to get even the kids that are the quote-unquote 'honors kids' to get into the classroom on time and be ready to go."

This basic difficulty in controlling the class frustrated and demoralized both Bernie and Esther. Bernie confided that when he decided to teach, he had not anticipated the amount of time he would spend "battling" with students: "I've been in control of anything I've ever done, you know? . . . And I just don't like the feeling of the loss of control that I once had. I could have an entire boardroom at my command—people that were twice my age had to listen to me and do what I say. . . . Going from that to having young girls talk back to you when you tell them they can't leave without a pass. It's just a little bit too much right now."

Students' Skills and Engagement

Bernie and Esther also were taken aback by the low skill levels of the students in their classes. Their dreams of shared inquiry into heady problems faded, and they changed their instructional approaches. Halfway through his first year, Bernie remarked, "I'm surprised at the writing level of all the kids, and their level of where they should be right now, in terms of basic skills. . . . Some of the kids really can't read." His original teaching plans had relied heavily on students' reading the history textbook on their own, which he quickly realized would be a problem. He scrambled to find teaching approaches that would be effective, asking other teachers for advice about how to teach history to students with low reading skills. He recalled, "I tried pair-reading and reading groups, but a lot of the kids can't stand each other anyway, and they won't get into pairs or groups." By mid-year, Bernie had settled on a strategy of having the stronger readers read aloud to the entire class. He was not especially proud of this teaching strategy, but said, "They seem to enjoy it."

Esther knew students' low skill levels made it difficult for them to succeed in her class, but she also felt that they simply were not trying. She contrasted her students' efforts to her own as a child. She remembered feeling motivated to do well in school, and wondered why her students did not behave as though they felt the same way: "I've never taken a test where I didn't try. I have kids come in, I'll be giving them a quiz: 'Ah Miss, I can't do this today,' and they'll give me their paper back, and they'll put their head down, take a zero. I let them come in and make it up, but you know most of the time they won't come back in. They'll just take the zero."

The Role of Collegial Support

Although Bernie and Esther encountered similar difficulties adjusting to their students, they had access to different levels of resources and support. Bernie did not find much in the way of schoolwide structures to support him, but he did learn some things from the people around him. For example, colleagues shared ideas for instructional strategies they thought might work well and showed him common procedures, such as how to document classroom incidents. Esther received little help in reaching students from the teachers and administrators in her school. She said her ineffectual principal—whom her colleagues openly mocked in the teachers' room—did not seem to like her, and other teachers kept their doors closed before and after school. Aside from another new teacher with whom she shared ideas and one veteran who offered informal advice when they met during hall duty, she felt she was on her own in learning to reach her students.

Identification with Students

Bernie was surprised by the realities of teaching, yet he felt that fundamentally his students were like him. He capitalized on his sense of connection to the community. He said, "I like the type of kid that I get. When I say 'the type of kid,' I mean, I guess, their demographic make-up. I come from a working-class, middle-class town, and I think [the community in which I teach] pretty much is diverse. And I like the fact that it's diverse." Although Esther came to like her students over the course of the year ("they get nicer as you get to know them"), she found little common ground: "I was just 'What am I doing? . . . Why am I beating myself up with kids that don't care?' And it is a shame that they don't. But I couldn't make them. Maybe if I were more experienced, just a different kind of teacher, maybe I could make them."

Both Esther and Bernie had much less success in reaching students than they had originally hoped for, but Bernie found more moments of connection than Esther did, and those moments kept him engaged and optimistic. Bernie said, "Believe me, there are days when the class grooves, and the kids are engaged and they're with you, and there are no behavioral problems. In general, I think that all my kids respect me and like me. But their idea of respect sometimes really doesn't jive with what it actually is. So there are days where I feel great about what's being done in my classroom."

Esther had few such shining days. She sometimes felt that she was doing the students a disservice, and often felt frustrated by her interactions with them. "'You're not a good teacher.' They tell me that all the time. 'You're not a good teacher.' I don't understand.

They've been dozing. They've been talking with their friend." The students blamed her when classes did not go well, though she believed they were not giving her a chance. How could a student criticize her lesson when he had been talking to a friend throughout the class period? With no help from administrators or colleagues, Esther felt that she alone shouldered responsibility for engaging the students, and she did not know how to do it. Learning to teach was hard enough; learning to teach on her own, with students whose disengagement and behavior so surprised her, was overwhelming.

The Decision to Stay, Move, or Leave

As his first year of teaching drew to a close, Bernie signed on for another year at his school. He had not been as successful a teacher as he would have liked his first year, but he felt that he was making progress. He said,

> I'm not sure that I have [the skills and resources]—and I'm not sure if anybody does—to do the job right . . . meaning how you deal with the kids, how you reach them. Because the kids come from all different walks of life, and all different emotional backgrounds. . . . You know, you try to reach a kid and get him motivated, and do it in a variety of different ways. And I'm learning how to do that. And hopefully having some success—maybe I don't know how successful I am. Maybe I am doing it, and I just don't know.

Though Bernie saw room for improvement, he felt successful enough to want to come back.

Bernie's second year went much more smoothly than his first. He was more comfortable in his role and more prepared for what might happen in his classroom: "I think it was 90 percent me being better, and 10 percent having a different schedule. . . . It was definitely much more enjoyable, less hectic. You know, I was able to be more proactive in my classroom management stuff right at the beginning of the year, and the beginning of every class. And that just led to it being a nonissue, really, for the whole year." With classroom management under control, Bernie could focus on refining his lessons. Three years later, Bernie was still teaching history at the same high school.

Esther did not stay. Feeling exhausted and defeated in the spring of her first year, she decided to leave her first school and look elsewhere for work. "It was too hard emotionally. There was nothing I could do. I needed something good. Somebody needed to learn— want to learn something. . . . I think I would have tried it another year because there were kids there that were very nice, but the administration was not overly supportive." Esther found a job teaching math at a more affluent high school near her home. As she left the vocational high school she was surprised and touched by the students' reactions. "It was funny. When I quit the last day of school last year . . . when I told the kids I wasn't coming back, they said, 'Why are you leaving us? What did we do to you?' I am thinking, 'What did you do to me? What did you call me? What did you do?'" Their dismay at her departure was genuine—"They were really deadpan about that"—leading Esther to reconsider her sense of failure to reach them, but not enough to make her want to stay.

At her new high school, which served predominately white, middle class students, Esther found a more familiar community, supportive colleagues, and administrators and achieved a much greater sense of success. As she continued to learn how to teach, she had mentors and resources available to her. In this setting she also found it easier to connect with the students, whom she described as "more respectful and more there for learning" than the vocational education students she had taught her first year. She recalled that at the end of the year at her new school, "I had several students say 'You have to keep teaching. You did a good job.'" The positive feedback heartened her, for reaching students was a key reason she had switched careers in the first place.

Esther regarded her decision to leave the vocational high school with some regret, wishing she had found a way to succeed with her students there. She deemed her decision to transfer "unfortunate, because a part of the [Massachusetts Signing Bonus Program was that] they wanted people in the inner city. But I think they need to do a better job preparing them to get there, if that is truly what their function is."

Had she decided to stay at that high school, Esther might or might not have found greater success over time, but her story illustrates an important phenomenon. Learning to teach is difficult, complex work; learning to teach students from markedly different backgrounds is even more complex. New teachers need support and guidance in order to achieve success, yet that support is often hardest to come by in low-income urban and rural schools, which very often have few institutional resources and low levels of student achievement. Those schools, in turn, have a harder time keeping teachers. The result is the steady turnover of teachers in high-poverty and high-minority schools and a staffing disparity between the low-income and high-income schools in the nation (Haycock, 1998).

Teacher Turnover and Student Characteristics

Esther's decision to leave her urban vocational school for a suburban high school is not unusual. Recent work by researchers studying teacher turnover in Texas and New York State (Hanushek, Kain, & Rivkin, 2001; Lankford, Loeb, & Wyckoff, 2002) reveals that teachers in those states who changed schools consistently moved to schools with "higher achieving, non-minority, non-low income students" (Hanushek et al., 2001, p.12). Those higher-income, higher-achieving schools tend to be in the suburbs; studies of teacher turnover paint a picture of new teachers' urban flight.

A pattern that looked like urban flight emerged in the career decisions of the fifty new Massachusetts teachers, as well. One of the most striking aspects of their career decisions is that every teacher in the sample who voluntarily transferred moved to a school serving wealthier students. Sometimes this change was dramatic and involved moving from a high-minority, low-income inner city school to a wealthier, whiter suburban school; sometimes it involved moving from a racially diverse or predominately minority, low-income urban school to another in the same district that served a slightly higher income population of students.

Research conducted with large quantitative datasets, such as the studies mentioned above, shows overarching patterns of who moved, where, and when. In our study, teachers explained *why* they moved from school to school. Achieving success with students—building positive relationships and fostering academic achievement—was paramount. As they spoke about their experiences, it became clear just how many factors came into play. They explained that they were transferring not in search of wealthier students, but in search of more supportive work environments. Achieving a sense of success was related less to the characteristics of the students than to the character of the school.

Keisha moved from one low-income, low-performing, high-minority school to another school with similar demographics and found stark differences between the two. The lack of structure and administrative support in her first school made the job seem impossible to her. In December of her first year she remarked, "All of my issues with the situation are not with the kids. . . . because the kids are the reason why we are all here. That is not going to change. But some [structures of support] clearly need to be put in place . . . as a first-year teacher there are so many things that you're dealing with." She left a school where she felt isolated and frustrated for one in which the environment was "really inviting and really supportive." At her new school, she was confident that she would not be left to struggle alone. "There is an expectation that you're a professional and you're going to do the best job that you can possibly do. If you need help, we're here to help you and support you." That sense of shared responsibility and the consistent focus on learning have been important for Keisha's sense of success and satisfaction.

Although many teachers migrated toward higher-income schools in search of environments in which they could teach successfully, a few of our teachers took their first jobs in high-minority, low-income schools and chose to stay. Four white teachers in our sample stayed in schools in which more than three-quarters of students qualified for subsidized lunches and more than half were students of color. They attribute their satisfaction to a host of school-level factors that buttress successful teaching: supportive administrators and colleagues, schoolwide emphasis on learning, clear expectations for students, and safe, orderly environments. Amy, one of those four teachers, called her school "the best school" in the city. The school has a reputation as a serious place, where learning is valued and students do well. Amy did not have as many resources available to her as did teachers in more affluent schools, but she became savvy about finding them. She felt very successful with her students, and she planned to stay at that school for the foreseeable future.

School Cultures and Conditions Facilitate Teachers' Success

The environment of the school ultimately mediates teachers' ability to find satisfaction in succeeding with students: what courses are taught, how students are grouped, what supports are available for students and teachers, what kinds of behavior are encouraged and discouraged. The fifty Massachusetts teachers consistently sought schools where the cultures and conditions facilitated student learning. That they often found those schools in high-income, suburban communities probably points to inequity in the distribution of resources among schools and an associated disparity in schools' capacities to support teachers. Yet as Keisha's and Amy's stories demonstrate, supportive conditions for successful teaching can be found in schools that are often thought of as hard places to teach. When those schools maintain orderly environments focused on learning and build in supports for teachers, the teachers are, in turn, better able to achieve a sense of success with students and perhaps are more likely to stay.

Chapter Five

Schools That Support New Teachers

Some schools are organized to support new teachers in succeeding with their students. These schools not only celebrate learning and promote hard work but also provide teachers and students with the infrastructure needed to work together productively. They organize time and space so that teachers are well connected with regular opportunities to exchange ideas and information.

Such schools have present, active, and responsive administrators who develop personal relations with their new staff, assign them an appropriate set of courses, and arrange for them to receive constructive feedback about their teaching. Experienced colleagues in the school are available so that new teachers can observe and consult with them in an ongoing way.

In addition to supportive colleagues and current curricula, such schools have sufficient supplies and equipment so that teachers can do their job without having to forage for basic resources or fund them from their own pocket. Also important, these schools have schoolwide expectations for student behavior and they uphold the same approach to discipline throughout, thus enabling new teachers to manage their classes effectively from the first day. They offer an organized set of student support services, which new teachers can count on in addressing the many needs of their students.

Some teachers we interviewed described working in schools where such supports make success not only possible but likely. Many others told of schools that failed them in many regards, failures that would be likely to increase the rates of teacher attrition and transfer. Brenda was one.

Brenda's School

Brenda's experience teaching Spanish in an urban middle school was one of the most dramatic and troubling in our study. A native Spanish speaker with no training in how to teach a foreign language, Brenda was assigned to teach 210 students in ten classes. Her sixth grade students met twice weekly; her seventh and eighth graders met three times. Because each grade was tracked, Brenda had many more preparations than her colleagues in math or English, who typically had no more than three preparations for their five classes. Brenda remarked, "Just thinking about the work, what I was given as a first-year teacher coming in, I mean, two hundred-plus students. I mean, realistically, how well could I have done? It just seems like a complete setup."

Although most of her colleagues had time set aside for team, or grade-level, meetings, Brenda's assignment and schedule made it impossible for her to attend all the meetings she thought she should: "I go to eighth grade cluster meetings. . . . I mean, obviously, it would be one of my [planning periods]. But, then, that meant that I didn't have a prep that day. So, in the beginning I didn't [go]. . . . But it turns out that it seems important just to go with the grade that is the most difficult, just to kind of know where the students are at and what may be going on."

Brenda wanted feedback about her teaching, but found it hard to come by. She had initially expected help from her principal, who had encouraged her to apply to the school. She had expected her principal to be invested in her success but seldom found her available: "She's very busy. She's very busy. . . . It's hard for me to say, though, what specifically she does." She wished her principal would visit her classes more often: "Every once in a while, especially at the beginning of the year, she would just stop in, walk by and come in and see how things were going." But over time, the principal's visits ceased, and Brenda worried that her principal had given up on her.

Brenda's formal foreign language supervisor, who was located in another school, did visit her periodically, but she did not find his visits helpful. In his own classes, he kept candy in his pockets and threw pieces to students who answered correctly. After observing Brenda, he suggested that she break her class period into ten three- to five-minute segments and move quickly and enthusiastically from topic to topic, an approach Brenda dismissed as "trite." She acknowledged that "in some ways, you could see [his classroom observation] as support, but it didn't feel that supportive to me."

Despite having worked in a nonprofit organization that was never flush with resources, Brenda was surprised that her new workplace was so spare and provided so little to support her work:

> You know, it's not like I'm in awful conditions, like rats running around the room or anything. But I come from nonprofit, a research organization, not making a lot of money but social issues, researching, working with adults. But if I needed to photocopy something, there was a photocopier there. There were computers. There were phones. And to think that we expect to educate kids not having any—we have one copier at the school. And, of course, no phones in the rooms—that goes without saying. So put that together with just feeling kind of beaten down and so exhausted at the end of the day, every day. I think it's a wonder that anyone stays.

Brenda encountered discipline problems in her classes, most dramatically when two of her students called her a "bitch" in class. She realized that "things [felt] sort of out of control" and that she could not resolve the problem herself: "I just felt like I needed help." But her requests for help went largely unanswered. She spoke with her principal who "indicated that she would come and talk to the class." However, the principal "didn't show up when she had said she would. And I mentioned it to her again, and she said she would come at another time, [but she] didn't come. . . ."

One morning as Brenda walked by one of these students in the corridor, she again heard her say "bitch." She recalled: "I was so frustrated and just sort of at the end of my rope. And I went in the teachers' room and there were a couple of colleagues there who I trusted, one teacher who had been teaching for thirty years. She said, 'Good morning. How are you?' and I just burst into tears and explained what had happened." Brenda said that her veteran colleague, who was outraged, was adamant that this had to stop. Brenda explained that the veteran colleague "went down to the office and let them know that this student was not welcome on the second floor until she had a meeting with the principal." With no formal responsibility to do so, "this other teacher just kind of took things under control." However, soon the student arrived back in class saying, "Well, the principal told me just to come back." Eventually, the principal called a meeting with the student's parents. Brenda was invited to attend, but then was asked to leave before the meeting concluded. Looking back, she said, "I just never felt like I was really supported."

The sum of these shortcomings and the relentless day-to-day demands of teaching her classes moved Brenda to the brink of quitting throughout her first year: "I have found it very difficult. Yes. I just keep trying to get through the first year, I think. I've several times been pretty close to stopping. So I just keep telling myself, 'It's the hardest year. Just stick it out to the end.' And I'm not one to stop things, to quit things very easily, but it's been very difficult." The experience of getting through each day was emotionally draining: "I would come home and keep working until I couldn't keep my eyes open any more. And be upset about things that had happened with certain students, and just be crying and get up the next day and go—always . . . trying to keep it together."

Although Brenda's experience certainly was not typical of the fifty teachers we studied, many of them encountered less extreme versions of these same problems. Threaded through the new teachers' stories were accounts of negative school cultures, inappropriate or unfair assignments, inattentive or abusive principals, misused time, inadequate supplies, lack of outreach programs for parents, ad hoc approaches to discipline, and insufficient student support services. New teachers who worked in schools that lacked these basic supports were demoralized and often felt ineffective with their students.

Roots in a One-Room Schoolhouse

In making sense of Brenda's experience, it is important to understand that the schools our new teachers entered had evolved from the one-room colonial schoolhouse, where a lone teacher was responsible for educating students of all ages from a community. In the mid-nineteenth century, local communities, faced with growing student enrollments and emerging beliefs that students should be grouped by age, created the so-called "egg-crate school," a metaphor describing both the building and the organization it housed. Such a school was essentially a cluster of one-room schoolhouses. Education historian David Tyack (1974) describes the Quincy School of Boston, built in 1848 to accommodate fifty-six students in each of twelve age-graded classrooms. With its four stories and auditorium, the school looked far more complex than its one-room progenitor, but within that building the process of teaching and learning was not much different from what it had been in the single-cell structure. Although students were grouped by age, teachers continued to work in isolation. Sociologist Dan Lortie (1975) observed that officials dealt with schools as "aggregates of classroom units, as collections of independent cells," rather than as "tightly integrated organisms" (p. 16).

The Egg-Crate School Endures

Across the nation, this cellular growth of schools has had far-reaching implications for management, teaching, and learning. Local officials found that a school composed of identical cells could be managed easily during episodes of growth and decline, since a school (or a district composed of schools) could add or close classrooms one unit at a time. This meant, however, that teachers had to serve as replaceable parts, prepared to do the same task, with modest adjustments for students' age or for subject specialty, wherever they were assigned. For students, this organization meant that their formal education was never a carefully integrated experience.

This egg-crate structure, which persists today in most schools, requires that teachers begin their careers with a clear understanding of what they should be doing in their classrooms, since they are expected to be self-sufficient from the start. There might be superficial coordination of their work—assigning playground duty to ensure sufficient coverage or dividing up Shakespeare's plays so that *Macbeth* would only be taught in grade 12—but within the classroom, teachers are expected to function independently, largely in isolation. Often, new teachers are welcomed briefly, then left to sink or swim.

For decades, educators and the public convinced themselves that this disjointed approach to schooling worked, despite evidence that it worked best for students from wealthy families and barely worked at all for students from low-income families. However, recent evidence about student performance has made it clear that schools cannot successfully educate all students with this structure, which promotes, even requires, such separation. Careful attention to when and how skills are taught, informed by ongoing monitoring of individual students' learning and progress, requires a teaching faculty whose work is interdependent, not simply in theory but in practice.

The Challenge of Reforming Schools

In the past fifteen years, education researchers have carefully studied schools that succeed in educating all students, and they have repeatedly found that such schools have moved well beyond cellular organizations. Michael Rutter et al. (1979) identified the characteristics of effective urban schools where, against all odds, high proportions of low-income students succeed academically. Subsequently, Judith Warren Little (1982) studied desegregated elementary, middle, and high schools and found teachers more likely to collaborate in successful than in unsuccessful schools. Similarly, Susan Rosenholtz (1985), reinterpreting the findings on effective schools, concluded that these schools were far less likely to be isolating work settings for teachers. She explained that for teachers as a group "to adopt student achievement as their primary mission" required steady interaction over time: "Norms of collegiality do not simply happen. They do not spring spontaneously out of teachers' mutual respect and concern for each other. Rather, they are carefully engineered by structuring the workplace with frequent exposure to contact and frequent opportunities for interaction" (p. 367). Researchers repeatedly have confirmed the need for teachers to work together if they are to meet the needs of their students (Bryk, Camburn, & Louis, 1999; McLaughlin, 1993; Newmann & Associates, 1996).

Given such compelling evidence, it may seem surprising that more schools have not reorganized effectively to improve instruction. However, fundamentally changing the internal structure of an established organization—particularly one so deeply rooted in history and perpetuated by generic roles that keep costs low and simplify the work of administrators—is very challenging (Fullan, 1991). Alternative approaches, which would involve team teaching, job-embedded professional development, and differentiated roles for expert teachers, have proven both controversial and fragile. Redrawing the organization chart has not translated directly into changed practices, particularly when the new arrangements were not managed well or supported with sufficient time for meetings and differentiated roles for teachers (Elmore, Peterson, & McCarthey, 1996). Such changes call for principals to be astute leaders. They require redefining teachers' roles and rethinking compensation systems. They challenge the notion, supported by union rhetoric and most teacher contracts, that all teachers are equal and, therefore, should be treated the same. They oblige teachers, themselves, to relinquish what comfort they might find behind their classroom doors and to welcome the experience of being observed by peers or reviewing their students' work with colleagues.

In many schools, changes that had been adopted enthusiastically sputtered and fell into disuse when essential supports—such as shared planning time, stipends for curriculum coordinators, released time for classroom observations—were eliminated during budget cuts. Many schools that once optimistically adopted reforms subsequently reverted to the security of the egg crate, and the vestiges of change were apparent in labels but not in day-to-day practices.

Public demands for accountability gradually have exposed the failings of schools that resist change and persist in conducting business from the separate cells of their egg-crate structures. Pressures to do better are mounting, and evidence continues to accumulate that doing better requires work for teachers that is differentiated and interdependent.

Schools That Are Organized for Learning

Those who talk and write about good schools sometimes mistakenly focus on superficial features of the school environment. Freshly painted corridors, orderly lines of students moving from class to class, or a posted logo affirming that "All Kids Can Learn," may convey the school's sense of purpose but not be matched with structures that make it possible for teachers to work in a collaborative fashion to monitor students' progress. The new teachers in our study described in considerable detail the internal workings of their schools, explaining the ways in which those schools succeeded or failed to support learning.

The Principal's Influence

These new teachers' accounts reinforced the finding of repeated research studies that the principal is central in shaping how, and how well, a school works (Murphy, 2002). Like Brenda, other teachers we studied spoke intently about how their principals related to them personally and professionally. They wanted administrators to be present, positive, and actively engaged in the instructional life of the school. They expected their principals to anticipate their needs as new teachers by making appropriate and fair teaching assignments and helping them forge productive relationships with their new colleagues. They counted on their principals to maintain an orderly school and to support them in classroom management.

Although more new teachers reported being disappointed than pleased with their principals, certain principals stood out as particularly successful and supportive. For example, Fred said of his principal: "She's an innovator. She's an example. . . . She's constantly looking for new ideas and new ways of solving old problems, which is unique. . . . No problem is too large [for her] and. . . you don't have to guess where she stands on the issues." More often, though, the principals failed to meet these teachers' expectations. Most were said to succeed in some things but fall short in others. A surprising number were, in these teachers' views, ineffectual, demoralizing, or even destructive.

Experiencing Instability at the Top. Some respondents worked in schools that had experienced repeated turnover in the principalship, and the effects of instability at the top reached deep into their classrooms. There had been seven principals during the prior eight years at Bernie's high school. A new one had just arrived as Bernie was being hired: "They finally hired a gentleman who seems to really be well-suited for the job. . . . So, hopefully, there will be some stability there." Five months into his first year, though, Bernie had not yet met his new principal. Similarly, Esther said her large, urban vocational high school had "been in a big flux," first because of weak leadership and then because of a leadership vacuum when the principal left abruptly. Soon after she began teaching, the principal left. He was, she said, "very nice, very cordial . . . but he didn't set a strong enough tone for the school." The hallways were chaotic and her fellow teachers, she said, "had no respect for him at all" and "mocked him in the teachers' room." Like Bernie, Esther had hope for her new principal, who was "setting a stricter tone" in the school.

Seeking a Personal Relationship. While teachers like Bernie and Esther were waiting to see what their new principals might do, others, like Brenda, were hoping for some level of positive, personal interaction from the principal who had hired them. Experienced teachers often have lived through several rounds of turnover in the main office and consequently may not count on their principals for personal support. New teachers, however, often look to these administrators as their main source of entrée to the professional life of the school. They hope for a cordial relationship and helpful advice. Amy praised her principal for being "very fair," but said: "I don't perceive her as someone I could just go up and talk to. She is very cold." Similarly, Carolyn found her principal "a little gruff," and said she was disappointed to see her keep such a distance from the staff: "She has bulletins that she sends out. It's really her main form of communication with us." As a result, Carolyn explained, "there is a sense of the administration being higher and separate from the teachers."

Fred's principal, who had founded the professional development school and was deeply involved in making it work, stands in dramatic contrast. "She's very good at telling us what kind of job we do and how she appreciates it. . . . She's willing to put her confidence in the hands of the professionals that are teachers here." She "expects highly of them, but respects them highly." Fred explained, "That type of freedom and confidence creates a good feeling amongst the faculty."

Looking for Instructional Leadership. Given the flat, compartmentalized structure of many schools and the fact that experienced teachers and new teachers officially have the same roles, many of these novices looked to their principals for guidance. Often, however, their expectations went unmet. Teachers frequently said, as Brenda did, that the principal was preoccupied and did not make time for them.

Carolyn looked to her principal for direction, but said that she often took problems out of Carolyn's hands with a brusque "I'll take care of it," rather than recommending how she might respond. Like other new teachers, Carolyn wanted to learn from her principal: "So a lot of time, I'll have to keep probing her [by asking], 'In another scenario, how would I handle this then?' or 'What are the consequences [for the student] that the school has for this?'"

At her first school, Keisha had wished that her principal were "the leader of the pack." She wanted him to say: "This is what I expect," but also to explain, "This is how we get there." She emphasized that, "'This is how we get there' is really, really important. Don't throw things out there and just expect people to do them. You need to show them the steps to get there. . . . I want him to be more of a mentor. I want him to be more of a role model for teachers."

In particular, new teachers hoped for constructive feedback about their teaching. For Amy, whose principal rarely offered praise, the messages were implicit. By the end of Amy's second year, the principal was bringing guests to observe her class: "And I'm always the first room she brings them in. So, obviously, she's very happy with me, but she does not show that. I mean, she's the kind of person that will tell other people what a great job I'm doing, but she won't tell you specifically. I have a problem with that, I think." Carolyn appreciated receiving direct assessments from her principal but wanted more: "The principal comes in informally every now and then . . . once a week, sometimes more, sometimes less, but she stays for ten minutes tops." Although some might view weekly visits by a principal, however brief, to be evidence of instructional leadership, Carolyn was critical of the "very minimal" feedback her principal offered when she stopped by.

Mary's principal, like Fred's, had founded the charter school where Mary worked, and she admired his many accomplishments and contributions: "He sort of has this amazing capacity to figure out how to solve all these sorts of problems with getting a building and making—creating a new school. That's been his role." She said, however, that he did not observe her teaching: "[M]y principal is an entrepreneur. Now, what I need is not—personally, I don't need an entrepreneur. I need someone to come in and to give some really concrete feedback. . . . I can't judge him for that, because he's doing exactly what we've needed for these children." Nonetheless, Mary's principal was the only individual who had the authority to supervise her teaching, and she was deeply disappointed that he did not observe her and offer advice: "The intention is to make this a very professional environment. But it is extremely devaluing to not have administration coming into your class, looking at how kids are learning, asking you how you're doing, treating you like a human being. . . ."

By contrast, Victoria's established, suburban elementary school had enough administrators to support the staff, and Victoria thought they coordinated their work and used their time well. Her principal evaluated her, and her vice principal provided ongoing supervision, which she especially appreciated: "She'll check on me to see if I need anything, and just to give me whatever I need. And she's just right down the hall here, so I can just come and talk to her." Victoria thought that this was exactly what administrators should be doing: "They should be visible. They should give support. . . . They have to know what you're doing and to see you in action, and to give you feedback, and to support you."

It was not only elementary principals in the suburbs who took time to give new teachers feedback. In his urban secondary school, Fred's principal also stood out as a model: "She is great about [observing]. She's constantly ducking in her head, and I think that's great." He explained that "there's no requirement or expectation that she comes in, but she makes it clear to the teachers that she wants to know what's going on in the classroom. I encourage it." Significantly, this principal is known by teachers to be an expert teacher, herself. "She's taught for a long time. And so she's got the tools to back it up." Also, given the relatively small size of Fred's school, it was possible for his principal to be present often in the classes.

It is important to acknowledge that a principal—particularly one heading a large school—has an enormous scope of responsibility, a dizzying set of demands, and very limited time to meet them. The flat, undifferentiated organization of many elementary schools means that the principal is the sole supervisor and source of support for all teachers in the school. Middle and high schools often have additional administrators, but since these schools usually are larger and more complex, new teachers are no more likely to receive personal attention there. It is no surprise that new teachers yearn for more interaction and are disappointed when it is not forthcoming.

Appropriate Teaching Assignments

No teacher in our study had a reduced teaching assignment, designed to make the first year more manageable. Bernie's high school load in the history department was typical: "I have two honors classes and three of what they have labeled as 'open' classes [for low-achieving students]. Open classes also have special ed kids. . . . Five classes, five times a week. The kids have seven periods. I have one free period a day. Otherwise, I'm on hall duty, or bathroom duty, or what have you." Bernie, whose time as a corporate lawyer had been billed by the minute, was dismayed to find that his time as a teacher was used to "make sure that nobody smokes in the boys room."

Preparing and teaching a full load of classes is an immense challenge for a first-year teacher. Not only was Bernie's assignment not reduced, but he, like many in our study, actually had a more difficult assignment than his more experienced colleagues. "I have the highest class size of any open [lower track] classes. All the other open classes in the school, I found out this week, are all like ten kids. Mine are thirty and twenty-five." Moreover, Bernie had no classroom or desk to call his own and moved from room to room during the day as an itinerant instructor. Throughout the study, teachers described assignments that, although technically comparable to those of their colleagues (the same number of students, the same number of classes), were actually far more challenging. They included a preponderance of low-level classes, grade-levels in which students would take the state exam, split grades, or assignments that required traveling from classroom to classroom or school to school.

Keisha had done her student teaching in a well-staffed urban classroom that assigned three adults (teacher, paraprofessional, intern) to work with twenty-two children. As a new teacher, she was startled to discover that she was entirely on her own with her twenty-five second-grade students: "Here there is one adult and twenty-five [students], at a minimum. When I first started [in September], I was at twenty-seven [students], which is already over the cap for second grade." Keisha spent her first year learning to teach second grade, which she found very hard despite her extensive preparation. In fact, she was so troubled by her lack of success during the first months that she handed in her resignation, which she eventually withdrew at her principal's urging. As she approached the end of the school year, Keisha looked forward to a second, where she could refine her teaching. However, her principal decided to reassign her to the fourth grade, where the state standardized test, Massachusetts Comprehensive Assessment System (MCAS), was administered. Keisha knew that experienced teachers often avoid teaching tested grades because those assignments bring extra pressure. She thought that asking her to take a new grade with a different curriculum was an unfair request to make of her as a new teacher who had just begun to find her footing.

Other teachers were given unusually challenging assignments, which made their first years especially difficult. Although schools rarely protected new teachers from such assignments, there was no evidence that the principal and teachers deliberately tried to make things difficult. Rather, these assignments seemed to be the inadvertent consequence of a delayed hiring process or seniority-based transfer provisions in the teachers' contract. Typically, experienced teachers request a specific grade or set of classes in March or April, well before many new teachers are hired. Before leaving for the summer, these experienced teachers know what they will teach in September, what room will be theirs, and even sometimes who their students will be. When new teachers enter the scene, frequently in late summer or early fall, they usually get whatever is left. Although a few principals made a deliberate effort to ensure that new teachers' assignments were manageable and fair, that was unusual. Most who did were located in suburban districts, where hiring was less likely to be delayed by budget uncertainty, central office procedures, or seniority-based transfers.

Sufficient Supplies and Equipment

There was wide variation as well in the equipment and supplies provided to the new teachers. Again, there were predictable differences between urban and suburban schools, although some teachers in urban schools said that they had all they needed. Other teachers, particularly those in high-poverty schools, reported shortages of paper and other instructional supplies. Like many who had entered teaching from other careers, Esther was stunned to see how ill-equipped her school was, particularly compared to the suburban school where she had done substitute teaching. She recalled a time when there was no paper available and "the secretary was taking out her secret stash." With no classroom of his own, Bernie had to rely on photocopied handouts rather than blackboards to convey important information to students. He called it "just ridiculous" that he was allotted three reams of paper per quarter: "I go through that probably in, you know, a week and a half, two weeks." He said only somewhat wryly, "Some of the most useful tips I've gotten from veteran teachers have to do with font size, and making sure I copy on both sides of paper . . . to save on my paper." Bernie, like many others, complained that the photocopiers in his school never worked. He observed, "In the business world, they would have a photocopy center where you could either do it yourself, or have somebody on staff [do it]."

A few teachers were satisfied with their supplies. Amy said that, although her inner-city school did not provide a curriculum, she could get the supplies she needed: "Supplies, yes. They were actually really good. . . . They kind of gave me anything I wanted because I was new. . . . That was the only thing that my mentor did. She showed me the supply closet and said, 'You can get any of this stuff.' And I had asked for an easel and I got it." Victoria also had all the resources she might need. New teachers in her suburban school had allowances of $250 to spend in each core subject—science, math, social studies, and language arts. Given what they were expected to teach, this was not an excessive allocation. However, most respondents complained that they lacked the basic resources they needed to do their job—adequate lab equipment and materials to conduct experiments in science classes; full class sets of books in literature classes; or current maps and globes in geography classes. The schools' lack of equipment and supplies, coupled with the unspoken expectation that teachers should cope without them or buy what they needed with their own money, demoralized many new entrants. Keisha told about how her principal had criticized another new teacher because she had no posters in her room. Keisha asked rhetorically, "But are you providing money for her to buy any of that stuff? She is a first-year teacher. She is still working on her master's degree. She has zero money."

A Comprehensive and Flexible School Infrastructure

One of the most important supports that schools can provide new teachers is a comprehensive, yet flexible, approach to the work that they and their colleagues do together. Teachers in our study complained about schools that were at two ends of a continuum—those that were woefully haphazard and disorganized and those that were excessively rulebound and rigid. Start-up charter schools, such as those Derek and Mary taught in, were especially challenging because so little had been defined about how the school should operate.[1] In his second year at his school, Derek explained, "We create everything in our school. . . . The theory is the more we work, the less we will have to do later on." A year later, however, Derek said teachers in his school still could not count on explicit processes or predictable procedures: "Our school is a school where things just get done sometimes and there is no rhyme or reason. There is no practical explanation. We don't have a system in place for things to get done." Derek said that as a new teacher he expected to cope with some uncertainty: "That you feel like a rookie is fine. But [if] the reason you feel like a rookie is because you're just as confused as everyone else, that's problematic. The school needs to not be so confusing for everybody."

Mary described similar disorientation in her charter school. She had anticipated that working with inner-city students would be challenging. However, "what I did not expect was the day-to-day operational difficulties in the school environment that impact how I do my job with the students, and how important the consistent operations and structures are, in terms of how the school operates day to day." Mary said that this lack of order affected instruction. "[W]hat the kids are learning in class every day has been put aside because we're dealing with our discipline system that we have not yet established, because we're a new school. We're dealing with our schedule that's new. We're dealing with our building that's new. We're dealing with our lockers that we just got. . . . and all these things that people sort of complain about in established schools." Mary saw little improvement over two years: "You know, we have a lot of things we do well, but there are some things we're failing miserably at. And what are we doing to change that? There's very little attention on that, and there's no sense that the administration understands that."

By contrast, Keisha was troubled by the excessively structured setting in her first urban elementary school. For example, she found the procedures for getting special services for students "convoluted." She described the school as regimented in discipline and curriculum, making her feel "really stifled." Her principal, she said, focused on whether students were wearing a uniform. "Appearances are extraordinarily important to this administration. I could give a crip and crap about appearances, as long as learning is happening." When she had interviewed for the job, she had been told that the school was trying to become more progressive, but "when I tried to do more progressive things, I was told 'No, no, no.'" All of this made her question whether this was the right teaching environment for her.

Using Teachers' Time Well. One component of the school's infrastructure that was very important to new teachers was how their time was scheduled, particularly whether their preparation periods—usually one per day—were coordinated with those of other teachers who taught the same subject or students. New teachers, who arguably most need information and regular feedback from colleagues, praised schools that deliberately arranged their schedules so that they could plan classes or review students' progress together.

Secondary schools that featured project-based learning, interdisciplinary classes, or team-based instruction often arranged time for teachers to collaborate. In his professional development school, Fred had ninety minutes four times each week for preparation and work with fellow teachers. Mary's charter school, which had failed to create much infrastructure, did organize teachers' schedules to accommodate planning time for each team: "So I see people on the seventh grade team every day, for anywhere from an hour to an hour and forty-five minutes, because we have that extended period."

In more traditional secondary schools, preparation periods often seemed haphazardly assigned, more likely the byproduct of a computerized scheduling program than the result of deliberate planning. Bernie was dismayed that teachers—particularly new ones—did not have the benefit of their peers' knowledge and advice. He thought that the teachers in his school would have worked more closely together if their assignments had made that possible: "There's no common planning time. There's no thought given to scheduling. There's people that are teaching the same stuff, or have the same level, or whatever, and didn't plan together, you know. And you really just kind of do your interaction on the fly."

At the elementary level, teachers were even less likely to have coordinated planning or grade-level meeting time. Keisha wished that there were opportunities to observe other teachers in their classrooms, "but we don't have that type of release time. Our [paraprofessionals] are hung up doing whatever. We can't get subs." However, Victoria said that in her suburban school, time was reserved for weekly meetings with other third grade teachers to "just go over what's happening."

Establishing Schoolwide Standards for Student Behavior.
There is no more immediate and worrisome challenge that new teachers face than establishing and maintaining order in their classrooms. Effective classroom management must come first because, without it, teaching and learning cannot proceed, no matter how imaginative a teacher's pedagogy. Although teachers may accept responsibility for maintaining an orderly environment in their classrooms, the possibility of doing so is either greatly enhanced or severely compromised by what the school does.

Some new teachers worked in schools that deliberately focused everyone's efforts on instruction and systematically discouraged disruption and distraction. These are not schools that impose regimen or exact obedience at the expense of good teaching and learning, but schools that support instruction respectfully with a calm and purposeful environment. Typically, such schools set high learning goals for students and define standards for appropriate behavior, as well as explicit procedures for enforcing them. Teachers repeatedly said that it was much easier to maintain classroom order within the context of an orderly school.

The mission of Fred's urban secondary school was to have all graduates attend college. Given that these students had varying levels of academic skills and primarily came from low-income neighborhoods, the administration and staff had set their sights high. Fred explained that he and his colleagues adopted an approach to managing student behavior that helped everyone focus on the goal of academic success. Both the faculty and the administration, Fred said, "treat every problem, no matter how minute, as a significant disciplinary issue. And because of that, we don't have the typical problems that other schools do. I mean, problems that other schools would laugh at in terms of discipline are dealt with pretty harshly here. But I think that has created an atmosphere that is conducive to good discipline." In the school's three-year history, there had been no fights among students. "And that's pretty remarkable when you think that it's seventh, eighth, and ninth graders who spend as much time as they do together." He credited the principal with setting the standard: "Things are dealt with immediately by the principal. She's got a good relationship with the kids. They know not to disappoint her. She doesn't bite their heads off, but she has a very good way of dealing with discipline here."

Far more often, however, teachers talked about coping on their own, without the benefit of a schoolwide approach to discipline that was endorsed and upheld by teachers and administrators alike. Many teachers, like Brenda, complained about school administrators who failed to follow through on discipline. Often new teachers reported being reluctant to ask for administrative help, in the belief that their requests would evoke disapproval. Bernie said that he had "tried every move that I know of to deal with behavioral issues in class on my own. . . . You set up an environment, but you know the kids don't care, because if you just send them down to the vice principal's office, they may get a detention, or the vice principal might just come back down and tell them to tell you that they have to serve two detentions with you." Bernie was not confident he could rely on administrators for support: "I'm not sure that they back people up. I've heard stories that have made me really nervous, about teachers being called to the mat . . . for something as simple as removing a kid from the classroom because they're disruptive. . . ." He said that this had never happened to him, "but I'm a little bit surprised at the fact that it seems as though it's a pervasive fear amongst teachers that have been in the system. So it must have happened, with the kids being able to run the circus, so to speak." Bernie thought that even though "the climate is relatively OK at the school," there should have been more order. "If a kid's just being a continuous disruption in class or goofing off or something like that, something has to be done other than just giving him a detention, you know?"

Keisha, too, said that teachers in her first school were expected to handle all discipline problems themselves. She could go to her principal with certain concerns, but "not disciplinary problems, because we have enough memos on that. Kids are not to be sent to the office." In conveying the gist of her principal's expectation, Keisha jokingly exaggerated his message: "'Don't do it unless blood is streaming from their head or your head!'"

For new teachers with particularly difficult teaching assignments, the importance of maintaining order is heightened. One novice teacher in our study who worked at an urban magnet school remarked about her school's consistent discipline policy, "It makes teaching so much easier. It takes so much of the guess work out of it." However, the challenge of creating and sustaining school environments that maintain a focus on learning requires more than just voting at a faculty meeting to adopt a code of behavior. Principals, teachers, and parents must together develop, not only responses to misbehavior, but also preventive strategies that keep students focused on their studies.

Providing Coordinated Student Support Services. Schools that foster positive, productive relationships between teachers and students also support teachers as they try to address the many needs students bring to the classroom. Amy described an array of support services available to her students. Some were provided by the school; some Amy had enlisted herself. The school employed a full-time social worker and bilingual specialist who pulled students out of classes and worked with them individually. Amy had marshaled an army of helpers who had been recruited by the school: an AmeriCorps worker three times a week, a volunteer mentor who provided in-class support for students two days a week, a Junior Achievement volunteer who taught lessons to the whole class, and another tutor who worked with two of her lowest-achieving students twice a week. With their help, Amy felt she was reaching most of her students most of the time.

Victoria, who taught in a much more affluent environment, could count on the school for the instructional support her students required: "There's reading specialists, there's math specialists, there's gifted and talented, there's speech therapists, there's occupational therapists." Because most of Victoria's students were functioning well, she did not need to call upon most specialists but was glad to know that they were there if she did.

Building Bridges with Parents.   Although parents have often been kept at a distance from schools, there is increasing recognition among teachers and principals that establishing strong relationships with parents is essential if children are to be well educated (Mapp, 1999). Many schools ask their teachers to phone parents or visit homes, yet few administrators provide guidance or support about how best to do this. As more than one teacher observed, their rooms have no phones, making it difficult for parents to call them back. When schools maintain ongoing programs and opportunities for parents to become involved in their children's education, a teacher's phone call or note home is far more likely to be understood as part of that larger school initiative (Mapp, 1999). One midcareer entrant in our study, a parent herself, was dismayed by the lack of a support for parents at her urban middle school. Parents did not attend meetings of the school site council, which were held in the middle of the afternoon when many parents worked. "There's an attitude in this school that no one wants to come, no one will come. No matter what they do, no one. But I see it differently. And I actually think I've had some success with my kids' parents." She had hosted families at a year-end reception where they could view their students' posted writing and take home a portfolio of work from the year. She judged the event a success. "The parents come at night, you know." She was planning to organize regular potluck suppers the following year and hoped to encourage other teachers to do the same, although she was not optimistic that the administration would support her venture.

There are many ways, therefore, in which the school can be organized to support the work of new teachers. Those in our sample whose schools were more than collections of classrooms, whose principals and colleagues made decisions day to day with the entire school in mind, tended to report greater success and satisfaction.

How the School Influences Teachers' Career Decisions

The extent to which the school provided organized support for new teachers influenced our respondents' decisions to stay, look for another school, or leave teaching altogether. Admittedly, individuals' career decisions are complex and rarely result from a single factor. However, during our second round of interviews, conducted in 2001, we asked teachers to explain their career decisions. They often spoke about whether the school was organized effectively to support their success. Even—perhaps especially—when the new teachers planned to stay in teaching for only a few years, the school's role in their achieving success with students was key. All new teachers believed that schools could either facilitate or impede good teaching. When they were reasonably hopeful that they could become effective with their students, these teachers were likely to stay in their schools. However, those who thought that their schools interfered with successful teaching often moved on.

Teachers Who Left

By the third year of the study, eleven of the fifty teachers had left public school teaching, having decided that, as they experienced it, this was not the career for them. Derek, alone, left primarily because of pay, but he also expressed many dissatisfactions with being a teacher in his school. Overall, the teachers who left were dissatisfied with their schools or overwhelmed by the demands of the job and saw few prospects for improvement or success, either in their current or in other public schools. They listed similar factors that drove them out, although individuals weighed those factors differently in their decisions. They described principals who were arbitrary, abusive, or neglectful, and they spoke with disappointment about the isolation and lack of support they experienced.

Some, like Brenda, were overwhelmed by unrealistic teaching assignments or excessive teaching loads, and they resented the paltry

provision of resources in their schools. Believing that her assignment was unfair and undoable, Brenda requested a different schedule for her second year. Assured that her teaching assignment
would be modified, she planned to return. However, in September,
Brenda found that her schedule was still unchanged. After several
months of further dissatisfaction, Brenda resigned and took a temporary position teaching Spanish part-time in two suburban elementary schools. Although the working conditions there were far
better in many ways, the split schedule left her even more isolated
than she had been. At the end of the year, Brenda left teaching and
returned to her work in public health.

Teachers Who Moved

There were eight other teachers who felt ineffective in their classrooms or dissatisfied with their schools, and chose to transfer to
new schools rather than leave teaching. (There were also three
teachers who changed schools involuntarily, two because of staff
reductions and one because she was not reappointed.) Notably, this
group of eight voluntary movers included six midcareer entrants
who had already changed jobs at least once when they entered
teaching, and knew that work sites could vary tremendously. They
did not regard the problems they encountered as inevitable or
endemic to a career in public school teaching, and thus looked for
a place where they could give teaching another chance.

Those who moved transferred from schools where teachers
worked in isolation and where novices were left to sink or swim,
and sought schools offering organized support for new teachers and
schoolwide, collegial interaction. Those who moved left schools
where student disrespect and disruption were taken for granted and
looked for schools that had well-established norms about respect,
effective discipline systems, and deliberate approaches to parental
involvement. They left schools where teachers were routinely given
the most difficult assignment or workload, and moved to schools

where assignments were more fairly distributed and appropriate to teachers' knowledge and experience. They left schools that had scant curricula and scarce resources, and looked for positions in schools that had sufficient curriculum and materials to do the work they needed to do.

Prominent in the accounts of the teachers who chose to move were stories of principals who had been absent, punitive, or controlling. In seeking better work settings, the teachers looked for administrators who understood the challenge of being a new teacher, were fair and encouraging, and created structures of support and interaction among the school's teachers.

Esther, who transferred from her low-income, vocational high school after just one year, was dismayed not only by the disrespect among students and teachers that pervaded the school and left her feeling unsuccessful in her classroom, but also by the absence of any meaningful schoolwide response. She looked for a school with a strong leader, supportive colleagues, and an orderly, respectful environment, since in her first school, energy and resources were not focused on creating an environment conducive to student learning, and she lacked the skills to succeed without support.

Mary, who had been dissatisfied with the weak infrastructure and lack of supervision at her urban charter school, transferred after two years to what she called "a more sane environment." She reported realizing, "If I was going to sustain teaching, if I was going to keep thinking of this as a career and stay with teaching, I was going to need to make a change. . . . I knew I needed some more structure, but I was also at the same time really nervous about being in a super-traditional setting." She had been disappointed by the lack of supervision from the principal of her charter school. At her new school, she said, she could get advice from her vice principal or a counselor about how to handle the situation: "I don't know if I handled this right. What do you think?" She was confident that she would get a helpful response: "You send a kid to the office, they send you a note back [stating what they would do]—after school for this amount, a parent phone call. It's like right in your box immediately." Moreover, her department chair observed her teaching, met with her regularly, and offered her suggestions for improvement.

Where Esther and Mary sought more order in their second schools, Keisha sought more flexibility. Her principal's plan to move her from second grade to fourth grade when she only had begun to feel confident prompted Keisha to look for another school: "That was kind of the straw that broke the camel's back. . . . I was just figuring out the second grade curriculum and getting my feet wet and really getting this thing together. And now all of a sudden you want me to make what is a huge jump to fourth grade, and a high pressured grade." Keisha moved to a low-income charter school that allowed her to teach second grade and work closely with faculty colleagues.

Teachers Who Stayed

Of the twenty-eight teachers who remained in their original schools, fifteen were not fully satisfied with their school or with the profession. We came to call them the "unsettled stayers." Although their complaints resembled those of teachers who had transferred, these individuals also listed things they liked about their schools. The weight of dissatisfaction had not yet prompted them to leave. One who taught in an urban middle school said she had considered changing schools at the end of each of her first three years, but she always decided to stay. "[I] still definitely feel committed to the kids," she explained. "I'm not sure if I'm fully committed to the school itself. . . . I think I'd be looking for a place that has more structure that is visible, a place where it would be easier to see who makes the decisions, how the decisions are made, and why."

Among the fifty teachers, there were only thirteen who, during their second interviews, expressed overall satisfaction with their schools and the profession and, therefore, could be expected to stay in teaching and continue in their first assignment for some years to come. We called them the "settled stayers." For some, their favorable view of their school allowed them to look beyond reservations they might have about the profession of teaching. In some cases, their commitment to teaching enabled them to downplay features of their school that disturbed them. In general, many "settled stayers" had found opportunities for growth and development, and with increasing competence felt more effective and confident in the classroom. These teachers spoke of principals who were fair and informed educators, and who understood the idea of continuous improvement. Especially important, their schools were organized to support them as they found their professional footing.

Fred and Victoria had few misgivings about their schools and expressed confidence that they were achieving success as teachers. Both felt well supported by their administrators and colleagues. They could count on shared expectations and established procedures to provide orderly environments for teaching and learning. Fred made it clear that, were it not for his urban secondary school, he might have left teaching: "If I weren't at this school, I wouldn't be a teacher. I really don't think I would be." After her first year in her suburban elementary school, Victoria said, "I didn't just get by. I felt like I accomplished a lot, and I knew what I was doing. So I wasn't struggling, or I wasn't always trying to play catch-up."

In Search of Better Schools

Although federal and state officials are central in setting education policy that affects teachers, and the local school board and district administrators make important decisions about curriculum and student services, a teacher's chance for success with her students is bound up with the features of a particular school. It was in this setting where the teachers of this study decided whether or not to continue teaching. Although a few brilliant and heroic teachers may triumph despite decrepit and dysfunctional settings, most teachers must rely on their school to be a place that makes steady, good work not only possible but likely. They need institutional resources to support and sustain their personal resources.

Many of the teachers in this study said that their schools fell far short of what they needed. Inappropriate or overwhelming assignments, isolating schedules, lack of schoolwide systems for discipline, inadequate supports for student services, and disregard for teachers' views interfered with new teachers' efforts to make a difference in the lives of their students. Principals who failed to recognize their needs and to organize support for new teachers' work disappointed, even demoralized, them. When the school failed them, some teachers left the profession for good, whereas others went searching for better schools.

Such "better" schools—those that these teachers said worked for them and their students—had moved beyond the egg-crate structure of isolated classrooms and independent work. They were in the process of becoming complex, interdependent organizations. At these sites, there were no generic teachers. Rather, these schools recognized the needs of new teachers and the expertise of experienced teachers. Differentiated roles and responsibilities—sometimes formal, often informal—increased the capacity of the school to do its work and heightened the chances that teachers would achieve success and satisfaction.

The next chapters closely examine two very important factors that shape teachers' satisfaction with work in their schools—the curriculum and their colleagues.

Chapter Six

Filling the Curriculum Void

Coauthor: David Kauffman

New teachers face the daily challenge of planning and delivering lessons, usually for several subjects or courses. These lessons must fit together meaningfully over the course of a year, connect to what was taught in prior grade levels and what will be taught in coming years, and attend to the particular learning needs of the individual students in the class. Also, many schools and districts issue guidelines about what content students should learn in particular subjects and grades, and, to a greater degree than ever before, states require teachers to administer standardized exams that test whether students have mastered state academic standards.

Today's new teachers enter schools with various levels of content knowledge and pedagogical training. Some have academic majors or work experience in the subjects they teach, training in how children at various ages make sense of new knowledge and skills, or extensive experience with lesson planning. Others do not. Regardless of the skills and experience they bring to their first years of teaching, it is difficult to plan instruction effectively, and most new teachers need and expect curricular support.

A school's curriculum, defined simply as what and how teachers are expected to teach, is a mechanism for providing such support and guidance. It is usually conveyed to teachers through instructional materials that come in various shapes and sizes, including curriculum

The ideas in this chapter expand upon an earlier article: D. Kauffman, S. M. Johnson, S. M. Kardos, E. Liu, and H. G. Peske (2002). "Lost at sea": New teachers' experiences with curriculum and assessment. *Teachers College Record, 104*(2), 273–300.

frameworks or testing information issued by the state, textbooks and teacher's guides purchased from publishers, and lesson plans or teaching units developed by teachers at the school.

Curricula vary greatly in how much detail they provide about content and pedagogy and the extent to which teachers are expected to follow precisely what is laid out in the materials. A complete curriculum can assist new teachers with the essential and challenging work of designing instruction. It provides direction by identifying important content, skills, and topics and describing how they are connected to each other. It facilitates long-range planning by suggesting the sequence of units a teacher might follow and reasonable amounts of time to allocate for each. It can ease the burden of daily preparation by recommending particular instructional activities, possibly even detailed lesson plans, to use in the classroom. If well developed, it can also give new teachers insight into how students make sense of key concepts and the misunderstandings they may have along the way to comprehension.

Although a detailed curriculum can support new teachers, a curriculum that is too rigid can reduce teachers' sense of professionalism and curtail some of the intrinsic rewards of teaching. Lortie (1975) found in the 1970s that although teachers tended to accept many of the curricular responsibilities assigned them, they expected to have some discretion so they could "add something personal" (p. 111). New and experienced teachers in the past have generally rejected so-called "teacher-proof" curricula that prescribed lessons in great detail, because they felt that such materials undermined their chance to exercise professional judgment (Johnson, 1990).

One might expect the next generation of teachers to have intense concerns about teacher autonomy. Since the early-1990s, many states have introduced educational standards laying out the content teachers are expected to cover. State-level accountability measures, including sanctions and rewards based on student achievement, have introduced greater pressure, and some schools and school districts have responded with tighter controls over how teachers teach. These pressures and controls are likely to increase, as the federal No Child Left Behind Act of 2001 compels all states to assess students more frequently and to use test results to hold schools accountable.

When this study began during the 1999–2000 school year, it was unclear what the impact of standards-based reform would be. Would it reassure new teachers with clear guidance about what to teach? Or would it constrain new teachers, thus compromising the autonomy that past generations of teachers have valued? The new teachers we interviewed supported neither viewpoint. The state standards and associated curriculum changes did not provide them with curricular clarity; nor did the new teachers report feeling stifled by the top-down expectations about what to teach. Indeed, these new teachers expressed a desire for more, not less, structure and guidance. They expected, however, that within that structure there would be enough flexibility to adapt curriculum to their students' needs.

The Curriculum Void and Its Effects

Mary started her teaching career at a school that had, in her words, "no set curriculum." The expectations were that teachers create extended, interdisciplinary learning projects and that they prepare students for the state's standardized test. Mary had no textbooks, teacher's guides, or other instructional materials to follow. On the contrary, she said, "There's a big focus on creating your own, because there's a sense of nothing else out there works, that all these other schools out there failed. We are going to fix it."

Mary had chosen to teach at this urban charter school partly because of the flexibility and responsibility she would have. She had done her student teaching there, and found the small, non-hierarchical organization of the school appealing. She felt that "It was really nice to be in a place where people really do have a voice, and what you felt could work for these children would be heard."

Mary endorsed the instructional philosophy of the school and understood the importance of innovation and trying different approaches. However, she soon found the lack of curricular guidance and materials unmanageable.

For two years, Mary spent hours every week "seeking, copying, [and] reading through lots of different materials to figure out what's going to work." There was no library at her school, so she would go in the late afternoon and on weekends to her graduate school library and to a nonprofit organization that made history materials available to teachers. In addition to time and energy, Mary spent her own money to buy atlases and other instructional materials for her classroom.

When other teachers did give Mary teaching materials, they proved to be of little use. For example, in her second year of full-time teaching, she was hopeful that she could use a project-based history unit developed the year before by some colleagues. She received a box with "a thousand Xeroxes on Colonial America" and a warning from her colleagues that "there's a whole bunch of stuff that didn't work about it." There was no opportunity to discuss the unit with the teachers who developed it, so it was unclear what the problems had been and how she could avoid them. Mary explained that she and her teaching partner "ended up having to find all kinds of other things, because while [other teachers] taught it last year, much of the material was insufficient." She said, "It was not at a reading level that our students could understand. So in many ways we had to sort of reestablish the project and the curriculum." Mary resented spending a week of her vacation at the library copying information on Colonial America, calling it "a ridiculous waste of my time."

Mary became concerned that she was shortchanging her students. The time spent frantically gathering materials prevented her from developing "the depth of knowledge and the tightness in the lessons" necessary to help her students learn. She believed that there were effective instructional materials that other teachers had developed before her and that it was "insane" for an inexperienced teacher to have full responsibility for deciding what to teach when "there are all these other people that have already done it." More important, she said, it was not fair to students to "be trying all kinds of new things on them to see what works."

Mary did not expect a foolproof curriculum filled with easy answers, and anticipated learning some things through trial and error: "No one can really tell you that this is the way to do it. You have to experience it. You've got to screw up. . . . And, you know, you take risks, and you figure out what works." But she thought that was "a tough way to do it all the time." Even with a master's degree in education, a state teaching certificate, and more than a year of teaching behind her, Mary was deeply troubled by the dearth of curricular support she received at her school. As a new teacher, she expected more guidance about what to teach and how to teach it.

"Lost at Sea" Without a Curriculum

Although Mary worked in a charter school that sought to do things differently from other schools, her experience with curriculum was by no means unique. Even at more conventional schools where the use of textbooks and other instructional materials was encouraged, new teachers found limited curricular guidance. For example, Carolyn described the curriculum at her urban elementary school as "very hard to work with." She was surprised that district learning standards were vague and came with no specific guidance about how to teach them. Similar descriptions appear repeatedly in the accounts of the fifty new teachers we interviewed. All but two described a curriculum void in some, if not all, of the subjects they were expected to teach (Kauffman, Johnson, Kardos, Liu, & Peske, 2002). As a result, many felt, as one new teacher put it, "lost at sea."

Many of our respondents encountered a curriculum that specified topics or skills to be taught but provided scant detail about the content and little or no guidance about how to teach it. Mary, whose humanities classes combined history and language arts, knew only that she should teach about Colonial America; which information to teach and how to teach it was up to her. Some English teachers knew which novels to teach but received no guidance about how to approach them or which themes or literary elements to emphasize.

As an elementary school teacher, Carolyn was responsible for teaching several subjects each day. She had more curricular resources to draw on for some subjects than for others. In math she was able to "just follow the math textbook straight through." However, for social studies she only had "a few pages about American studies," which left her to create complete units and lessons on her own. Language arts fell somewhere in between math and social studies; Carolyn had a long list of topics to cover and books to choose from in the district curriculum guide for language arts, but there were few materials and resources. Encountering these expectations without support frustrated her.

Some of our respondents described having various unrelated books, teachers' guides, and worksheets, but not being sure how to organize them into a coherent curriculum for the year or even an effective lesson plan for the next day. A second grade teacher in a suburban district explained that "sometimes when you get all this material, especially a lot of written stuff and books and things, it can be overwhelming because you're looking at it all and thinking, Where do I start? What do I begin with? There's no handbook." Without guidance about how to organize and use the materials, having too much may be as disorienting as having too little.

Another challenge that many new teachers encountered was that the textbooks and other materials they received did not align with the topics they were expected to teach. For example, Esther found at her urban vocational high school that the math book did not cover trigonometry, a topic included in the state curriculum frameworks for that grade. This placed her in the difficult position of deciding whether to follow the available curriculum materials or to address the learning standards.

For ten of the teachers we interviewed, all of whom taught in middle or high schools, the curriculum void was particularly stark. Either they had no curriculum at all or, at best, a loose list of themes to cover. For example, one middle school teacher at a suburban charter school was simply told the title of his course, physical sciences; it was up to him to decide what to cover. For these new teachers, the curriculum was a blank slate. One high school teacher described his charter school's curriculum as "frustratingly open" and asked, "How are you supposed to come up with curriculum while you teach?"

A Mad Scramble to Prepare Day to Day

In response to having little or no curriculum, our respondents said they spent an unreasonable amount of time identifying appropriate content and developing teaching materials from scratch. This occurred amid expectations that they would learn to maintain discipline, facilitate class discussions, communicate with parents, grade papers, and negotiate the complicated red tape of school. Consumed by the mad scramble to prepare day to day, they had little time or energy for long-term planning or for critical reflection on the effectiveness of their lessons.

Like Mary, many new teachers we interviewed had little guidance about which details to emphasize and how much depth to pursue. They purchased books, searched the Internet, and spent evenings in the library. For example, a science teacher at a suburban charter middle school anticipated teaching about "geology, plate tectonics, and earth science stuff" the following trimester. Since her school did not "go by textbooks," she tracked down three textbooks on her own and read them at home in order to determine the most important concepts to teach. An elementary teacher in an urban school described preparing to teach her first graders about the history of religion, which she identified as one of the required topics from her district's social studies curriculum. She said that she bought a book and "read like crazy."

In isolation, each of these examples may not seem problematic. Surely it is desirable for teachers to conduct research and learn more about the subjects they teach. However, the time required for these efforts might have been better spent choosing and adapting appropriate content from prepared materials and planning how to effectively teach it to their own students. As Mary said, "[I spend] way too much time getting those things which we should already have, instead of focusing on what we're teaching."

Not only did these new teachers spend considerable time planning what they would teach and how they would teach it, but they also had to scavenge, create, and buy instructional materials to use with their students. Engaging a class of students is particularly challenging without appropriate materials, especially for new teachers. Many of our respondents lacked the class sets of novels, workbooks, textbooks, worksheets, science equipment, and manipulative math materials that they felt they needed.

These new teachers described spending a great deal of time creating instructional materials, such as worksheets, for their lessons. Some had none at all, whereas others found that what they had inadequately covered the particular content they were required to teach. A teacher at an urban elementary school described how hard she worked to create units and worksheets for math topics that were not included in the materials provided. She acknowledged that teachers should create some materials, so she was "not bitter about that." "But," she said, "having no resources at all for that, it's very difficult. And then, imagine having to do that for every subject."

Although these new teachers were willing to conduct research and to prepare materials for their classes, they recognized their own limits. It was overwhelming to do that for every subject, every day, or even for a single subject every day, when they were also learning to do the other complicated work associated with teaching.

The Curricular Support That New Teachers Want

As described in Chapter Five, Mary left her first school after two years and moved to a suburban middle school offering greater structure and support. At her new school, she still did not have the binders and materials that she expected from a complete curriculum, but she did have a textbook, a pacing guide that listed the topics to be covered and the approximate amount of time to spend on each one. She also had access to the school's "beautiful library" where she could find additional information. She concluded that it was "a better use of time" to think about how to teach those materials than to repeat the work that others had done before her.

Mary missed some of the curricular freedom she had at her first school. Nevertheless, she knew she "needed some more structure . . ." and "less craziness if [she] was going to be an effective teacher." Thinking back, Mary said she felt that there should have been a better balance of guidance and autonomy within each school. She was grateful for her experience at the project-based charter school, because it helped her develop more creative ideas about how to teach, but she also needed the curricular structure that her second school provided.

Greater Structure

Although prior research found that new and experienced teachers value their autonomy and do not want to be told what to do (Johnson, 1990; Lortie, 1975), nearly all of the fifty new teachers we interviewed appreciated what curricular guidance they had and most wished for more. They would have welcomed a clear, focused, and detailed curriculum. Specifically, they sought information about the facts, concepts, and skills they should address and detailed pedagogical guidance with actual lesson plans and worksheets they could draw from, or at least specific ideas about how to teach the content. As one high school history teacher said, "If they had the lessons in the curriculum guide, I'd be all over it." Some teachers said that their textbooks and teacher's guides provided this type of structure, but several considered those to be insufficient, since they rarely met their particular students' needs or aligned fully with the state standards that students were expected to learn.

The new teachers said that they probably would not religiously follow a detailed curriculum, but would use it as a starting place for

their own efforts and a backup plan when their own ideas or preparation fell short. One new teacher described a detailed curriculum
as a "crutch" to lean on, and another referred to it as a "central resource" to draw from.

In the midst of the uncertainty that is inevitably part of the
early years of teaching, these novices were seeking something they
could count on. They wanted to use and adapt lessons and materials that had proven successful for teachers before them. As a suburban high school history teacher said, "If you want to help a new
teacher get off to a good start, . . . don't make him feel like he has
to reinvent the wheel." These new teachers were not looking for
easy solutions, but they suggested that they were not yet well qualified to design curriculum from scratch. They believed that there
were materials available somewhere that provided, as one teacher
said, "a plan that seems to work."

Even new teachers who were teaching subjects in which they
had strong content knowledge, academic majors, or professional
experience longed for guidance about how to convey concepts to
students. One middle school science teacher we interviewed was a
science major with professional experience as a lab manager. He
acknowledged that his strong command of science only partially
qualified him to teach the subject and that "a lot of other people
have a lot better ideas [about teaching science] than I do, because
they have been doing it a lot longer than I have." He appreciated
that his teacher's guide provided detailed day-to-day guidance on
teaching an experiment-based curriculum. Many of the new teachers we interviewed believed that veteran teachers had much to
offer them in lessons that had worked in the past.

Flexibility

In calling for greater detail, however, these new teachers stopped
well short of asking that their every move be dictated. They were
willing to exchange some of their creative license for greater struc-

ture, but they were not looking to simply follow orders. Instead, they wanted to retain autonomy within a supportive structure.

Victoria felt that her district provided a clear, established curriculum that still allowed her to exercise her own judgment. She received a district curriculum guide for each subject, including expectations and goals for students in third grade. She also had curriculum materials, including textbooks for math and language arts. It was clear to Victoria that the district provided these resources precisely because they addressed the district curriculum guidelines.

The curriculum and instructional materials provided Victoria with structure and guidance, but did not constrain her ability to adapt her teaching to the particular needs of her students. She could follow the sequence and use the specific lessons provided in the curriculum materials if she chose, but she could replace, supplement, or modify them as she saw fit. Victoria explained that it would be difficult for her to teach in a district that offered little curricular support, even though "some people might find that exciting and build a whole new curriculum." In her opinion, starting with the available materials was the only responsible choice for a first-year teacher. She said, "I'd be an idiot if I just threw everything away. . . . I use what's there, and I use my judgment, and I pull other stuff in."

Like Victoria, most of the new teachers in our study reserved the right to adapt the prepared curriculum and materials to the specific needs of their students and to their own unique teaching styles. Although the new teachers generally acknowledged their limited expertise as classroom teachers, they also believed that as the classroom teacher they were well positioned to make curricular decisions that would best serve their students.

A Balance of Guidance and Freedom

These teachers believed that guidance and freedom could coexist, so they pushed for more structured curricula that they could adapt as they saw fit. Striking the right balance of guidance and freedom is an important challenge; too many requirements can constrain adaptation and creativity, whereas too much freedom can lead to indecision or misdirection.

Ambivalence About Freedom.   Some schools reject the use of textbooks and other curricular resources because of concern that they limit students and teachers. They believe that if teachers follow textbooks closely, students will be subjected to dull, impersonal lessons that fail to address their particular interests and needs. Furthermore, they fear that if new teachers have such structure, it will curtail their development and prevent them from seeking creative solutions to the educational challenges they face. Yet the new teachers in our study reported the opposite: detailed guidance helped them serve their students and develop as teachers.

In his first year, Derek was one of a handful of teachers in our sample who said he appreciated having a very loosely defined curriculum. He chose to teach at a charter high school because of the freedom and influence he expected to have there. Derek said that the freedom to determine his own curriculum was "the best thing" about teaching at his school: "It vibes with my personal style. I don't have to use somebody else's techniques to teach a course and take a class. [The students] can really connect with what I'm about." He chose this school over another where he thought he would have been told, "You are teaching this page and this page." Although he regretted not yet having "an expanded repertoire of things to just draw upon," he believed that the remedy was experience, not a structured curriculum.

Derek suggested in his second year, however, that the lack of curricular resources was frustrating, rather than liberating. He and his colleagues decided they wanted to order textbooks "to help orient" themselves and their students, but the school director refused at first because he felt that textbooks were "very limiting." Derek countered that textbooks could be helpful references and that there was "nothing wrong" with teachers using them strategically and sparingly. After a "big fight" with the director, Derek and his colleagues got their textbooks.

Derek did not see a conflict between curricular guidance and his own development as a teacher. On the contrary, he felt that having access to a structured curriculum scaffolded his learning, making the work manageable while giving him opportunities for healthy doses of exploration and experimentation. Derek reflected on the value of his textbook: "It provided, I think, key reference points and key ideas for my students. I mean, it's much better than me having to go out and get a piece of the Constitution, or get it off the Internet. This is a high school textbook, which is geared toward students at this age, and I can discern what's necessary, and what's not necessary. But it's given me a guide. It's helping me put my curriculum together." Derek thought that having a textbook enhanced the instruction he provided his students and his own development as a teacher without detracting from the curricular freedom he so highly valued.

Derek's story highlights the difference between the curriculum void and curricular freedom. Ironically a detailed curriculum may actually enhance new teachers' autonomy. For instance, Brenda, who had only a six-year-old binder of worn and dated photocopies to support her teaching of middle school Spanish, explained: "I feel like if I had more guidance in what the areas are that I need to be teaching, . . . I could then have more freedom as far as how I teach it." Brenda did not speak of the curriculum void as a welcomed opportunity to generate creative solutions or to develop as a teacher. For her, the lack of curricular guidance was negligent and harmful.

These teachers also did not expect to rely on a structured curriculum indefinitely. They tended to take a developmental perspective, saying they would no longer need as detailed a curriculum when they gained more experience. As beginners, they were unfamiliar with the age-appropriate content, had a limited repertoire of teaching ideas to draw from, and lacked the experience to distinguish what works from what does not; but they expected this to change over time. Research on the professional life cycle of teachers by educational researcher Michael Huberman (1989) supports these new teachers' predictions of growing self-reliance. He found that teachers' attitudes toward curriculum change over the course of their career: what begins as a struggle to master the curriculum develops over time into greater confidence and assertion of professional autonomy.

Ambivalence About Scripted Curricula. Some educators advocate prescriptive curricula that *require* teachers to follow rigid lesson plans or even to read from a script. Although critics of scripted approaches say they are futile and demeaning attempts to "teacher-proof" the curriculum and that they demoralize teachers and harm students, advocates point to evidence of increased student achievement in schools that use scripted curricula and argue that teachers are most demoralized when their students fail to learn. Given new teachers' desire for curricular guidance, they might be expected to appreciate such curricula, or at least to accept them.

Two of the new teachers we interviewed taught at a charter school that uses a scripted reading curriculum with rigid rules for instruction. One disagreed with its approach to teaching reading and took advantage of the lack of supervision at her school to modify the curriculum considerably. However, this teacher's aversion did not prevent her from staying a second year. Reading was only one of the several subjects she taught, and she appreciated the overall balance of structure and freedom she had across all subjects. Upon moving to a different state, she found work at a school that used the same curriculum.

The other teacher was ambivalent. She explained that, as a novice, she appreciated the guidance provided by the prescriptive curriculum: "Right now, being a first-year teacher, it's wonderful to have all these things in place for me." Even so, she reported that both she and her students found the reading lessons to be boring and she questioned whether the curriculum really would lead to success for all of her students. Nevertheless, she said that she would follow it in subsequent years if she felt that it worked; her decision would depend on student achievement, not her own enjoyment. Other research supports the idea that new and experienced teachers may be willing to relinquish their own freedom and creativity if they believe a prescriptive curriculum will benefit their students (Datnow & Castellano, 2000).

Teachers' responses to scripted curricula are complicated, and there is no clear verdict on the appropriateness of such curricula in classrooms with new teachers. The evaluation of a scripted curriculum, like any other curriculum, should consider its effects on both students and teachers. Schools should seek the right balance of guidance and autonomy, a balance that is likely to differ somewhat from one new teacher to the next depending on the knowledge, experience, and training they bring.

The Limits of Standards and Accountability

Most of the teachers in our study of fifty Massachusetts novices who had a curriculum of some sort said that it addressed, at least in part, state standards—the Massachusetts curriculum frameworks, the state test (MCAS) objectives, or both. In general, however, our respondents reported that these policy instruments introduced more confusion than support for them as new teachers. They offered three major reasons for this. First, teachers often were expected to use the state curriculum frameworks in lieu of an actual curriculum. Second, if schools had curriculum materials, such as textbooks and teachers' guides, they often did not fully address the standards listed in the curriculum frameworks. And third, the state frameworks covered too much content.

One of the Massachusetts documents that many teachers had available when our study began in the 1999–2000 school year clearly states that "[a] curriculum framework is not a curriculum" (Massachusetts Department of Education, 1997, p. 131). The framework communicates the state standards, while the "schools and their teachers" determine the curriculum and methods to be used.

The authors of the framework encourage teachers to plan collaboratively within their schools and to rely heavily on textbooks and other available resources to provide content and sequence. These statements echo the language in an essay by education policy analysts Marshall Smith and Jennifer O'Day (1991) that helped define and inaugurate the standards-based reform movement. However, Smith and O'Day also recommended that districts offer professional development for new and experienced teachers, sponsor curriculum development, and provide adequate materials at the school level. The curriculum frameworks, they contended, "should provide a way of organizing a coherent instructional guidance system" (p. 248). The new teachers we interviewed described little evidence of access to a "coherent instructional guidance system."

Because veterans and novices alike may be encountering new expectations, standards-based reform might provide an ideal opportunity for them to collaboratively develop new curricula in the manner suggested in the state curriculum frameworks. Everyone might benefit from the wisdom of the veterans and the fresh perspective of the novices. However, very few teachers said this was happening. Instead, veteran teachers appeared to be left alone to adapt to the new requirements or ignore the changes, while new teachers were left alone wondering what to do.

Many new teachers said they received copies of the curriculum frameworks but no advice about how to implement them. Esther, for example, said that the guidance she received from her department head was "teach everything on the MCAS in the frameworks for sophomores." Our respondents lamented that the frameworks, by themselves, were inadequate to guide their decisions about what and how to teach. A second grade elementary teacher in an urban school summarized the problem: "State frameworks, by definition, are very general. . . . 'This is what you should be covering.' It doesn't give you any idea of how to do it, or what the timeline is, or how other people are doing it, what works, or what didn't work." Receiving few specifics about what to teach and no suggestions about how to teach it, these new teachers had to devise their own plans for addressing the state standards.

Lacking resources and recommendations to translate the curriculum frameworks into curricula, many new teachers were frustrated by state standards and accountability. Anticipating the content that her fourth grade students would face on the state test in the spring, one teacher lamented, "You want me to teach this stuff, but I don't have the stuff to teach." The frameworks and high-stakes test introduced pressure without proven pedagogy and a mandate without materials.

In situations where new teachers did have materials such as textbooks to accompany the curriculum frameworks, they often said that the two were not aligned; the books or other materials did not cover the same content as the state's frameworks. A science teacher at an urban middle school described the problem succinctly: "Either I am reading the standards wrong or the book; [they don't] match." However, this challenge extended beyond the alignment of books to standards, for this teacher had examined the state frameworks, her own district's standards, and the MCAS questions and found a woeful lack of alignment.

The vast number of topics covered by the state standards also frustrated many new teachers; they resented being asked to do the impossible. A history teacher at a suburban high school expressed the view of many when he called the standards "mind-bogglingly comprehensive and vague." Bernie said that he was required to cover world studies from Rome through the French Revolution in one high school history course—"just about two thousand years of history in one hundred and eighty days or less." Even a first-grade teacher, whose urban school placed great emphasis on MCAS scores, described how the social science standards required her to teach "all the way from the Ice Age with hunters and nomads coming over the land bridge into Vikings and Explorers, Native Americans, first three colonies, all thirteen in the colonization, and then the Revolution into how we became America." Although she realized that she was not expected to cover every topic in detail, no one told her which topics to emphasize or the specific content to teach for each.

Thus, new teachers faced heavy demands with inadequate support. Many novices described haphazardly trying to cover everything by piecing together test-related materials and by using specific MCAS questions as the basis for instruction. Nineteen of our fifty respondents had been assigned to teach subjects and grade levels where the MCAS was administered, and many more said that the state assessment affected their instruction even though their grade or subject was not tested. The pressure to successfully teach the material in the frameworks was overwhelming in the absence of greater clarity and support.

The Importance of Curriculum

The new teachers we interviewed often were overwhelmed by the responsibility and demands of designing curriculum and planning daily lessons. They entered the classroom expecting to find a curriculum, yet many found little guidance about what to teach or how to teach it. Their confidence was undermined daily as they realized that they did not really know what information and skills to teach, that they had insufficient instructional guides, that they lacked ready access to resources that might enhance their own subject knowledge, and that their own private knapsack of instructional strategies was virtually empty.

Providing inadequate curricular shortchanges both new teachers and their students. It is important to provide new teachers with a basic set of instructional strategies and materials so that they respond to students' needs from day one and refine their own teaching style over time. Regardless of the particular curriculum that schools and districts choose, they should consider new teachers' needs for both day-to-day support and longer-term professional development.

The environment of new standards and accountability intensified new teachers' need to find out what to do and how to do it right.

They reported feeling pressure to teach something, but being unsure as to what that something was or how they should do it. Although curriculum has traditionally been a local responsibility, our findings suggest that state officials must go beyond simply developing standards and assessments. If they accept the premise of standards-based reform, then they must take seriously their responsibility to support its implementation in districts and schools. The development of curriculum and instructional materials, both with and for teachers, and ongoing high-quality professional development are essential (see Smith & O'Day, 1991). It is not enough to impose higher standards and tougher accountability without also offering the practical, day-to-day support that makes success attainable.

Instructional materials, including textbooks and teacher's guides, can be concrete and valuable sources of curricular support. However, simply providing new teachers with a textbook is not enough. At a bare minimum, new teachers should receive an orientation to the curriculum and the available instructional materials prior to starting work at their new schools. Better yet are long-term professional development opportunities that regularly engage new teachers and their colleagues in discussing the content they are teaching and investigating how and how well their students learn it. High-quality curriculum materials can be an important part of such professional development because they provide teachers with concrete support for implementing what they learned (Kauffman, 2002; Russell, 1997).

The potential of curriculum goes beyond simply mapping out the content and skills students need to know. It can also be a powerful tool for teacher development through which new teachers gain a more sophisticated understanding of academic content, pedagogy, and student learning. Rather than simply a list of topics to teach, the curriculum can include detailed information that supports teachers in making their own instructional decisions, such as "concrete examples of what student work might look like, what reasoning might underlie students' work, and what other teachers have done in similar situation" (Ball & Cohen, 1996, p. 8). New teachers working in isolation can find the wisdom of experienced colleagues within the pages of such a curriculum, and teachers working collaboratively can use it as a resource to deepen their professional conversations.

A small number of our respondents worked in settings that were structured to encourage regular discussions about curriculum and instruction among teachers at all levels of experience. In such schools, veteran teachers engaged with their novice colleagues in developing the very kinds of supports that new teachers said they needed. It is likely that experienced teachers also benefit from the continuous process of developing and refining curriculum and instructional strategies. Such school-based collaboration around curriculum development may be the most promising approach to orienting new teachers to their curriculum and helping them figure out what to teach and how to teach it. In Chapter Seven, we explore why such meaningful collaboration is rare in schools and how it can be encouraged.

Chapter Seven

Professional Culture and the Promise of Colleagues

Coauthor: Susan M. Kardos

New teachers yearn for professional colleagues who can help them acclimate to their school's unique culture, help them solve the complicated, daily dilemmas of classroom teaching, and guide their ongoing learning. When the fifty teachers in our study chose teaching, they envisioned the stimulating classroom they hoped to create and the buzz of their students engaged in learning. In the ideal, they also hoped for colleagues and administrators who would be committed to student learning and would help them, as new teachers, achieve success with their students.

Among the ten teachers featured in this book, only two, Fred and Victoria, began their careers in schools where their colleagues adequately supported them and the workplace culture fully included them. The others—Keisha, Amy, Bernie, Brenda, Carolyn, Esther, Derek, and Mary—were left alone, or with other novices, to make it on their own. The schools in which Fred and Victoria taught had structures in place to assist and support them (such as mentoring, classroom observations, and teacher meetings). Moreover, these structures were embedded in professional cultures that valued interaction and exchange between novices and veterans. Thus, despite the persistence of the "sink or swim" paradigm in schools, we found that when new teachers are buoyed by a professional culture that

---

The ideas in this chapter expand upon an earlier article: S. M. Kardos, S. M. Johnson, H. G. Peske, D. Kauffman, and E. Liu (2001). Counting on colleagues: New teachers encounter the professional cultures of their schools. *Educational Administration Quarterly*, 37(2), 250–290.

encourages professional interaction, they are more likely to feel supported and successful in their work with their students and may be more likely to stay in teaching.

Professional Culture and Why It Matters

Professional culture is the blend of values, norms, and modes of professional practice that develops among teachers in a school. The professional culture of a school has an enormous impact on new teachers, since they look toward their colleagues for signals about how best to do good work. Professional culture can be schoolwide, or it can exist in subunits within the school, such as departments, grade-level teams, or clusters.

Regardless of the quality or duration of a new teacher's preservice preparation, novice teachers must continue to learn long after they enter their first classroom. They continue to improve their skills and adjust their strategies for delivering engaging lessons. They learn about the philosophy of their school and what administrators, colleagues, and parents expect of them. They learn about the students, their families, and the community. They learn to keep order in their classroom, better manage their time, and differentiate instruction in response to students' learning styles. They become better at involving parents more effectively, fostering student responsibility, and assessing student progress. They learn to create curriculum, integrate technology into their teaching, and better prepare students for standardized tests. Leaving new teachers on their own to address these complex and dynamic challenges is both unreasonable and unnecessary, particularly since they are surrounded by colleagues doing similar work. Indeed, the quality of new teachers' interactions with their colleagues may determine their success as teachers (Bryk & Schneider, 2002; Feiman-Nemser, 1983; Louis & Marks, 1998; McDonald, 1980; Rust, 1994) and their decision whether or not to stay in teaching (Adelman, 1991; Feiman-Nemser, 1983; Gold, 1996).

The fifty new teachers in our study described the workplace cultures of their schools and the ways in which those cultures did or did not support them. Keisha, Amy, Bernie, Brenda, Carolyn, and Esther experienced what we called a *veteran-oriented professional culture*, where the workplace norms were set by veteran teachers who protected individual autonomy at the expense of professional interaction. In this culture, new teachers did not benefit from the accumulated wisdom of their experienced colleagues because there was little exchange between new and experienced teachers. Derek and Mary experienced what we called a *novice-oriented professional culture*, where the values and work modes were determined by a predominantly novice faculty. Again, new teachers' work was uninformed by experienced colleagues' expertise because there were few opportunities for these novices to interact with experienced teachers. Fred and Victoria experienced what we called an *integrated professional culture*, where there was ongoing professional exchange among all teachers across experience levels (Kardos, Johnson, Peske, Kauffman, & Liu, 2001).

Keisha's Experience: "Survival Mode"

Keisha's first teaching job was in a second grade classroom of an urban elementary school. As we saw in Chapter Two, she left her job in higher education because she was troubled by the weak literacy skills of many college students with whom she worked. She wanted to teach in the primary grades, where she thought she could address literacy problems at their roots. Most of the teachers in her school were veterans and seemed to greatly value their privacy and autonomy. Like other new teachers who find themselves in a veteran-oriented professional culture, Keisha was on her own, trying to decipher the unexplained code of her school and trying to meet the daily, unpredictable challenges of her classroom. By the middle of her first year, she said, things were actually getting better: she upgraded her status from "going nuts" to being "in survival mode."

Although she entered teaching with experience in another career and a master's degree in elementary education, Keisha still faced many challenges as she learned to teach. As she soon realized, much of the complex craft of teaching is developed in practice and can more easily be learned with help from experienced colleagues. She explained: "I'm starting from ground zero as a new teacher. . . . Other teachers are pulling stuff up; they're going through their repertoire, 'Let's use this. Let's use this.' I didn't have that." So Keisha sought support, advice, and opportunities to collaborate with the veteran teachers at her school. They were not responsive, and instead she relied on a few other novice teachers in the building.

Keisha genuinely liked her students and her colleagues, but the professional culture of the school was oriented toward the needs and norms of veteran teachers, with little recognition of what she needed as a new teacher. Teachers worked behind closed doors and did not share the materials they had accumulated over the years. Keisha explained: "I am a first-year teacher. I cannot do what she does next door. . . . She has been doing it for twenty-five years. I expected to be pulled in here before the rest of the teachers got here. . . . I thought they'd say, 'Oh you're new. Let me tell you about this job. Let me tell you about the expectations in the building.' Still, I find out things as they trickle down."

While Keisha was waiting for things to trickle down, she was desperately trying to figure out how to do the best job she could for her students. She and three other new teachers formed an informal support group because, despite the fact that they had all been assigned official mentors, they "felt that [they] weren't getting" the assistance with instruction and classroom management that "[they] needed from the school." One of Keisha's novice colleagues told her that if she needed anything, she should just come upstairs to her classroom, which Keisha did every single day, some days crying. Even though the novices had formed a group, they still felt alone in their work. Although they did try to take care of each other, they had little teaching experience to draw upon and no expertise that had stood the test of time.

Keisha's isolation was not the result of veteran teachers' deliberate efforts to marginalize her and other new teachers from the professional life of the school. There was simply no structure in place to assist her and no norm or expectation that expert teachers would deliberately or systematically support new teachers in their work. Furthermore, she bemoaned what she perceived to be the lack of a team approach toward achieving a shared goal. Keisha explained that "overall the faculty was very nice," but she did not get from them the kind of help she needed as a new teacher: "They weren't, on the whole, where I needed them to be for me professionally." Her hopes of working with the experienced teachers on her faculty were never realized. Instead, she encountered a firm norm of privacy and noninterference: "I think any collaboration that is done is strictly on an individual basis. . . . You are kind of in your own little classroom, and your space is kind of your world. Literally, I could probably close that door and teach here until June, and be unaffected by other people, if that's what I wanted to do—unfortunately."

It was unfortunate for Keisha because, whereas autonomy and noninterference may signal professional power or administrative trust, for Keisha it meant consignment to isolation. The egg-crate model of schools, which today's cohort of veteran teachers inherited from their predecessors, is public education's time-worn version of the modern office cubicle. In schools, however, the separating walls are higher and more permanent. Furthermore, in public schools like Keisha's, there may well be no reliable common meeting time or space where teachers are expected to engage in collaborative projects or problem solving.

After her first year, Keisha quit her job to take a teaching position at an urban charter school where the professional culture was integrated. In contrast to her first school, she described it as, "not so terribly isolating. It's a much more supportive environment." She explained that, at her new school, the administrators and teachers had created a culture where "there is an expectation that you're a professional and you're going to do the best job that you can possibly do. If you need help, we're here to help you and support you, but we're all pushing at the same level for the same goal." This is what Keisha had hoped for, but never found, in her first school.

Veteran-Oriented Professional Culture

As Keisha's case illustrates, in veteran-oriented professional cultures the workplace culture is set by the experienced teachers at the school. In this type of culture, veteran teachers operate independently and go about their work with little attention to the professional needs of the small numbers of novice teachers in their midst. These veteran teachers may be masterful in their classrooms; they may be burned out and ineffective; or they may be somewhere in between, doing a solid, if not remarkable, job. Regardless of veteran teachers' abilities, skills, or dedication as teachers (or even their kindness as individuals), independence and privacy are the dominant work mode among veterans (Little, 1990b), and new teachers' needs and special talents are mostly ignored. In these cultures, professional interaction among new teachers and their veteran colleagues rarely occurs, and thus new teachers do not benefit from their wisdom and expertise.

The Price Paid in a Veteran-Oriented Professional Culture

In veteran-oriented professional cultures, new teachers receive little mentoring and experience few useful classroom observations accompanied by constructive feedback. When they occur, observations are usually evaluative, rather than designed to provide assistance or support. Thus, new teachers in veteran-oriented professional cultures suffer from professional isolation and lack the sheltered status they need as beginners. The cost to schools is often frustration, confusion, and attrition among their new teachers.

Mentoring and Classroom Observations

Most teachers in our study, Keisha among them, reported having been assigned an official mentor. But the success of most of these mentor matches was apparently left to chance, and rarely did they yield the level of support the new teacher needed. Keisha's mentor offered little curricular or instructional assistance, although she did provide some help and emotional support. Esther was assigned a mentor who was a special education teacher and knew little about the math that Esther was teaching. She described their relationship: "I've spoken to this lady twice, maybe for five minutes. . . . She's very nice and stuff, but she kind of goes by and kind of gives me a worried look [and says], 'How's it going?' I say, 'OK.' And then, that's it." But Esther had hoped for curricular and instructional support from someone who knew how to teach math. One person she logically looked to for help was the math department head. However, the department head explained that she could not step in as Esther's mentor because she was responsible for evaluating her, and she could only observe her class for the purpose of formal review.

Brenda, who entered teaching with little formal preparation, expected to have a mentor at her school but did not. This left her yearning for feedback and support in her first year of teaching: "I just really wanted feedback on . . . what I'm doing. . . . 'You could be doing this a little bit different.' 'I think that wouldn't have happened if you had done this.' . . . I just kept saying, 'I want anybody that wants to come in and observe. I mean, I don't care. I don't care what they think; I just want some feedback. I don't care if it's a horrible lesson and they see me—I just need to know.'" Many of the new teachers echoed this sentiment; they were committed to teaching their students well, and they knew that direct observation, feedback, and advice and critique would help them improve. But was hard to come by.

Like Brenda, Bernie did not have a mentor in his first year at his urban high school. The experienced teacher with whom he shared a room offered little support, even when Bernie went to her with specific questions or concerns. Bernie believed he could have benefited from a mentor in his second year, as well, but explained, "I'm just kind of, you know, getting my mentoring where I can. In the hallway, or in the lunch room, or what have you." He said that he would have liked to have had a mentor but doubted the quality of the matches and advice: "They have the home ec guy mentoring the first-year social studies guy. All he's telling him is, you know, 'This is a corridor pass,' you know, nothing really substantive."

Thus, merely having one-to-one mentoring in place did not guarantee that new teachers would get the assistance they needed. The success of one-to-one mentoring rests on multiple factors, some of which are impossible to control. First, some schools simply do not have the capacity to provide every new teacher with an on-site mentor who teaches the same subject in a similar grade level. Second, some schools are unable to provide new teachers with a mentor who teaches in close proximity or who shares common planning time to meet or collaborate. Third, a good match depends upon compatible personalities, similar styles, or shared values, all hard to arrange. Finally, simply having a mentor promises little unless the relationship is nurtured in a professional culture that takes mentoring seriously and supports work norms that make these relationships useful to new teachers.

Not Recognizing New Teachers' "Newness"

The fact that new teachers in veteran-oriented professional cultures are not given special consideration as novices has implications for them both in what they receive from their colleagues and what they contribute. In the name of equity and professional independence, most schools expect new teachers to assume a full teaching load (and often extra assignments) from day one, without any additional assistance or time. New teachers realize, however, that this situation compromises their potential for achieving success with students. Brenda offered a solution:

> I think first-year teachers should have less students. I think they should have more time to prepare. I think they should be paired up with someone that comes in and observes them. . . . They shouldn't be expected to do a lot of extra things. I think that the expectation should be for them to get used to things, at least for the first year, and just to learn how to manage the classroom and be part of the school community. And then, you would just feel so much more positive about taking other things on, just so much more prepared for it.

When Carolyn said of her urban elementary school, ". . .pretty much right when you start . . . as a teacher you have full responsibility, whether it's your first year or your thirtieth year," she was referring not only to new teachers' assignments, but also to their treatment. Equal assignments and equal treatment meant that her school did not acknowledge that new teachers' professional needs are *real* and differ, in important ways, from the needs of their experienced colleagues. This is a problem for those new teachers who have been carefully and extensively trained, as well as for their colleagues who enter teaching with little or no preparation. Teaching well—especially in the context of high standards and high stakes for students—takes more than just content knowledge and the sheer will to be good at it. Most new teachers in veteran-oriented professional cultures are not only on their own, but they are expected to assume the same roles and responsibilities with at least the same effectiveness as their colleagues with ten, twenty, or thirty years of experience.

New Teacher Isolation

Teachers in a veteran-oriented professional culture work within a norm of privacy and noninterference, which, for new teachers, translates to isolation. For some veteran teachers, professional privacy and autonomy allow them to teach well without distractions from out-side the classrooms. For others this independence provides a way to hide ineffective teaching or unruly students. Regardless of the reason, in the best cases, new teachers in veteran-oriented professional cultures are welcomed and spoken to, but never included or assisted. In the worst cases, their veteran colleagues hoard books or lesson plans, dismiss or even ridicule new teachers' ideas, sabotage improvement efforts, and constantly complain and criticize. New teachers describe these scenarios of professional isolation as frustrating and troubling.

Many new teachers in veteran-oriented professional cultures (and some of their veteran counterparts) do not believe that independence among teachers is an ideal worth perpetuating. Keisha described, with some dismay, the grade-level autonomy that exists in her school: "I will tell you that this floor doesn't know what that floor is doing, and that floor doesn't know what this floor [is doing]. The upper elementary is upstairs. I don't know what the heck is going on up there. We never even see them because we have different lunch periods. Never even see those teachers, except at the copy machine." She was pleased when she crossed these borders, albeit only to interact with other novice teachers.

It seems that even where there is the will among veteran teachers to interact with and support new teachers and each other, there are both cultural forces (values, beliefs, and norms) and structural factors (school size and teachers' schedules) that make it hard to create and maintain meaningful professional exchange. Brenda talked about some teachers who have supported her, but then explained that she mostly felt alone:

> I think there's only so much they can do, though, as far as being supportive, because they all have their own classes, and their time is so, so busy also. . . . It's hard to be able to talk to other teachers more than just in passing or in the lunch room. Most teachers are just gone at 2:30. . . . And they've set up things in such a way that maybe after years and years of doing it, they don't have to plan as much or they

have their systems down for homework, that it's just easy. But I find myself being there a lot. So, it would be nice to be able to see teachers after school, and I find that that's not really possible.

Bernie also explained how teachers in his school hole themselves up in their rooms for the day and then leave as soon as they finish teaching: "Everybody's in their classrooms. There's not much opportunity to really—maybe one of the things I'd love to do is to sit in on a few of the classes and, you know, I have the one prep, and it's the first period of the day, and that's like gold to me, because I need to use that. . . . And then you have a hall duty, and you have a fifteen, twenty minute lunch. And then pretty much everybody's gone."

Despite the dearth of structured collegial support, some new teachers manage to survive that first year because they band together with other novices at the school (as in Keisha's case), they have an outside network of support, they win the kindness of a single colleague, or they have a lucky assignment that brings them within earshot of someone willing to help. Esther, for example, had the good fortune of having hall duty at a time of day that enabled her to get a few minutes of support—in front of the boys' bathroom—from a colleague who was leaving her post. Esther explained: "There is an English teacher who's kind of been, not my mentor for my subject and stuff, but I mean, she's helped me—I guess I would consider it as a mentor. I mean, we have duty back to back. You know, she's getting off duty as I'm going on hall duty. So, we tend to chat, and you know just about the kids and about the environment. And that's helped, just having someone who's been here for a while." Modest as it was, Esther appreciated the interaction. But when her veteran colleagues rejected her attempts to collaborate or they withheld books and supplies that she needed, Esther decided to find another place to teach: "As a first-year teacher, I needed someone to help me out a little bit. And there was no one. So I needed to be elsewhere if I was going to continue."

For Carolyn, the struggle was to sustain her idealism and motivation in the face of a teaching staff who had lost much of theirs.

She explained: "Sometimes I'm feeling hopeful and optimistic, wanting to come up with some strategies: How can we fix this? How can we change the way things are here? And teachers laugh, you know, 'Oh, come on, Carolyn, you know better than that, to do that here.' And it's not because they don't want a better school, or things to work well; it's because I think they've all spent so much of their own time trying to make things work, and have seen things fail so many times that they're just—have had enough." Similarly, Brenda's colleagues frequently deflated her idealism. Her requests for help, or even sympathy, were often met with indifference. When she asked subtly for support, she was sometimes made to feel silly for needing assistance in the first place: "I often feel like if I say something to them about 'I had a hard time with so and so today,' [veteran teachers respond], 'Oh, he never gives me a hard time.'" Thus, working in a veteran-oriented culture can demoralize new teachers who need support and assistance in learning to teach effectively.

In the first year of our study, twenty-one of the fifty new teachers taught within veteran-oriented professional cultures. Of those twenty-one, nine (43 percent) left their schools at the end of that year, and five (24 percent) left public school teaching altogether. Among our ten featured teachers, Esther and Keisha switched from schools with veteran-oriented professional cultures to schools where the professional culture was integrated. Amy, Bernie, Brenda, and Carolyn stayed in their schools, but Brenda, faced with the same overloaded schedule as the previous year, quit by November.

Derek's Experience: Running a Sprint

In his first two years teaching high school history in an inner-city charter school, Derek expressed a deep and palpable commitment to his colleagues, his students, and his school. By year three he was exhausted, disillusioned, and considering new job opportunities outside the classroom and outside the school. He was concerned not only about the low pay, but also about the intense school climate in which he was expected to do his work.

When asked to describe his school, Derek said he could not explain it in words; it must be experienced first-hand. He referred to the faculty, the majority of whom were in their twenties, as "a family." His colleagues, he said, were "more than just co-workers." They worked hard together during the school day, they spent time together on weekends, and they shared a philosophy about teaching. They were all, according to Derek, "moving in the same direction."

Teachers at his school interacted constantly with each other, planning major projects and classes, making schoolwide decisions, and having fun. They treasured the premium put on innovation, creativity, collegial interdependence, and friendship. Their commitments and loyalties to each other were, in Derek's words, more like "family to family" or "good friend to good friend." And it was this, he said, that "facilitate[d] a true understanding and a movement." However, this intense set of relationships did not entirely fulfill new teachers' needs, for they had no senior colleagues to ask for advice or suggestions, and no one to provide perspective or wisdom. This mode of operation came at a cost. Derek summed up his early experiences when he said, "Our school is like a cult."

Within this cultlike context, which Derek called "crazy and hectic," he and his mostly novice colleagues worked long and hard hours in a relatively new school. As a result, teacher turnover was high. The administration gave new teachers little formal support about curriculum and instruction, and there was no on else they could look to for guidance and wisdom. Furthermore, because of the crisis mode in which the school operated, there was little, if any, room for "rookie mistakes." In his second year of teaching, Derek remained optimistic: "I'm single. I'm young. Got a lot of energy. And I can do it for [the students]. I don't necessarily think I'll always be able to do it, but I can do it for now." However, by his third year, eleven of the sixteen teachers had announced they were leaving, and Derek was seriously considering doing the same.

Among other things, Derek described ambiguous processes for decision making and shaky systems of implementation and said that the "school was not really setting up structures for teachers to do the best job." In his view, it was difficult to articulate to newer teachers the reasons behind certain school policies and procedures, and it was difficult to even find the time to try. By year three, he said, the stability of the school was in jeopardy and teachers were feeling "rubbed raw." Derek explained with resignation and sadness, "We had a young staff that was really dedicated and committed, and we just—it went out of control. It spiraled out of control." He had foreshadowed this when he told us the previous year: "We must remember that it's not a sprint. It's a marathon. But some of us go to work like it's a sprint." Indeed, Derek and his colleagues did not pace themselves at all, and by the third year they were spent.

Novice-Oriented Professional Culture

Derek's experience, in many ways, typified that of many new teachers who find themselves in schools with novice-oriented professional cultures, which occur most often in charter schools, redesigned or reconstituted schools, or low-performing schools with ongoing teacher turnover. Each year in such schools, there are high proportions of inexperienced teachers who determine the values and work mode. Youth and idealism prevail, and long hours, innovation, reinvention, and frenzy rule the day. Although the tenor of novice-oriented professional cultures is quite different from that of veteran-oriented professional cultures, the consequence for new teachers is the same: they fail to benefit from the wisdom and expertise of experienced colleagues. There may be intense professional interaction among novices in these cultures, but the absence of experienced teachers leaves unassisted novices spinning their wheels and retracing old paths.

The Price Paid in a Novice-Oriented Professional Culture

As we learn from Derek's experience as a new teacher in a novice-oriented professional culture, the price paid by schools, teachers, and ultimately the students they aim to serve is extremely high. Although new teachers might praise the mission, excitement, and social-emotional bonds they experience in novice-oriented professional cultures, they often bemoan the overwhelming challenges of their many responsibilities and the lack of support they have in meeting them. The cost to new teachers is exhaustion, frustration, and disillusionment, while schools pay a price in new teacher attrition.

The Absence of Mentors and Mentoring

Since schools with novice-oriented professional cultures are staffed predominantly by new teachers, often there simply are not enough mentors to go around. Often new teachers are left completely alone or are assigned to all-novice groups to plan their lessons, manage their classrooms, decide on curricula, create tests, meet with parents and community members, and improve their teaching. There is also little guidance about school policies and procedures, mostly because the schools are newly created, reorganized, or reconstituted, and established policies and procedures are not yet in place.

Despite their sincere commitment and worthy intentions, there is clearly a need for mentoring of new teachers in novice-oriented professional cultures. Derek described as "problematic" the fact that in his second and third year at the school he was expected to assume the role of experienced teacher. In his second year, he took on a vast array of responsibilities, including mentoring two student-teachers. He recognized, however, the inherent problem of being a new teacher in a new school who is responsible for the induction of even newer teachers. He explained, "When a new teacher asks, 'How do we do this?' And you go, 'We do this, we do that, we do a bunch of things. . . .' 'Well, you don't really know that much more than I do. . . .' 'We're all in the same boat.'"

In her first year of teaching, Mary taught humanities in a charter middle school, which had a prototypical novice-oriented professional culture, in which teachers struggled—unguided—to learn to teach. After two years, Mary left her school. She was attracted to her second school, she said, because she would get experienced supervision there. In her novice-oriented school she said she often felt that "this is not working, these kids are failing. . . . I don't know how to fix it." In short, she was deeply bothered by the fact that she did not think she was serving her students well, and she saw having access to veteran teachers' expertise as a possible solution. Mary compared the professional cultures of the two schools, describing first the novice-oriented one: "There were no veterans. The veterans at my old school. . . . The most experienced teacher probably had seven years of teaching. My principal only taught for a couple of years. The oldest person was in the late thirties. And . . . a couple . . . were in their early thirties. In my new school there is probably, it's about a split, although maybe 40 percent are veterans, and 60 percent new at this point. So, for example, in my team, there are three teachers who had taught over twenty years. . . . I have a mix really, it's a mix . . . which is good for me, which I've appreciated." In her second school, the mix helped ensure that supervision, support, and mentoring were available to her.

Scarce Classroom Observation and Feedback

Because there are few experienced colleagues to observe and offer feedback, new teachers in novice-oriented professional cultures often do without. Many of the teachers say that their schools have an "open-door policy" where anyone is welcome in any classroom. That policy, coupled with collaborative planning and decision making, often replace much needed classroom observations and direct feedback about instruction. However, for the most part, declaring an "open-door policy" does not yield frequent visitors because teachers are just too busy. When new teachers in novice-oriented professional cultures participate in peer observation, they often observe colleagues who, like them, have little experience. And when observations do happen, there is rarely structure or time for meaningful debriefing and problem solving. Mary explained how observations happened in her first school: "We have a peer professional development program. So, you're matched with a partner, and you observe each other's classrooms. . . . That piece has not been as supportive, in the sense of really concrete advice, really concrete feedback. It's been really weak. . . . The structures really weren't there. . . . And in terms of administration? Not a lot of feedback. Very little feedback. . ." Mary explained, "And it's been up to you. We have a protocol we could use if we want. If not, we just go in, and observe and talk later."

Although meaningful observations seldom occur, new teachers in novice-oriented professional cultures stave off some of the isolation experienced by new teachers in veteran-oriented professional cultures because they interact among themselves all the time. Derek explained that working in "clusters" (planning curriculum, projects, and trips in teams of three teachers: humanities, math, and science) enabled him not only to get to know the other teachers well, but also to talk more easily about students or rearrange schedules to accommodate a teacher's special request. He described the cluster as "a situation where we create support."

However, social-emotional support and group decision making are not the same as direct assistance in teaching. As Derek explained, "It's more of a personal connection that provides and lends the support. And I can't explain necessarily how that works. But it works in a different way than a professional relationship." In novice-oriented professional cultures, personal support often substitutes for professional support. Furthermore, Derek explained, these intense personal commitments can take their toll: "It also contributes to that overworked mentality, because you feel like you are trying to work for people that you really, really care for."

Chaos and Frenzy

Many factors contribute to an atmosphere of chaos and frenzy at novice-oriented schools. In addition to the intense personal commitments described above, they include the absence of established school policies and procedures; the value placed on innovation, creativity, and hard work; organizational uncertainty; and the lack of experience of the majority of the staff. Mary explained about her first school:

> It's a new staff. I would say we're all a young staff. Not that many experienced teachers. . . . It's sort of an intense kind of energy there. A bit of a chaotic sort of feel, because of the number of transitions we've been through, I think. . . . And so there's sort of an energy of wanting to make things better for these children. That's like the whole energy of the school. But a lot of sort of anxiety and frustration about how we're not really at that place yet. . . . Sort of the frustration of the lack of progress that we're making with some of our students is taking its toll on people. And some of that is, you know, people do come in a bit weary looking, . . . people are feeling a little bit worn down, I think, from the challenges.

Derek described the intense work ethic in his school as self-imposed, but no less problematic for teachers or for the school itself: "We overwork ourselves to the point where people get sick, which makes the machine break down." But there is little choice; in Derek's school fledgling teachers are charged with not only teaching their classes, but also creating or re-creating the vision, programs, and policies of a school. Of course, innovation and hard work are generally applauded in organizations; however, in novice-oriented professional cultures, the context often is chaotic, the pace is relentless, and the casualties are the students and their teachers. Derek likened his school to an emergency room: "it's all crisis, so there is no room for rookie mistakes." That makes for intense pressure for new teachers but little support.

New teachers in novice-oriented professional cultures value their professional "freedom" and "influence" and their ability, as Derek said, to "all sit down together and decide what it is we would like to teach, what we think would be good for our kids." But underlying this independence is the assumption that new teachers have the skills and experience to do this complicated work—that they will not, or even cannot, make rookie mistakes. However, the truth is that they do not have the skills and experience of seasoned veterans, and they need sheltered opportunities to improve their craft.

Twelve of our fifty teachers, including Derek and Mary, began their careers in novice-oriented professional cultures. Of those twelve, four (33 percent)—including Mary—left those schools after the first year of the study and two (17 percent) left public school teaching altogether.

Fred's Experience: Remarkable Support

Fred began his teaching career at a small, urban secondary school. He was deeply committed to his students' success and to the excellence and continuing development of his school. When we first met Fred, his school included grades seven, eight, and nine, and school leaders planned to add one grade every year through grade twelve. The school, a neighborhood public school, draws its students from the low-income community that immediately surrounds it. It is a Professional Development School, the result of a unique partnership between a local university and the city school district. The faculty includes both highly experienced teachers and newer teachers. Most of the newer teachers have traditional teacher preparation, master's degrees, and internship experience at the school. Frequently during his interviews, Fred attested to the vibrancy of the school's professional culture. He said, "It's really quite remarkable here, the support." Moreover, teachers, students, and administrators at Fred's school are committed to a single goal—that all students will go to college.

To Fred, his school is about high expectations, collaboration, and ongoing teacher learning, all in the service of high student achievement. As he explained, "the expectations are so clear . . . we're gearing these kids to college, that that's our ultimate goal: to get the kids ready for college." The expectations are high for student and teacher performance, but neither is left alone to achieve the mission.

Fred and his new teacher colleagues received consistent support from their school as they learned to teach. In fact, new teachers were treated in ways that not only recognized their particular needs but also valued their special skills and knowledge. In particular, Fred appreciated both the assistance that he got as a new teacher and the recognition he received for his expertise in developing history curriculum. He said that the school acknowledged that new teachers needed support and provided it by "affording me the professionalism that was important to make me feel like I was part of the faculty, but still not leaving me there to sink."

According to Fred, the fact that the faculty included a mix of new and experienced teachers "promotes the best type of situation for faculty." He described the interaction among novice and veteran teachers this way: "So we have a nice blend of veteran teachers who have been in the system for a long time and know the art of teaching. Then we also have a nice core of . . . young teachers like myself with less than five years of teaching experience. And that creates a really good atmosphere. So I think the young teachers learn from the veteran teachers. And I think the veteran teachers get sparked a little bit from the young teachers coming in, you know, a new, fresh attitude. So it's mutually enriching in that sense."

It is important to note that there is nothing inherently beneficial about simply having a mix of novices and veterans within the same school. What is exceptional at Fred's school is that teachers interact regularly about teaching across experience levels, both formally and informally. Fred described a typical situation: "If I have a question or if I had something happen in class that perplexed me that I didn't know how to deal with, then I go down to [Sue] or [Tom] and say, 'I'm having trouble, how do I deal with this?'" He explained, "People take the lead from the people who know what's going on here."

Fred said the school's culture emphasizes "teachers as learners," and it is expected that teachers learn when they work together. Learning to teach is an ongoing process; a teacher masters the art by practicing, over time. Thus, administrators and teacher leaders at Fred's school realized that it serves their school well to recognize that new teachers grow in skill and expertise from day to day and from year to year: "There's an expectation that you would mature as a teacher and develop new strategies in various arenas that you may not have had in your bag of tricks to begin with. . . . I don't think I can really narrow it down to one particular thing or one particular pedagogical component. But . . . there is a great expectation for understanding things—for instance, like students who need LD [learning disabled] services and IEPs [individualized educational plans]—to understand those better, and how to provide accommodations better than I did my very first year."

Fred also explained that the teachers in his school feel and act as if they are collectively responsible for the school, the students and each other. He said, "we're all in the same game here together." He explained that he believed it was "[his] responsibility, as it is everybody else's, to share in the burden" of achieving the school's mission. In speaking of his duty to all of the students in the school he said, "I'm not primarily a social studies teacher here; I'm a teacher here primarily."

Integrated Professional Culture and the School Site

In contrast with veteran-oriented and novice-oriented professional cultures, integrated professional cultures offer new teachers an environment of inclusion and support. There are no separate camps of veterans and novices; instead, new teachers have ongoing opportunities to benefit from the knowledge and expertise of their experienced colleagues. In general, this type of culture, like the ones found at Fred's and Victoria's schools, is grounded in a belief that teachers hold knowledge and power in the school, and that students are best served when teachers assist each other and share responsibility for their students' learning as well as their own. In integrated professional cultures, mentoring is organized to benefit both the novice and the experienced teachers, and structures are in place that further facilitate teacher interaction and reinforce interdependence. Schools with integrated professional cultures are organizations that explicitly value teachers' professional growth and renewal.

The Advantages of an Integrated Professional Culture

Integrated professional cultures benefit both new teachers and their veteran colleagues. New teachers are supported in their efforts to teach their students well, veteran teachers are continually renewing themselves, and the entire faculty is united in its pursuit of student success and school improvement. Furthermore, those who teach in integrated professional cultures seem more likely to stay. In our full sample of fifty new Massachusetts teachers, seventeen, including Fred and Victoria, began their careers in integrated professional cultures. Of the seventeen, fourteen (82 percent)— including Fred and Victoria—stayed in those schools after the first year of our study (compared to 57 percent in veteran-oriented and 67 percent in novice-oriented professional cultures).

Mentoring and Classroom Observations

Fred, Victoria, and the other new teachers in our study who worked in integrated professional cultures had mentors who took their responsibility as teacher-of-teachers seriously and whose work as mentors was supported by their schools. In Victoria's school, "All new teachers, we are assigned a mentor. . . . It could either be in the same grade or it could be someone in the field, of course. So that person guides you through the year. If you need anything, you can go to that person." And in most cases, where the mentor was unable to help, the new teachers had other experienced teachers to turn to for assistance. Fred explained, "There's never a time when I don't feel like I can go to . . . the veteran teachers and say, 'It's not working, I need help with it.' And the suggestions they've given always seem to deal with the problem." Not only is a formal one-to-one mentoring program in place, but veteran teachers, too, assume responsibility for supporting new teachers.

New teachers get direct help with their classroom instruction, as well. Fred arranged to have his class videotaped, and he analyzed the tape with his experienced colleagues. Victoria was observed and given feedback by the vice principal, who is not responsible for evaluating her or directly determining whether she will be rehired. In addition, the new teachers have ample opportunities to observe other teachers teach. Victoria observed her colleagues teach when her students were in their noncore classes. She explained, "I'll walk into the other classes just to sit down at one. I'll walk into the hall, and I peek in, and I just stop by for a few minutes just to see what they're doing. I get to do that. . . ." Similarly, Fred described doing "a lot of stepping in and listening to other teachers." He said, "I still like going down and seeing . . . the science teacher teach. He's been doing it for thirty-four years and he's really got a knack—just very good at what he does." Both of these schools had open door policies that worked.

Novice Status

In integrated professional cultures, not only are teachers supported in their development, they are also granted some level of protected "novice status" during their early years, when their particular needs as new teachers are recognized and met, and they are given sheltered opportunities to develop teaching skills. For example, they might experiment with a new pedagogical strategy, after planning the lesson with an experienced colleague. They might make a difficult call to a student's parents, but with a counselor standing by. Of course they are held to high standards, but the anxiety that Derek described about not making "rookie mistakes" is moderated. New teachers in these settings are not left alone to sink; instead, they are kept afloat by a culture of support—to the benefit of their students.

Conversely, new teachers in veteran-oriented and novice-oriented professional cultures spoke of feeling in over their heads. Bernie, for example, recalled that in his first year, "I was probably as overwhelmed as I've ever been." And Carolyn was surprised that there was no differentiation between what was expected, regardless of "whether it's your first or your thirtieth year." Although they hoped for reassurance that they would not be expected to be experts from day one, there was, in fact, no such acknowledgment from administrators or colleagues in their veteran-oriented professional cultures that learning to teach is a hard, gradual process.

In contrast to Bernie and Carolyn's experiences, Fred said of his school, "There's an expectation that you would mature as a teacher and develop new strategies in various arenas." And the norm in Victoria's school was that experienced teachers constantly offered support and assistance to new teachers. She explained that in addition to her mentor and her colleagues, she had direct, ongoing contact with specialists at the school so that, "[If] they have anything that they think that I could use, they'll share it with me." She reported that curriculum supervisors at the school visit classrooms to "do lessons, and come in . . . just to see what we need. And then we have this internal e-mail system that when we need something, we just e-mail, and they'll get back to us right away, or send us pretty much anything we need." Finally, she had classroom visits from the principal and vice-principal, which she experienced as supportive rather than threatening. She explained that they occasionally "walk through the classroom . . . to see how we're doing, anything we need."

New teachers come to the profession not only needing to be granted appropriate status as novices, but also wanting to be recognized for their expertise. They bring to the profession useful skills, talents, and experiences that they are eager to share with their colleagues and adapt for use with their students. Newly prepared teachers often arrive prepared with the latest training about cognitive development or how to teach in inclusive classrooms. They may come with in-depth knowledge about how to integrate technology into classrooms, how to interpret test score data, or how to co-plan or team teach. Midcareer entrants arrive at their schools with rich experiences from diverse fields, such as science, technology, journalism, and the arts. Thus, new teachers also have much to offer their colleagues, their students, and the institutions that hire them.

Collective Responsibility and Interdependence

In integrated professional cultures, new teachers communicate and cooperate with each other and with their more experienced colleagues in the service of improving schoolwide instruction. Integrated professional cultures cultivate a close sense of collective responsibility and community among teachers. When Fred said, "I'm not primarily a social studies teacher here; I'm a teacher here primarily," he meant that teachers share responsibility for all students in the school, not just the students in individual teachers' classes.

In veteran-oriented professional cultures, the adult community is split into camps of novices and veterans or it is diffuse, with individuals camped out in their private classrooms; in novice-oriented professional cultures the commitment to the community tends to be intense but is not necessarily focused on developing the craft of teaching. However, in integrated professional cultures the community is "close knit" and "intimate," without an overbearing sense of personal obligation. Fred explained: "I think it's a fun place to come to work. The people are nice. There's a feeling of togetherness that I don't think always exists in other schools. I think that's important. I consider these people to be more than just professional colleagues, but many of them friends. But in the same respect, there's a nice disconnect. . . . It's nice because we spend a lot of time here with the faculty. I get along with them very well. We have a good relationship. And then at the end of the day, we go home."

In integrated professional cultures teachers are *interdependent*. Although they have professional power and autonomy, they do not work in a culture of privacy and noninterference. Instead, there is a powerful belief that schools best serve students when teachers of various experience levels work together, when talents and skills are optimized, and when challenges are jointly met. Fred explained that "teachers in the classrooms are the experts in their fields, and have the rights and responsibilities to do their job." At the same time, he described the web of teachers he works closely with and the "supportive collegial atmosphere" in which they work. For

Fred, the supportive atmosphere is a result of the mix of novices and veterans on the faculty: "I think it [the mix] adds a great deal of excitement and fresh ideas and new ideas. And the kids relate well, I think, with teachers who are that age. But I also think it's nice to have the veteran teachers, too. I know on a number of occasions, more than I can count, you go to them and say, you know, 'look, I'm having this problem, what should I do?' So you can't have a school that's too heavy either way, I don't think."

Victoria also described the formal and informal ways that she and her colleagues work together. She told of formal schoolwide and grade-level meetings where topics related to teacher work are discussed, such as how to handle teasing and bullying, how to assess student learning, and how to deal with issues related to diversity. She described meetings for new teachers in which they got support in their planning and teaching, such as "how to teach this unit, . . . what to expect, what to look for, what to leave out, what to include." Her grade-level teaching team met weekly to "go over what's happening," and they also worked together as a team to plan and teach. Finally, Victoria explained, "there are things that I can just knock next door. You know, 'Can I borrow this?' 'What do you think about this?' . . . We do things together, like go on field trips together. So that is really—that's nice." She added, "Even down in the copier room, where you see someone copying something, and say 'Hey, that looks great. Could I use it?' They'll just make another copy and hand it to us."

Simply, Victoria liked her school and its professional culture, and she particularly liked the teamwork:

> We have a good team. The third grade team, we try to plan together. We teach pretty much the same curriculum, but we, within our own room, we do our own style of teaching it. So, we stay with the same units, and we plan the same field trips. So that part is good. You feel like you're supported. So that was good, especially last year, too, because it was nice. And then this year, I feel like I can stand on my own two feet. . . . And the team is good; it's strong. . . . I do my own thing, but I also, I'm a team player and that's what you need

here. And you can't come here and say, 'Well, I'm going to do everything my way' and survive here. And it's a lot of teamwork and you
have to be a team player.

Keisha too, after leaving her first school and its veteran-oriented
professional culture, was thrilled that her second school had a "team
model" approach to teaching and that she was placed on a team
with other second and third grade teachers. She explained, "We
have block amounts of time, actually two hours each week that
have been carved out. So we have the opportunity to sit down and
actually plan and work together. We plan curriculum together; we
implement curriculum together; those sorts of things are happening.
No one is quite working in isolation."

Fulfilling the Promise of Colleagues

Novice teachers desperately need their colleagues. According to
educational researchers and analysts, it has long been the case that
new teachers' early years in the profession are characterized by anxiety and trauma (McDonald & Elias, 1983), feelings of disillusionment and intense pressure (Gold, 1996), and dashed expectations
(Wideen, Mayer-Smith, & Moon, 1998). But as the environment
of teaching becomes increasingly complex and dynamic, new teachers depend on having access to existing expertise and craft knowledge in order to make sense of enduring obstacles and solve new
problems. When novice teachers work with their experienced colleagues on curriculum and teaching they are more likely to know
what is expected of them, how to meet those expectations in the
context of their schools, how to solve problems in their classrooms,
and where to go for assistance. As one new teacher explained, "I
think teachers become better teachers by just sitting down and
talking to another teacher and say[ing], 'These are the things that
are confronting me; how do I deal with them?'" Indeed, it appears
that new teachers are most likely to survive and thrive when they
work in schools where support structures are embedded in integrated professional cultures.

Chapter Eight

Making Better Matches in Hiring

Coauthor: Edward Liu

Teaching general science at a racially and socioeconomically diverse urban middle school is a very different job than teaching Advanced Placement chemistry at an affluent, suburban, and largely white high school. Each position requires a unique set of dispositions, skills, and knowledge. Teaching positions also differ in less obvious ways. For example, teaching in a school that has adopted a school-wide math curriculum presents opportunities and demands for a new teacher different from those of teaching in a school where every teacher decides for herself how to teach math. Because no two teaching positions are alike and no two teachers are alike, everyone is better served if the hiring process leads to a deliberate match between a new teacher and his or her first position.

For new teachers, finding positions that closely fit their particular skills, knowledge, and interests is important, because it influences their prospects for achieving the success and the personal rewards for which they entered teaching. Unfortunately, the ways in which schools and districts hire new teachers often make it unlikely that a good match will emerge. Amy's story illustrates some of the problems that bedevil effective teacher hiring.

Amy's Hiring Experience

During the winter break of her senior year in college, Amy worked for a few days as a substitute teacher in the large urban district where she was about to begin student teaching. A few people had told her that "it's a really good idea to substitute teach during that time so your name is in [the district]. You will get your name in the door." In January, Amy saw a bulletin stating that substitute teachers applying for full-time jobs would automatically get an interview with the district. Amy went to the initial screening interview at the district central office, where she met a principal who was "extremely nice" to her and seemed impressed with her teaching portfolio. She sent this principal a thank you letter with her contact information, in case any positions opened up at her school. Although the principal had no openings at the time, she kept in touch with Amy throughout the spring, calling her five or six times. Each time she would ask Amy, "Have you heard anything from [the district]?" The principal told Amy that she had given her a "highly recommended" rating and was mentioning her name to other principals. Meanwhile, two other principals in the district were also trying to help Amy find a job—the principal at the school where she was student teaching and one of her college instructors who was also a principal in the district.

Spring passed, summer was ending, and for all her efforts and connections, Amy still had no job offer. Not much had resulted from her initial screening interview with the district, and her paperwork seemed to be languishing downtown in the district personnel office. She recalled, "I had all these principals helping me, but nothing was coming out if it. . . . I didn't get any interviews from them. All the interviews I got [came] from me pushing my name around with other people."

About three weeks before the start of the school year, things finally started to pick up. Principals from three schools in the district called Amy for interviews. Through her best friend's mother, Amy met yet a fourth principal in the district (the one who would eventually hire her), who asked for her résumé and scheduled Amy for an interview. Soon after, Amy heard again from the principal who had kept in touch with her throughout the spring. She now had two openings and wanted Amy to interview at her school and nowhere else. Unwilling to cancel the interview she had already scheduled with the other principal, Amy attended it and was immediately offered a job teaching second grade. The school had a very good reputation in the district and was a short commute from her home, so Amy accepted the position. It was Labor Day weekend, only a few days before school would start, and Amy finally had a job.

The Importance of Hiring

Amy's story illustrates how outmoded and inefficient many teacher hiring processes are. Amy was a strong candidate in many respects. She had nine years of rich and relevant experience working in an after-school program; she was fully credentialed; she had completed her student teaching within the district and was familiar with its curriculum; and she impressed three principals enough that each was trying to help her find a job. Yet the district's approach to hiring frustrated Amy's efforts to find a position. Her paperwork seemed stalled in the central office, and many teaching positions did not officially open until just a few weeks before the start of the school year. Given its late start, the district was quite lucky that by Labor Day Amy had not given up and bolted for the suburbs, where hiring is usually completed much sooner. One wonders, however, how many other talented individuals had.

The hiring process that Amy experienced was also problematic in that it provided her and the school that eventually hired her with relatively little information about each other. Because it was late August, the hiring process was rushed and Amy was hired on the basis of her résumé and a single interview. She was not asked to teach a sample lesson, nor did she have the opportunity to meet her future colleagues or observe the school in action to see if it would be a good place for her to begin teaching. As a result, both the school and Amy made decisions about her employment that were not well informed. It turned out that Amy did fit into her first school, but this was in spite of the hiring process rather than because of it.

Amy's story is not unusual. Late hiring and inadequate information are pervasive, particularly in large, urban districts. All too often, new teachers spend months navigating the central office bureaucracy, filling out paperwork, and attempting to obtain information about where openings might be. Ironically, principals are often in much the same position, waiting to find out how many teachers they can hire. Staff allocations might depend on a variety of factors— student enrollment projections, state and district budget decisions, retirement notifications, and the completion of teacher transfers within the district. Suddenly, it is September and yet another last-minute hiring frenzy ensues, for in the end, the district must put a teacher in every classroom.

In part, the late and haphazard hiring practices that many schools and districts employ are relics from a bygone era and a legacy of the "egg-crate" organization of schooling. In many respects, schools are still modeled after factories, which were designed around the use of unskilled labor. There remains an underlying view of teachers as interchangeable, replaceable parts and of teaching jobs as identical. This view is quite problematic, for it often leads both schools and individuals to underestimate the great variation in teaching positions and the importance of matching individuals to positions that fit their interests, needs, and skills. This fit is particularly important given the diversity within the next generation of teachers. As we saw in Chapter Two, this incoming generation is diverse in terms of age, experience, preparation, expectations regarding the workplace, and conceptions of career. Many teachers today approach teaching tentatively or conditionally, rather than as a certain, lifelong career. If their first teaching position does not provide a good fit with their interests, needs, and skills, teachers may choose to leave the school or the profession altogether after a short time. Improving teacher hiring and the eventual fit between new teachers and their schools would be likely to lead to better initial experiences in the profession and thus reduce teacher turnover.[1]

The Problem of Late Hiring

Late hiring is quite common in public education. In a random-sample survey of almost five hundred new teachers in California, Florida, Massachusetts, and Michigan, we found that approximately one-third of new teachers in the four states are hired after the school year has already started. Including these individuals, almost two-thirds of new teachers (62 percent) are hired less than a month before the start of their teaching responsibilities (Liu, 2003). Although we do not have full accounts of all of the hiring experiences of the fifty Massachusetts teachers whose careers we followed, many said their hiring experiences were "last minute" or "down to the wire."

Why Hiring Happens So Late

New teachers are hired late for several reasons. First, some districts have a difficult time predicting student enrollments, which determine appropriate staffing levels for each school. Second, even if they do have fairly stable and predictable school enrollments, many districts remain at the mercy of budget decisions made by the state or municipality, which are often delayed due to political wrangling. The level of state funding also fluctuates from year to year, creating additional uncertainty. Indeed, some districts routinely hand out layoff notices to every nontenured teacher when budget cuts threaten. Usually, most or all of these teachers are called back, but this process generates rampant anxiety and delays the hiring of new teachers, which often has to follow the recall of pink-slipped teachers. Finally, some districts and schools are constrained by collective bargaining agreements requiring that within-district transfers by tenured teachers be completed before new teachers can be hired.

One first-career teacher in our study described how the hiring process worked in the district where she wanted to teach: "The way it works in [this district] is the list of job openings comes out, maybe in May. Then it's sent . . . to all the schools. . . . Already contracted teachers can bid on those positions. If anyone wants to transfer, they are given first opportunity. Then a second bid list comes out. That is sent around to the schools again. Anyone who is a long-term substitute can then bid. After that, it is open to new candidates." This drawn-out process meant that this teacher did not find a position until August, when, she said, she "was really freaking out."

The Consequences of Late Hiring

Late hiring has several negative consequences for teachers, students, and schools. First, it often frustrates and discourages candidates. When we interviewed our respondents, they were all classroom teachers who had successfully found positions. However, it is likely that late hiring discourages some individuals from entering teaching or leads them to take positions in other professions or industries that make their job offers much earlier.[2] Late hiring may thus put schools and districts at a competitive disadvantage for talent. Indeed several midcareer entrants among the fifty Massachusetts teachers were surprised by the hiring practices they encountered within education. One, who obtained her position quite late, sent out forty résumés and noted that she often received no acknowledgment from districts or schools that her résumé had been received. She commented, "I think it's just good business sense to at least send a letter, a form letter, saying, 'We received your information. We'll keep it on file,' or 'You don't meet our requirements.'" A former lawyer and Massachusetts Signing Bonus recipient was "flabbergasted" when he did not get a job until August, only a month before school was to start. Another midcareer entrant was surprised that so many schools continued to call her about openings after the school year started. She commented: "I'm like, 'Gee, I wish you had called before.' And that's why they have trouble getting teachers. Nobody hires anyone like that."

A second consequence is that new teachers often feel pressure to take the first position they are offered. As spring turns into summer (and as summer becomes autumn) candidates become increasingly anxious. Often they jump at the first offer, even if the school and position do not closely align with their interests, expertise, or teaching philosophy. As one midcareer entrant noted: "You get an offer, and generally the people demand a response within a couple of days. So, you really have no opportunity to compare. And you have to make a quick decision. . . . Basically, you go with the first acceptable job that comes along the pike." Another teacher, a first-career entrant, belatedly recognized the great demand for teachers and explained, with some regret, why she took the first position offered to her:

> I wish I really would have realized how vital and how important the need for teachers is, and especially having my background [in science], and being Latina, and having a lot of pluses. I didn't really realize that I could have had a choice. I just kind of felt like, let me take the first thing that looks good and go with it, because I don't want to be jobless and I don't want to have this hanging over me all the summer. So, I took it. . . . I kind of rushed into the decision, so to speak.

A third consequence is that even when candidates do find jobs, they often have little time to prepare their curriculum or classroom and begin school in a rush. One midcareer entrant, who found out only six days before school started what position she would have, said, "I didn't have much time to really prepare and familiarize myself with the work."

Finally, late hiring drives schools to rely on impersonal, noninteractive practices that fail to give them or the candidates good information about one another. When hiring occurs during the summer, it is often difficult for schools to round up teachers to join in on interviews with prospective colleagues. Moreover, candidates do not have the chance to observe classes and see the school in action. When hiring continues into September, principals are rushed to fill their positions and may not take the time for a lengthy and information-rich hiring process. Thus, they may hire candidates based on paper credentials and a single, hurried interview.

Hiring and Fit

Hiring typically is seen as a one-way process in which schools and districts evaluate candidates, yet it should properly be viewed as a two-way process in which schools and candidates exchange information and size up one another. Two important decisions need to be made. The employer has to decide whether to extend a job offer, and the teaching candidate has to decide whether to accept a job if it is offered. For these two decisions to lead to a good fit between the new teacher and his or her school, both must be well informed. The hiring experiences of Keisha and Mary illustrate how the hiring process influences the fit between new teachers and their schools.

Keisha and Mary: Movers in Search of a Better Fit

Keisha and Mary, both midcareer entrants, decided to become teachers because they encountered social problems in their previous work—Keisha worked in higher education administration and Mary did crisis work with adults. They both attended traditional teacher education programs leading to a master's degree and ended up teaching at a school that proved to be a poor fit. Both decided to make a change and sought out new schools, Keisha after her first year of teaching and Mary after her second. The second time around, Keisha and Mary had more personal and information-rich hiring experiences, and they ended up in schools that were better matches than their first ones.

When Keisha went through the hiring process for her first teaching job, it happened so quickly that she did not know what to make of it. In the final months of her master's degree program, she applied to teach in the large urban district near her home. She completed an initial screening interview with someone from the district personnel office and then "got on whatever list that you get on when you make the first cut." Next, a principal called her to interview with his school's hiring committee. At that interview, Keisha recalled, "They offered me the job on the spot, which really scared me." Although the job was in the school district where she "definitely wanted" to teach and at the grade level she was seeking, Keisha felt she knew "nothing about this school." Unsure what to do with the offer, she talked through her decision with her cooperating teacher from her student teaching, as well as with friends and associates. Keisha described their collective advice as: "You have nothing to lose. It's your first year. It's the . . . grade that you want. It's in the [X] public school system—which is an impossible system to get in, as everybody keeps telling me—you have nothing to lose. You hate it? You move on next year."

Keisha took the position but soon realized that the school was not right for her, and that there had, in fact, been something to lose by accepting the position. The school had few formal supports for new teachers, and the administration focused a great deal on discipline and the physical appearance of classrooms rather than on instruction. Moreover, when Keisha tried out some of the "more progressive things" that she had learned in her teacher preparation program, she was chastised. Keisha felt "really stifled" at the school and was disappointed by the lack of support for innovation. In late February of her first year, Keisha started looking for positions at other schools.

Keisha was exhausted from teaching and did not have the energy to do a comprehensive job search that spring. She figured that she could stick it out at her school for another year, if absolutely necessary. However, through one of her mentors from graduate school, Keisha learned of an opening at a within-district charter school and applied.

This school's hiring process was strikingly different from the one Keisha went through the year before. Instead of a single interview that included an immediate job offer, it involved multiple interactions with a wide cross-section of the school's faculty, students, and parents. Keisha had an initial interview with a search committee, observed classes, attended the school's math exposition, and interviewed with the principal. Keisha found the interviews very informative, covering instructional matters, as well as the history and culture of the school. The principal took the time to visit Keisha's school and watch her teach. Keisha noted, "The entire process of how they worked . . . impressed me." She came away with a good sense of the school and thought that she would like to teach there. When the school offered her a position, she took it. As of spring 2003, Keisha had been at the school for three years and was planning to return for a fourth.

Mary moved in the opposite direction from Keisha, from a less structured within-district charter school to a more structured conventional school. Whereas Keisha found the intense environment of a charter school exciting after feeling stifled in her traditional school, Mary, as we have seen in previous chapters, found her charter school too chaotic, and she sought a school with more predictability and support.

Mary had done her student teaching at her first school, but being a full-time teacher there was different than what she had expected, especially since the school believed that teachers should create their own curriculum materials for each of their courses. After two years she decided to move on. She considered leaving teaching and, in fact, interviewed for jobs outside of education, but others encouraged her to try another school before giving up on teaching.

The hiring process at her second school was information-rich. She met with the principal of the middle school, two vice principals, the department head, and the assistant superintendent of the district (a step that she described as "a rubber stamp"). Mary was looking for specific things. She wanted more support and a more experienced supervisor. She was happy to learn that the department head, who would be her immediate supervisor, had twenty to twenty-five years of teaching experience. She could tell "he was really kind, supportive, and experienced. He also was currently teaching . . . [a] class. So he was a supervisor, but also continuing to teach. . . . So that was a huge plus for me. It really was. I realized that I didn't have that [at my previous school], and I really needed that." The school environment was also important to her: "I could tell it was the type of environment that was what my old school was trying to achieve, but didn't have the order to pull it off. . . . This had both the structure and the care."

Mary had taken her teaching portfolio to her interview, where she "showed them basically the kind, the type of work I had done in my previous school, which they were very interested in. And I also realized, as I was showing them the work, that, as much as this was a . . . traditional public school, they were actually looking for someone who had some ideas in terms of projects, and some more innovative . . . things." Overall, Mary thought that the hiring process gave her an accurate sense of the school and what it would be like to work there. Looking back one year later, she commented: "The year has been very much like what my experience at the interview was." As of spring 2003, Mary had been at the school for three years and was planning to return for a fourth.

Between them, Keisha and Mary experienced several different hiring processes. Although the hiring process for Keisha's first job involved both the district office and the school, it gave her almost no sense of what her future school would be like. Hiring for her second position, though, was entirely school-based and gave her a vivid picture of the school, its culture, the students and families, and her future colleagues. In accepting her second position, Keisha was much better informed, and the school, presumably, had a more detailed picture of what she could bring to the school.

Both of the hiring processes that Mary experienced were largely school-based. Mary's first school hired her after she had completed her student teaching there. Those doing the hiring may have assumed that Mary knew what she was getting herself into and, as a result, did not try to give her a better sense of what it would be like to teach there as a full-time faculty member with a full load of responsibilities. Her experience with hiring at her second school was more information rich than what most teachers experienced. Although not as comprehensive as the hiring process at Keisha's second school, it nevertheless gave Mary a good sense of the position and school before she accepted the job offer.

It is important to note that both Keisha and Mary took a more active approach the second time around. They asked more questions, looked for specific school characteristics, and even made requests of the schools, all of which led to better matches.

How Schools and Districts Organize Hiring

School districts make important decisions about who hires teachers, decisions that affect how applicants experience the hiring process and the type and quality of information exchanged. Some districts rely on centralized processes, where hiring occurs at the district level, whereas others rely on decentralized processes, where hiring happens at the schools. As Arthur Wise (1987) and colleagues observe, districts are balancing two competing needs: "the central authority's need for efficiently managing school systems and effectively maintaining uniform district standards and . . . the local principals' need for effectively selecting candidates who best fit their particular schools" (p. 54).

District-Based Hiring

In district-based hiring, administrators at the central office carry out most of the hiring activities and have overall responsibility for assigning new teachers to positions in schools throughout the district. Centralized processes often reflect an underlying concern for control, uniformity, and efficiency. As a result, districts that centralize hiring typically rely on standardized procedures for processing large batches of applications, and they tend to use generic job descriptions, interview protocols, and criteria for evaluating candidates. Many of these procedures have been developed, in part, to combat nepotism, cronyism, and discrimination (Shivers, 1989). By rigidly specifying each step of the process, districts seek to eliminate subjectivity and politics and thus ensure that all applicants are fairly treated.

One of the consequences of adopting a district-based approach, however, is that it does not take into account the specific characteristics of teaching vacancies (for example, subject area or grade level) and the particular needs of local contexts (for example, the student population served and the professional culture of the school). With district-based hiring, these considerations are not factored into the hiring equation until the late stages of the process, if at all. District officials instead focus on candidates' formal qualifications and whether they match the general requirements of certain job categories (for example, elementary school teacher, reading specialist, high school math teacher). Indeed, in many cases, districts hire new teachers on the basis of their general qualifications and only later find a school for them. Thus, candidates may receive little or no information about specific positions and have little basis on which to evaluate the fit between their own skills, interests, and expertise and the positions to which they will be assigned. In accepting a job offer, they are agreeing to work with a district, not a particular school.

School-Based Hiring

In school-based hiring, individual schools review candidates and can, from the start, decide whether they fit the requirements of a particular position and the specific needs and culture of the school. School-based, or decentralized, hiring can incorporate concerns about local needs and the local context. The process is potentially more customized. Principals and teachers (and, sometimes, students and parents), who have the authority to hire, often devise their own criteria, activities, and interview questions for evaluating candidates. School-based hiring is one of the defining features of charter schools.

Between District-Based and School-Based Hiring

Many school districts fall somewhere between these two extremes of centralization and decentralization, dividing hiring activities between the central office and the school site. Typically, a district's central office performs early hiring activities, such as the initial screening of paper credentials, while school-based administrators make the final decisions regarding whom to hire.

These mixed hiring systems allow districts to maintain some systemwide control while also providing individual schools with a say in the hiring decisions, but they may be hard to coordinate. Timely communication is essential. As Amy's case illustrates, these systems also increase the layers of bureaucracy through which candidates must navigate.

The Promise of School-Based Hiring

School-based hiring puts the decision in the hands of those who will most directly live with it: principals and teachers (and, sometimes, students and parents). There has been growing consensus among researchers and policymakers about the importance of giving individual schools more control over how they organize their work (Little, 1990b; Murnane, Singer, Willett, Kemple, & Olsen, 1991; Rosenholtz, 1989). Control over hiring decisions may well be essential for building and maintaining effective teams and for increasing organizational capacity (Newmann, Wehlage, & Rigdon, 1997).

However, a school-based hiring process does not guarantee a rich exchange of information between candidates and schools. We found in the four-state survey that 75 percent of new teachers in California, Florida, Massachusetts, and Michigan are hired through a mostly decentralized process (Liu, 2003). However, we also found that most new teachers still have limited interactions with school-based personnel as part of the hiring process. Although the vast majority of new teachers in these four states do interview with the school principal, less than half interview with teachers, and fewer than one in six interview with department chairs, students, or parents at the school. This survey also revealed that the hiring process still relies heavily on paper credentials and interviews and that schools and districts make very little use of teaching demonstrations or observations. Very few new teachers in the four states are observed teaching a sample lesson as part of the hiring process—the individual state percentages range from 7 percent in California to 20 percent in Massachusetts. This suggests that very few hiring decisions are based on an authentic demonstration of a candidate's teaching ability.

It is up to schools to seize the opportunities created by a decentralized hiring process. Ultimately, it is what the school actually does that will determine whether the new teacher and those already at the school have a good understanding of one another. If a hiring process is to lead to good hiring decisions for both schools and teaching candidates, it must be interactive and information rich.

Information-Rich Hiring

Information-rich hiring processes rely on various activities, including interviews with a wide cross-section of the school community, teaching demonstrations, and observations of classes or staff meetings.

Keisha's hiring experience with her second school, which provided her with useful information about what it would be like to teach there, illustrates some of the benefits of information-rich hiring. Keisha recalled that the hiring process was informative from the very beginning: "I was called in by a search committee [that] consisted of teachers, parents, and administrators. I was actually called in on a Saturday, which at first glance impressed me—that folks were that dedicated that they were actually doing this on a Saturday." Keisha's early sense of the school as a place that engaged teachers and parents in important decisions was then confirmed by her experiences there. After her initial screening interview, she "went upstairs and there were teachers in the library, and teachers were kind of working on things. [Later] I went to this Friday night expo—I mean, this is after they had been teaching all day. They were doing this expo until 8 o'clock at night. So it was like, okay, what kind of intensity goes into making all of this stuff happen, making this stuff run?" Keisha's interview with the school principal covered a wide range of topics, and it seemed intended as much to educate her about the school as to elicit information from her: "We talked a lot about the traditional stuff of my philosophy of teaching, what would my classroom look like. . . what is my philosophy of discipline? What was my experience with various math programs, reading programs, things of that nature. We talked a lot . . . about the nature and the culture of the school . . . the involvement of parents and teachers and staff and students, and the creation and the continuation of the school." Although some candidates might have decided that a school with such demands for teacher engagement was not what they wanted, for Keisha this was just what she had been seeking. The culture of the school was "really inviting and really supportive" and the parent involvement at the school was "one of the biggest pluses for [her]." The school encouraged teacher initiative and innovation, which was important to Keisha, given the stifling nature of her first school.

Information-Poor Hiring

Unfortunately, as our four-state survey revealed, most hiring processes are information poor. Information-poor hiring processes use activities that either provide insufficient information or that transmit information in only one direction, from candidate to potential employer. Many districts and schools rely heavily on collecting and reviewing materials such as résumés, college transcripts, letters of recommendation, or writing samples. Although these materials are important and useful for evaluating candidates, they transmit information in only one direction. Information-poor hiring may include a single interview with the principal or a few administrators. As a result, teaching candidates may have little opportunity to interact with and form impressions about potential colleagues and students, and may receive scant information and a narrow perspective on the school.

How New Teachers Influence the Hiring Process

Despite the many problems that plague teacher hiring, new teachers need not be helpless. As they navigate the hiring process, they, too, make critical decisions about how wide to search, where to devote their efforts, whom to seek out, what questions to ask, what demands to make, what school characteristics to pay attention to, and how selective to be in choosing a job. They, too, influence the hiring process.

Targeting Individual Schools

Hiring does not always happen by the book and organization charts seldom reflect how things really work. Although districts may have official policies that say how hiring is supposed to happen, these policies are often ambiguous or not followed closely. Sometimes centralized hiring and decentralized hiring coexist within a single district, one as the official process and the other as an unofficial one. Savvy principals and teaching candidates understand this and take advantage of it.

Amy, Carolyn, and Keisha all found their first teaching jobs in the same district but their hiring experiences were quite different. This district had a moderately centralized system that split responsibility for hiring between the district office and individual schools. Keisha's first hiring experience conformed most closely to the district's formal process. She was hired after a screening interview by the district human resources office, followed by an interview at a school.

Carolyn, in contrast, started by targeting a specific school within the district. Her aunt told her about a school that "was a really good school in town," and so Carolyn sent the principal a letter in April, introducing herself and saying that she would like to meet her. When they met in June, the principal liked her. However, Carolyn still needed to take the state teacher test and get her certification as part of the Massachusetts Signing Bonus Program. Luckily the principal was willing to wait for her: "She was like, 'OK, read these books, you know, come back to me after you get the test results back.' So I did."

Amy, as we saw, began her job search by substitute teaching in the district, just to get her "name in the door." Although she did submit her paperwork and attend an initial screening interview at the central office, not much came of that and she took matters into her own hands, "pushing [her] name around with other people." In the end, this paid off.

Amy's case also illustrates how some principals try to be proactive. The principal she met at the screening interview kept in touch with her throughout the spring. Although there were no openings at the time, the principal probably anticipated that some would open up in the summer. Thus, she cultivated her contacts and kept in touch with candidates like Amy.

Influencing How Much Information Is Exchanged

At the school level, candidates can influence how much information is exchanged during the hiring process through their actions, questions, and requests. In her second job search, Keisha drew upon lessons that she had learned earlier. She realized that she had ended up at her first school because she "literally did not apply to any schools. . . . I applied to [the district], and then I got calls. . . . I didn't bother to put a call in. You live and you learn. I think that I probably should have done some research on schools. There are vast differences within the . . . system." The second time around, Keisha applied to a specific school and focused her efforts on learning as much as possible about it. She was pleased that the search committee invited her to the math exposition, but she "also wanted to kind of see the average, every day." So, Keisha sat in on first, second, and third grade classes, "just to kind of get the feel." Throughout the hiring process she asked about the support systems that were in place for teachers new to the school and about what professional development opportunities would be available. Experience at her first school made her realize that these were important to her.

Improving New Teacher Hiring

Schools and districts that are serious about attracting and retaining new teachers carefully consider the particular demands of each position and the unique qualities and skills of each prospective teacher. They understand the important role that hiring plays in establishing the initial match between new teachers and schools and for setting accurate expectations.

Starting Hiring Early

One of the most important things that schools and districts can do is start hiring early, so that (1) hiring decisions can be deliberate and well informed, (2) new teachers have sufficient time to prepare for their new positions, and (3) urban districts do not routinely lose strong candidates to other (often suburban) districts that make job offers in March or April. Of course, this is easier said than done, since many factors that contribute to late hiring are beyond district officials' direct control. Districts may need cooperation from policymakers and unions to make earlier hiring possible. For instance, state policymakers could help districts by providing more timely and predictable budgets so that districts can determine staffing levels earlier.

To take advantage of these changes, however, districts and schools will need to increase the efficiency and effectiveness of their personnel systems. Late hiring is not simply due to late and unpredictable budgets and enrollment forecasts; it also results from the accumulation of little delays and "slippages" throughout the hiring process. Had Amy's strengths as a candidate been well documented by personnel administrators and disseminated to those principals with openings, she might have found a position earlier and had time to prepare for her new job. Instead, she was not hired until after Labor Day. Finding ways to improve the information flow among the district office, schools, and candidates—that is, getting relevant hiring information to individuals when they need it—is essential. Many districts are beginning to use information technology in innovative ways to support their hiring efforts, from posting job openings online to processing and tracking applications using sophisticated databases to conducting interviews via videoconferencing technology, thus reducing the time and expense of travel.

Working with Unions to Reform Hiring Policies

Teachers unions are often blamed for the shortcomings of district hiring processes, and it is certainly true that collective bargaining agreements regulate staffing practices and limit the flexibility of management. In many districts, the transfer process for tenured teachers, which must be completed before openings are announced, poses one of the biggest barriers to early hiring. It is important to note, however, that union contracts vary a great deal and that in many cases the provisions pertaining to staffing decisions are much less comprehensive and restrictive than critics assume. Often delays have as much to do with slow bureaucratic processes as with union-imposed restrictions. Still, where the teacher transfer process poses a barrier to early hiring, school officials and unions can negotiate to start the process earlier or reduce seniority as a criterion in staffing decisions. In recent years, two urban districts, Seattle and Boston, have done so.

Seattle Public Schools and the 1997 Teachers' Contract. In its 1997 teachers' contract, the Seattle Public Schools and the Seattle Education Association agreed to major changes in how teachers are hired.[3] The district and union agreed to reduce the claims on open positions that veteran teachers could make solely on the basis of seniority. Today, from the beginning of the hiring process, a school may consider any teacher from inside or outside the district, including new recruits, for any position for which the applicant is certified. In exchange for this reduction in seniority-based rights, however, teachers now play a bigger role in hiring their colleagues. The contract calls for a site-based hiring process carried out by hiring teams at each school. These teams consist of teachers and, if the school decides, parents and other staff. At a minimum, the hiring team is responsible for screening applications and résumés and for interviewing candidates. The team then recommends three candidates, in order of preference, to the principal, who must choose one of them. As specified by the contract, all members of the hiring team must participate in training about how to interview, which is jointly sponsored by the district and the union. The contract also includes provisions that encourage the earliest possible posting of job openings.

Boston Public Schools and the 2000 Teachers' Contract. In Boston, attempts to reform hiring and personnel practices began in the early 1980s. At that time, teachers' seniority rights were iron-clad, and staffing decisions were based almost entirely on teachers' length of service. Sequential "bumping" of junior teachers by veterans with more seniority routinely slowed hiring and disrupted the opening of school. Through negotiations in the mid-1980s, the union agreed to eliminate sequential bumping. Union and management also agreed that teachers could no longer be assigned to program areas without demonstrating subject matter competence. Finally, principals were granted the right to choose from among the three most senior applicants for transfers (Johnson, Nelson, & Potter, 1985).

In 2000, the Boston Public Schools and the Boston Teachers Union once again agreed to significant changes in the hiring and transfer provisions of their contract, with the goal of enabling the district to compete more effectively with suburban districts for strong candidates. The changes included (1) an initial posting of all teaching vacancies by March 1, (2) the opening of the hiring process to outside candidates on March 1, three months earlier than in the past, and (3) the ability of principals to protect first-year, untenured teachers from being "bumped" from their jobs by tenured teachers. As part of these changes, the teacher transfer process was compressed from three months to four weeks.

Principals are now allowed to interview any candidate for any vacancy starting March 1, even if the within-district transfer process has not been completed. If they choose, they can also rehire any of their own first-year teachers at that time. To make a job offer to an outside candidate, however, principals still must wait until May 1, when all teacher transfers have been completed. This is a big improvement over previous contracts, when principals could not interview, let alone make job offers to, outside candidates before June 1.

In the first year of implementing these changes, it became clear that revisions of the contract language could not, in themselves, improve hiring. District office practices also needed to be revamped. Many changes were made, all major deadlines were met, and the Boston Public Schools made important progress. However, a subsequent report by a business watchdog group pointed to several missed opportunities and recommended that the district invest heavily in new personnel systems and management capabilities (Boston Municipal Research Bureau, 2002). In 2003, however, state budget cuts and delays made it impossible for the district to adhere to the schedule for the hiring process that labor and management had agreed to the year before, and many positions remained unassigned as school began.

Shifting Hiring Decisions to the Schools

In addition to starting hiring earlier, both the Seattle and Boston reforms sought to give principals and schools more flexibility and autonomy in making hiring decisions. Decentralized hiring puts the hiring process in the hands of those who will live with the decision—principals, teachers, and even students and parents—and also puts candidates in closer contact with their prospective colleagues. Although it does not guarantee information-rich hiring, decentralized hiring is an important prerequisite.

To be sure, there are certain tradeoffs involved in pushing hiring decisions down to the school level. Centralized hiring has certain advantages of scale; it may be more efficient, for instance, to screen paper credentials in the central office than to have each school do this separately. Also, the district may have an interest in enforcing similar standards throughout the district. Finally, there is the concern that individual schools hiring on their own may lead to staffing imbalances, since some schools may not have the organizational capacity to conduct hiring well. The schools within the district that are well led and well organized may be able to get the better teachers, while the remaining schools may get the leftovers. Competition for teachers among schools might thus exacerbate staffing inequities within the district.

On balance, however, the benefits of decentralized hiring outweigh the costs. Districts also have the option of creating mixed systems that split hiring functions between the school and the central office, though they should be aware of the communication and coordination challenges that mixed systems introduce. In designing their hiring systems, districts may want to err on the side of decentralization. If they have concerns about maintaining standards across the district, district officials can address these through training principals and hiring teams, by requiring each school team to include a principal from another school, or by reserving the right to review school hiring decisions.

Making Hiring More Personal and Information Rich

Even when hiring is decentralized, schools often do not take full advantage of its potential. Perhaps this is not surprising, given how labor intensive information-rich hiring practices are. Collecting and reviewing résumés is a relatively simple matter. Conducting group interviews or setting up teaching demonstrations, however, takes considerable time and coordination. Quality information does not come without a cost.

From an organizational standpoint, arranging a teaching demonstration by a candidate is perhaps the most difficult part of an information-rich process, for it requires time, a scarce resource in most schools. Principals have to find time to conduct the observation. Teachers at the school, if they are to be involved, need to be released from their classes and substitutes found to cover for them. Coordinating individuals' schedules, finding a place to hold the demonstration, and imposing on a teacher's class where the candidate will teach a lesson all require considerable effort. It is thus not surprising that so few new teachers are observed teaching a sample lesson as part of the hiring process.

Yet the benefits of teaching demonstrations are considerable. They are among the most authentic indicators of a candidate's teaching ability and potential. Requiring candidates to teach sample lessons can also send a strong signal to them about a school's values and priorities regarding teaching, thus making the school an attractive place in the eyes of the candidate.

Involving a wide cross-section of the school community in interviewing candidates also takes time and work, but has several benefits. First, it taps the expertise and insights of teachers (and perhaps even parents and students) to evaluate candidates. Second, it allows candidates to get to know potential colleagues and gives them access to multiple perspectives on the school. Third, it may generate in veteran teachers who participate an interest in assisting the new teachers after they are hired—a small step toward building, or reinforcing, an integrated professional culture. Finally, it may provide an opportunity for teachers at the school to discuss among themselves and articulate for job candidates what their school is about and what they expect from colleagues.[4]

Information-rich hiring, however, can pose particular challenges for administrators in low-performing, poorly resourced, or dysfunctional schools that have difficulty attracting applicants, for they may fear that giving candidates an accurate picture of what it is like to teach at their school might scare them away. Although principals may be tempted to shield candidates from some of the realities of daily life in their schools, the costs of dissembling can be high. By misleading candidates, they may set unrealistic expectations and lead new teachers to be disillusioned and depart early. A process that lacks candor may also make it more difficult to identify those candidates who are actually attracted to teaching in challenging schools. For these schools, it might make sense for principals to start by conducting hiring on their own (or with a small group) with the intention of gradually building the capacity of the school to engage in more information-rich approaches to hiring. Rather than just giving candidates a sense of the current state of the school, principals might aim to convey where the school is headed and what it might become with the prospective teacher's help.

Given how busy teachers and principals are, the prospect of carrying out an information-rich hiring process is daunting. The potential payoff, however, is great, and schools can be selective in which activities they use and when. For instance, they may use less labor-intensive activities (reviews of paper credentials or phone interviews) to sift through the applications and only use the more information-rich activities for evaluating finalists.

Equity and Improving Hiring

By starting hiring earlier, shifting decisions to the school level, and making hiring more personal and information rich, districts and schools can improve the fit between new teachers and their initial schools and positions. These changes are not easy to make, and they are also harder for some schools to adopt than for others.

The disparities in teacher qualifications between urban and suburban schools and between schools serving low-income and high-income students (Lankford, Loeb, & Wyckoff, 2002) reflect differences in how attractive some schools and teaching positions are relative to others—that is, differences in pay and working conditions. However, they may also reflect differences in schools' and districts' capacity to organize and carry out hiring. Indeed the two factors are related.

In addition to offering higher salaries and less challenging working conditions, suburban schools are often able to hire earlier than urban schools because their student enrollments and budgets are more stable. Well-staffed suburban schools may also find it easier to free up teachers and administrators to participate in information-rich hiring. Compared to their wealthier suburban counterparts, then, many urban schools may find it more difficult to improve new teaching hiring. Yet there are examples of urban schools serving high-need populations, such as the Murphy Elementary School in Boston, which will be discussed in Chapter Nine, and urban districts, such as the Seattle Public Schools, that have succeeded in carrying out early, information-rich hiring.

From Hiring to Induction

Although improving hiring is very important, it is only one of many things that schools must do to become finders and keepers of new teachers. After they are hired, new teachers still need extensive induction and support. In a sense, hiring is the first step of induction, the beginning of a dialogue between a school and the new teachers about what it means to teach at the school. The mutual exchange of information that begins during the hiring process must continue, as the new teachers learn how to teach effectively in a particular setting. Administrators and veteran teachers need to learn more about the professional learning needs of individual new teachers and build supports that help them find success in the classroom. They also need to learn about the strengths that particular teachers bring and find ways to tap into their talents and skills.

Chapter Nine

Supporting New Teachers Through School-Based Induction

Coauthor: Susan M. Kardos

No matter how much preparation a new teacher has, starting a first teaching job or entering a new school can be mystifying and unsettling. The pattern and pace of a routine day of teaching, coupled with the peculiarities of a particular school, always make entry a challenge. Schools differ in features that are obvious: some are large, others small; some are urban, others rural; some are well-resourced, others underfunded. They also differ in the ways they are organized internally: some are team-based, others departmentally organized; some have a single powerful principal, others have leadership distributed among members of an administrative team. Schools also differ in ways that take more time to discern: whether the staff really do have high expectations for all students; whether teachers share core values about schooling; whether a new teacher's request for help will be interpreted as a sign of strength or weakness. In order to find her way in a new school, a teacher must understand both the obvious and the subtle.

A new teacher's entry into the practices and culture of a school is almost always abrupt, rather than gradual. On the first day of school, the students arrive *en masse*, filling the classrooms with their energy and expectations. By the first bell, the new teacher is expected to perform confidently as a full-fledged agent of the school, doing difficult work in a new environment. Despite the range of demands placed on new teachers, few schools deliberately and thoroughly introduce new teachers to their work or their workplace.

The Need for School-Based Induction

Given the history of school organization, it is not surprising that few schools provide systematic induction for new teachers. If school officials assume that new teachers come prepared with generic teaching skills, ready to do predictable independent work in single-cell classrooms, there is little obvious need for school-based induction. However, given the variation among schools and the changing context of schooling and society, this assumption is outdated. A carefully tailored, comprehensive induction program is essential if new teachers are to teach their classes successfully, work interdependently with their colleagues, and meet a shared commitment to schoolwide learning. Without school-based induction, how would new teachers know what the school expects of them and how they can best do their jobs?

Keisha, who had extensive preservice preparation, soon discovered that she still had much to learn about her new school. She expressed disbelief at the absence of even modest attempts to orient her: "I expected to be pulled in here before the rest of the teachers got here, and gone through some new orientation, just in this building. I had never seen, for instance, a "cum[ulative] folder" before. I had never seen all of the massive amount of paperwork that had to be done in the beginning of the year. I thought I was going to lose my mind. I thought that there was going to be some orientation session, much like normal industry, that brings you in." Like Keisha, Esther was dropped into her teaching role with virtually no explanation or advice. She summarized the guidance she had: "Here are your keys, here's your room, good luck." Entering a complex vocational school with only summer preservice training behind her, Esther was bewildered and overwhelmed. A sudden and solo entry not only stymies new teachers, it shortchanges students. Success in a new assignment requires much more than having a set of keys and knowing where the classroom is.

Some facets of the new teacher's job are very complicated and, admittedly, such understandings take time to acquire. However, some of what new teachers must learn to do in their schools is straightforward and could be easily taught—how to record attendance or how to refer a student for special testing—but many schools neglect to convey even such routine information. When there is no organized, ongoing school-based induction, novice teachers must first identify what it is they do not know—both the mundane and the complex—and then set off to learn it all on their own. Given that good teaching is an exquisitely complex craft, and that good teaching within a particular context requires deep understanding of a school's people and practices, it is unreasonable to expect new teachers to take these first steps in the dark. As Amy explained, "Everyone is willing to help, but it's like, I don't even know the questions to ask."

School-based induction begins with the assumption that each school is unique and intricate and that in order to succeed, a new teacher must understand her school's particular mission, values, norms, traditions, curriculum, policies, and practices. Becoming a good teacher necessarily means becoming a good teacher within the context of a particular school and its community. Schools that approach induction in a proactive manner anticipate the needs of new teachers and provide programs to meet them.

Mentoring and Its Limits

Many schools or districts rely on one-to-one mentoring as the sole component in their induction effort. At its best, mentoring can provide new teachers with valuable, individualized professional and personal support. A mentor can answer a new teacher's questions, share lesson plans, observe classes, provide moral support, and offer a perspective on the school's community, history, and mission. There is good evidence that effective mentoring benefits new teachers (Darling-Hammond, 1999; Gold, 1996; Little, 1990a; Smith & Ingersoll, 2003).

However, as we saw in Chapter Seven, one-to-one mentoring has its limits. Some matches of mentors and new teachers work brilliantly, whereas many others never go beyond an early cup of coffee with polite but superficial conversation. Some matches fail because the school structures do not support them with common planning time, and mentors rarely have time allocated to do this important work. Others fail because the individuals' personalities are incompatible or teaching styles are divergent. The premise of one-to-one mentoring is that a "good match" can be made between an expert and an apprentice teacher—an aspiration that is worthy, but rarely met. Many factors come into play, and if a new teacher relies solely on his mentor for all that he needs, he is bound to be disappointed (Breaux & Wong, 2003). Although a few new teachers in our study said they would have been lost without their mentors, most provided little evidence that one-to-one mentoring offered much support.

Mentoring proved to be most useful to new teachers when their mentors taught the same subject as they did, had common planning time, and had a classroom close by. These conditions, of course, are hard to arrange in many schools, and the difficulty increases as the number of novice teachers rises. As new teachers replace veteran teachers in large numbers, most schools can expect to encounter a shortage of able and willing mentors.

The Importance of Professional Culture

Given the challenges of matchmaking, the limited supply of mentors, and the logistics of schedules and space, schools can never count on one-to-one mentoring for the effective induction of all new teachers. Paradoxically, the presence of a mentoring program may actually reduce the scope of assistance and support that new teachers receive, because when everyone assumes that a new teacher's needs will be met by her mentor, other experienced teachers are less likely to "interfere" when they see a novice in need. Likewise, new teachers are less inclined to seek out another teacher's advice for fear of seeming disloyal. A novice teacher is far less likely to be left confused or floundering when there is shared responsibility by all experienced teachers in the school for the induction of all new teachers. A novice need not depend on a single relationship to learn what she needs when the school has a web of professional support, as in a school with an integrated professional culture, discussed in Chapter Six.

Established Roles for Expert Teachers

A school where experienced teachers share responsibility for the induction of new teachers can become even more effective by creating formal leadership roles for expert teachers and granting them release time to organize or participate in new teacher induction. Experienced teachers can coordinate programs, create and lead seminars, or serve as master or mentor teachers. Rather than having to count on the goodwill of busy colleagues, a new teacher in such schools can feel entitled to the advice and support that expert teachers have to offer, since their roles in the program are formalized. A district's or school's commitment to the effective induction of new teachers can often be gauged by whether they formalize and compensate experienced teachers to provide that support.

Support and How to Find It

Although most teachers in our study discovered little organized induction at their schools, some felt welcomed and encouraged to ask for whatever they needed. Those working in integrated professional cultures, where there was easy and frequent exchange among new and experienced teachers, were less likely to feel isolated. Teachers in small schools also had a better chance of not being overlooked, but small school size did not guarantee that their needs would be met.

Some respondents described elements of support that they found helpful. For example, Mary's second school provided her with a mentor-supervisor who, as she explained, "meets with new teachers almost every week at the beginning, and then every other week. And I never felt like I was getting off track." Esther's transition to her second school was eased in a comparable fashion. She recalled, "I had a director who spoke to me. [She] said 'What can I do for you? Come to me with your questions.'" Moreover, Esther benefited from her department's deliberate introduction to the math curriculum. She explained, "At the beginning of the year, we sat down, and they told us what chapters to teach. You know, 'This is what we do. This is the order we do it.'" Though not comprehensive, elements of induction—such as the assignment of mentors, a regular opportunity to ask questions, and an explicit orientation to "what we do" and "how we do things here"—supported these teachers' entry to new jobs in new schools.

In marked contrast to what her first school offered, Keisha's second school provided one of the few organized approaches to induction described by our respondents: "There is also an orientation during the summer for all new staff, whether it's para[professional]s, interns, whomever, for all new staff that come in. For every event that comes up, there is a briefing for you. Because there are lots of events that happen. I mean, curriculum night and science expo and math expo and all of these things. There is a briefing that happens for new faculty before the event to say, 'This is what it looks like. Are there any questions? How can we help you?'" Keisha, like Mary and Esther, appreciated having a preview of what to expect and what was expected of her. She was glad for the chance to ask questions. And she liked that her new colleagues had considered in advance what she needed to know; the responsibility for anticipating her needs in this new setting was not solely hers. She said, "People are always kind of checking in with you and a step ahead of the things that they know might set off some bells for you." This attention and anticipation by her colleagues helped Keisha adapt more easily to her work and her new workplace.

Keisha's experience in her second school was very unusual, however. Most teachers said that orientation—if it existed at all— was district-based rather than school-based, and focused more on bureaucratic than educational concerns. We know from the previous chapters how crucial the school site is in new teachers' success with their students and their ultimate decisions about whether or not to stay in teaching. We know that a school's curriculum—when there is one—can present perils or support for new teachers. We know that relationships with colleagues play a crucial role in a new teacher's learning and satisfaction. And we know that new teachers enter their schools with different degrees of readiness to respond to the many and rapidly changing demands of the job. Thus, although one-to-one mentoring, a well-designed orientation, or even a set of meetings to explain a school's curriculum might be useful to new teachers, they only go part way in addressing a new teacher's needs. Not one teacher in our study had the opportunity to engage in a full-scale induction program at his or her school site. Organized, ongoing, school-based induction—with hiring as its first step—is critically important to provide thorough information and support to new teachers. Their success and their decisions about whether to stay in teaching may well depend on it.

School-Based Induction: Three Exemplary Cases

In the few years since we first began our research project, more schools across the country have begun to institute extensive and thorough school-based induction programs. These programs recognize that if new teachers are to be successful and satisfied in their work, they not only need help in becoming acclimated to their new school, its particular goals, and its unique context, but they also require ongoing support in becoming better classroom teachers.

In an effort to understand what a comprehensive induction program offers and how it works, we studied three schools—two high schools and one elementary school—each of which was reporting early success in the induction and retention of its new teachers. All three schools were committed to their students' high achievement, but they differed in size, the racial and socioeconomic composition of the student body, and the resources available to them. Each faced, or anticipated facing, substantial turnover among retiring teachers and the hiring of many new teachers. We visited these schools in the spring of 2003 and conducted a series of interviews with new teachers, experienced teachers, and administrators involved in the induction programs. We found the schools and programs to be quite different, but there were common elements in what they offered new teachers, and all three encountered similar challenges as they developed. Each is illuminating.

Brookline High School

Brookline High School (BHS), located just two short trolley stops from the town's border with Boston, has long been the pride of the Brookline community. BHS, with its nearly 1,900 students and 180 teachers, enjoys an excellent reputation both within the state and nationally for its uncompromisingly high standards and for the ambitious and innovative projects it undertakes within the community and with local colleges and universities. Families who can afford it move to Brookline so that their children can attend the public schools there.

The student body at BHS, which thirty-five years ago was almost entirely white, is increasingly diverse. BHS is unique in that it reflects the town of Brookline itself, which has both urban and suburban features. BHS does not have the sprawling campus enjoyed by nearby suburbs, nor is the student body homogeneous. At BHS, approximately 68 percent of the current students are white, 15 percent are Asian American, 11 percent are African American, and 5 percent are Hispanic. There is a large proportion of immigrant students enrolled at the school, particularly from the former Soviet Union and from East Asia. Thirty percent of Brookline families do not speak English as a first language.

Although the school enjoys ample resources and even has an alumni endowment, wealth varies within the town. It has spectacular estates, single-family houses, condominiums, rental apartments, and subsidized public housing. Slightly less than 10 percent of the BHS student body qualifies for free or reduced-price lunch. Observers are impressed by the school's high level of student achievement (85 percent of BHS graduates attend college), its well-educated and committed faculty, its highly regarded headmaster (principal), and the active parental involvement in the school.

On arriving at BHS, new teachers would probably sense among the faculty and administrators a deep commitment to the school and its students. New teachers would hear about expectations of excellence as their more experienced colleagues talked with pride about school programs and students' success. Perhaps they would hear about the Black Scholars Program, the new Special Education Tutorial, or the school's consistently large numbers of National Merit Scholarship finalists. They might also hear about the unusually large student support staff, who organize a wide array of resources on behalf of individual students. The school's commitment to all students becomes truly apparent in the details of how the school works. For example, a prospective teacher will learn that the most experienced and highly regarded teachers do not pad their schedules with only Advanced Placement courses and senior electives. Instead, all teachers are assigned courses at various levels. School leaders believe that all students at BHS deserve great teaching. A new teacher will soon be swept into this ethos, feeling the pride of being a member of the faculty, as well as the pressure that accompanies that pride.

New Teacher Induction at BHS

Brookline High School began its current induction program in 1999 when large numbers of new teachers joined the faculty. Experienced teachers realized there was no organized support for the incoming teachers beyond a brief orientation before school started. As in the preceding several years, thirty new teachers were hired onto the BHS faculty for 2002–2003. With the encouragement of the headmaster, Robert Weintraub, and the financial support of the BHS alumni fund, the Twenty-first Century Fund, two experienced, expert teachers—Gayle Davis in math and Margaret Metzger[1] in

English—designed the induction program they coordinate today. Many BHS teachers we interviewed concurred with a colleague who said, "Margaret and Gayle *are* the Induction Program." New teachers raved about the attentive and wise support they receive from these two committed teachers and from the program they designed and have coordinated for four years.

Hiring as the First Stage of Induction. When a new teacher interviews for a position at Brookline High School—often as early as February or March—it is no small matter. During a visit that often lasts two days, the candidate interviews with the curriculum coordinator (department chair), prospective colleagues, and the headmaster and also usually visits classes, observing teachers and students at work. There are many chances to ask questions and get a feel for the school and what it would be like to work there. The active involvement of so many experienced teachers in the hiring process signals to candidates that BHS faculty members take on important responsibilities and have a stake in who their future colleagues will be. It is during the hiring process that current teachers and administrators first convey what they expect and what they can offer new teachers. It is then that BHS induction actually begins.

Orientation. New teachers who sign on to teach at BHS—both those who have prior teaching experience and those who do not—can expect several kinds of support throughout their first year at the school. First, there is a two-day orientation before the start of school when incoming teachers become acquainted with the community, the district, the school, and other entering teachers. New teachers we interviewed especially appreciated the chance to meet, as one said, the "entering cohort of colleagues," and to establish relationships with more experienced BHS teachers. Most important, they met Margaret Metzger and Gayle Davis, who would then follow them closely and arrange personalized support throughout their first year.

Exhibit 9.1. Key Components of the Brookline High School Induction Program—Brookline, Massachusetts

Orientation. Before school starts in the fall, there is a two-day orientation for all new teachers, in which new teachers are introduced to the community and the district, complete district paperwork, and participate in a school-based program. The main purpose of the school-based portion of the orientation is to familiarize new teachers with their new colleagues, introduce them to the general culture and expectations of high school teachers at BHS, and prepare them for the opening day and the first week of school.

Retreat. The autumn retreat happened in year two of the program (2001) and is slated to happen again in year four (2003). The retreat featured two keynote speakers and provided new teachers ample time to share ideas with each other about the retreat's topics and about their teaching, in general. According to the program coordinators, one of the goals of the retreat is to allow the incoming teachers to bond as a group and to encourage friendships among them that will sustain them so that they enjoy coming to work. The retreat also offers an invaluable opportunity for incoming teachers to get to know second-year teachers, who also participate in the biannual event.

New teacher seminars. New teacher seminars, organized by the coordinators, are held twice monthly and cover cross-cutting topics such as student discipline, parent interaction, and support programs. There is an effort to link topics to upcoming responsibilities, such as deciding how to determine grades for report cards. The meetings are closed and, like all of the interactions between new teachers and the program coordinators, they are completely confidential.

Mentoring. All incoming teachers are assigned a mentor by the curriculum coordinators (department heads). These are one-to-one pairs. Through great effort, mentors and their incoming teachers share the same prep period, office space, and, when possible, course assignment. Mentors are released from one administrative duty and are paid over $400 by the district. Mentors receive a mentor handbook, but in general their obligations are loosely defined. The interactions between mentors and incoming teachers are designed to be strictly confidential. In addition, small groups of mentors meet with Metzger and Davis several times a year to share concerns, offer suggestions, and build

---

Exhibit 9.1. Key Components of the Brookline High School Induction Program—Brookline, Massachusetts, *continued*

---

their mentoring skills, such as how to offer difficult feedback in a supportive way.

Coaching from program coordinators. The program coordinators serve as sources of support for the new teachers. They advocate for them and help them solve problems of any sort. Again, these interactions are strictly confidential.

Classroom observations. Observations and feedback (twice per semester) by program coordinators are an important part of the induction program. Observations are always followed up by specific suggestions for improvement, subsequent observations, or recommendations to observe others. These observations and the feedback are kept confidential. In addition to these observations, new teachers also are observed (often informally) by their mentors, and they are formally observed and evaluated by the curriculum coordinators.

Observing others. During the second and third quarters, new teachers are released from one supervisory duty per week to conduct observations of other teachers. New teachers often observe particular teachers based on the recommendations of the Program Coordinators, their mentors, and sometimes the students. Each new teacher is expected to conduct 16 observations. Administrators in the school have volunteered to cover new teachers' supervisory duties so that they have time to observe other teachers.

In this initial orientation meeting, incoming teachers quickly learn about the high standards of BHS. Davis and Metzger provide examples of written expectations that experienced BHS teachers distribute to students on the opening day. The new teachers are then called upon to role play what they will say to their students at the first class meeting. This intense session conveys that BHS takes teaching seriously.

Seminars and a Retreat. For teachers in many schools, the conclusion of such an orientation session in August or September, if it occurred at all, would mark the end of induction, but at BHS there is much more to come. Throughout the year, Davis and Metzger run confidential bi-monthly seminars, open only to incoming teachers, which cover topics such as classroom management, lesson planning, student motivation, how to facilitate discussions, how to work with parents, and how to deal with discipline. The seminars, which give serious attention to the craft of teaching, ask new teachers to consider how students learn and, as one participant said, "why we teach the way we teach." Specialists visit the seminar to explain their programs and services. Some of the seminar time is dedicated to specific and timely topics chosen by the coordinators, such as Back to School Night in the fall. Some of the seminar time is dedicated to addressing the new teachers' concerns as they emerge. For example, one new teacher said he learned a lot from the "present-a-problem" approach, where a new teacher presents a real classroom dilemma and the others help work on the problem in a structured way. Another participant said that during the seminar she discussed her lesson plans for *Death of a Salesman* and explored, with others' help, the goals she had for her students. The strict confidentiality makes for candid discussion, which engenders trust among the participants; several new teachers described the seminars as a sanctuary. New teachers can also count on Davis and Metzger to serve as troubleshooters beyond the seminar. They advise and intervene, if need be, in the daily, delicate dilemmas new teachers encounter with students, colleagues, administrators, and parents.

Late in the fall of 2001, Metzger and Davis organized a two-day retreat held in a comfortable, off-site conference center. The event featured two speakers and group discussions. There was informal time, as well, when the new teachers could refuel and rekindle relationships that had lapsed in the rush of the first months of school, relationships that the coordinators believe are essential to ensure that new teachers enjoy coming to school. Although all accounts of the event were glowing, money to fund it was not available in 2002. Incoming teachers, who had heard about the prior year's retreat, were deeply disappointed, leading Metzger and Davis—with Headmaster

Weintraub's help—to secure funding for 2003 from the Parent Teacher Organization.

Mentors. Incoming BHS teaches are paired with departmental mentors for whom the district provides two days of training. New teachers said that mentors offered them various kinds of guidance: social-emotional support, curriculum planning, lesson planning, classroom management, personal affirmation, and advice about managing the professional pressures of working at BHS. Some, though not all, new teachers said they were observed by their mentors. Meetings between some mentors and incoming teachers were formal and scheduled; others were characterized as ad hoc and informal. The character of any particular mentoring relationship depended on the individuals involved, their strengths, preferences, needs, and access to one another. When mentors and incoming teachers taught the same course and had common planning time, which remarkably was the case very often, the relationship could provide valuable instructional support that a new teacher could count on. However, sometimes the personality or teaching style match was not right. As one new teacher said of her mentor, "We're just not on the same wavelength." Notably, new teachers whose mentor pairings were "not right" were not left unsupported, for the induction program at BHS is comprehensive, and there are always other experienced colleagues whom new teachers can count on for help. Although this new teacher did not feel like she was on the same wavelength as her mentor, in fact, she was extremely pleased with her induction experience at BHS and particularly liked that the program is "run by teachers for teachers."

Observation: Being Observed and Observing Others. In 2002–2003, Metzger and Davis observed each teacher teaching a class at least twice, sometimes more. Recognized as expert teachers, Davis and Metzger offered the incoming teachers extensive, candid feedback accompanied by recommendations for improvement.

At their suggestion or the incoming teacher's request, they often conducted follow-up observations. The new teachers repeatedly said that these observations were enormously helpful. One new teacher explained that she was interested in better understanding how she was interacting with her students. Metzger had explained to her that she was assuming too much responsibility for the myriad classroom tasks and helped her figure out how to assign students various roles in the classroom. In addition, all new teachers are observed—also several times—by curriculum coordinators (department chairs). In the science department, for example, these observations include detailed scripting of the class and in-depth debriefing. Although these observations are evaluative, they are also informative, and new teachers reported that they found them extremely useful.

Davis and Metzger also recognize that new teachers need to see different instructional approaches as they develop their own understanding of what good teaching means at BHS. The coordinators and school officials make time for new teachers to observe a colleague at work once each week during the second and third terms of the school year, for a total of sixteen observations. Administrators demonstrate their commitment to this part of the program by covering the administrative duty (hall or cafeteria duty, for instance) for each new teacher who is observing a colleague. Davis and Metzger often offer suggestions to new teachers about whom they might observe, because Davis and Metzger know the strengths of their colleagues and have identified skills that individual new teachers need to develop. New teachers might be looking for ways to make group work more efficient, strategies to promote more student-centered teaching, techniques for setting up and running a lab, or approaches to introducing new material. Incoming teachers are encouraged to observe teachers both within and outside their departments and to seek out colleagues who teach students of different ages and abilities and who rely on different instructional approaches. Ultimately, it is the new teachers who decide whom to visit. There is little formal debriefing after these observations, but the new teachers we interviewed did not see that as a problem and said that they found the observations extremely useful.

In many schools, new teachers are never observed by anyone other than their formal evaluator, and they rarely find encouragement or time to watch and analyze another teacher's pedagogy. At BHS, new teachers see and draw from many models and approaches to teaching as they expand their repertoire of effective techniques and refine what they do in the classroom.

Evanston Township High School

Evanston Township High School (ETHS) is located near Lake Michigan in Chicago's northern suburbs, about two miles from Northwestern University. The school and its campus are large and extremely well maintained, and the student body is racially and economically diverse. At ETHS, the front hall is a welcoming, open space with a huge fireplace and an impressive display of students' sculptures and modern artwork. Mixed groups of students lounge comfortably in common spaces throughout the school.

With portraits of graduates from previous generations decorating the hallways and a special section in the library housing books authored by ETHS alumni, it is clear that ETHS honors its history and traditions. However, this is a school that does not rest on its reputation, but faces its current challenges head on. ETHS has made a serious commitment to closing the minority achievement gap among its students. Upon entering ETHS, a new teacher will notice that the school hums with energy and purpose. A new teacher will soon learn that adults in the school seem to agree on three things: ETHS is a unique and special place, teachers at ETHS work extremely hard, and teachers and administrators have high expectations for themselves and their students.

At ETHS, 50 percent of the student body is white, 38 percent is African American, 7 percent is Hispanic, 2 percent is multiracial, and 2 percent is Asian. More than one-quarter of the school's students are classified as low-income. The nearly 3,100 students and three hundred teachers appear to interact with enthusiasm in the broad corridors, bustling cafeterias, and attractive open spaces. A new teacher will notice students and teachers actively engaged with each other about the work of the school.

ETHS, known for the caliber of its faculty and its challenging academic program, offers students a wide range of courses, including rarities such as American Sign Language and metal sculpture. The school believes that all students should have access to technology; thus, it has raised enough alumni dollars to support a laptop loan program for any student who wants to check out a portable computer from the state-of-the-art computer center. ETHS boasts not only a fine academic program, but also some of the finest high school facilities in the nation.

New Teacher Induction at ETHS

At Evanston Township High School, a new teacher's induction is designed to last "from hiring to award of tenure," according to Laura Cooper, assistant superintendent for curriculum and instruction, who oversees the program along with induction coordinators Renee DeWald and Anne Gilford. ETHS has hired forty to fifty new teachers each year since 2000, bringing the proportion of nontenured faculty to approximately 50 percent. As at BHS, both new teachers and experienced teachers who are new to ETHS participate together in all components of the induction program.

Hiring. An ETHS candidate's induction to the school begins, as it does at BHS, with hiring, an intense process conducted by the department head and teachers in that department. The amount of information exchanged during the hiring process depends on when the candidates are hired—the earlier the process, the richer the exchange. Although department chairs are committed to hiring early, the timing of the process has been somewhat delayed recently by the overwhelming numbers of openings in each department.

Nonetheless, the hiring process is thorough. In addition to interviews, prospective ETHS candidates may visit classes and be asked to teach a sample lesson (with some or all of the hiring committee observing) or demonstrate their content knowledge by, for example, writing an essay in Spanish when applying for a Spanish position. Like their counterparts at BHS, candidates come to understand quickly that teaching at ETHS is demanding but potentially very rewarding, as well.

Orientation. In late June, when many neighboring districts are just getting serious about hiring, new teachers at ETHS begin preparing for the fall. Orientation starts early with a four-day series of seminars called "ETHS 101." By scheduling this program with the summer break still ahead, ETHS gives new teachers plenty of time before school begins to consider and draw upon what they learn about the school and how it works. These sessions cover academic standards, course requirements, and teaching strategies. The presenters share ideas about how to get started and give advice about how to create an appropriate syllabus. New teachers meet the superintendent and veteran teachers who attend and lead the seminars.

Looking ahead to the school year, a new teacher at ETHS can count on a strong network of support. The induction program also provides each new teacher with a departmental mentor and the assistance of the department's staff developer. In addition, the new teacher can rely on new and experienced colleagues, as well as the department chair.

Mentors. Mentors, who are assigned by the department heads, provide new teachers with social and emotional support and subject-based, practical assistance in planning and teaching. One new teacher said his mentor "walked [him] through the curriculum" over the summer. Another explained that his work with his mentor is "more nuts and bolts ideas about teaching the subject. It's more planning discussions." New teachers also said they get good advice about ETHS procedures and policies. One new math teacher said

Exhibit 9.2. Key Components of the Evanston Township High School Induction Program—Evanston, Illinois

Hiring. At Evanston Township High School hiring is conducted and completed in the spring and considered part of the new teachers' induction. Each department hires its own teachers. A large-group interview with members of the candidates' potential department and classroom observations of those potential new colleagues seem standard practice across all departments.

ETHS 101. ETHS 101 (Evanston Township High School 101) is a four-day course for new hires, which they attend in June. It focuses mainly on how to build relationships with students across racial, cultural, and class lines; the ETHS culture; and classroom management and discipline. A summer Standards Institute, which introduces new teachers to the district's work on standards and assessment, is also part of ETHS 101.

Staff developers. Each department has one or two staff developers, who are recognized and appointed for their teaching mastery. These expert teachers meet new teachers in the summer to welcome them and integrate them into relevant summer curriculum projects. In new teachers' first and second years, staff developers observe new teachers in their classrooms and provide them with feedback. Staff developers aim to serve as department-based resources for new teachers. Staff developers also accompany the new teachers at their summer introduction to the school's technology resources. The staff developers have release time to work with new teachers.

Orientation and reception for new teachers. New teacher orientation, in August, is organized by the personnel director and involves district procedures and paperwork. It concludes with an evening reception for new teachers at a local bank.

Mentoring. Each new teacher is assigned a departmental mentor. The expectations and activities that occur within the context of this relationship vary from department to department and from pair to pair. It is primarily meant to serve as a source of social and emotional support.

The Mentor Program. The Mentor Program (not to be confused with mentoring) is a program that takes place during new teachers' professional development time (twice a month over the course of several months) during the first year of teaching. During these sessions, new teachers participate in seminars about parent

> **Exhibit 9.2. Key Components of the Evanston Township High School Induction Program—Evanston, Illinois, *continued***
>
> conferences, student discipline, closing the achievement gap between minority and nonminority students, and understanding the new teacher evaluation system.
>
> *Studying Skillful Teaching.* This course on pedagogy, adapted from *The Skillful Teacher: Building Your Teaching Skills,* by Jonathan Saphier and Robert Gower (1997), is for teachers in their second year at Evanston High School. The course is co-taught by Laura Cooper and other experienced teachers well versed in the practice of skillful teaching. Because of its rigor, teachers can earn graduate course credit or a monetary stipend for its satisfactory completion.

that her mentor helped her understand the department's expectations: how to start class with an "opener," how to make an assignment sheet for the whole chapter, how to grade students' work in honors versus regular sections, and how to organize her syllabus and classroom procedures consistent with the math department's mission.

As at BHS, the usefulness of the mentor match had to do not only with the styles and personalities of the individuals involved, but also with structural characteristics of the match, such as whether the new and experienced teachers taught the same courses or had common planning time. Mentor matches with common assignments and time to meet were less likely to happen at ETHS than at BHS.

Staff Developers. In each ETHS department, there is at least one staff developer, an expert teacher released from one course assignment to provide support for new teachers. One new teacher said that the staff developer's support included preparing him for "a lot of little things that would have caused some headaches the first few days of school" such as getting textbooks, completing paperwork, and acquiring a full set of keys. However, staff developers also observe new teachers and are observed by them, and they provide new teachers with much needed practice-based and subject-specific support. The content of observations, feedback, discussions, comments, and questions remains strictly confidential, and new teachers said that they felt comfortable enough to acknowledge weaknesses or fears and to seek assistance without worrying that such admissions or requests would affect their evaluations.

Some new teachers described differences across departments in what staff developers do. One new teacher described ample support: "My staff developer has never turned me down; she's never been too busy; she's always open; and she's been able to say, 'I don't know, I'll get back to you as soon as I can.' So she's been very helpful." Another said that her staff developer is "one of the reasons I'm still going." Not every teacher was equally satisfied, however. One new teacher, who did not have such useful contact with her staff developer, said, "At this school, you really need to be able to fend for yourself."

Structured Seminars for New Teachers. A new teacher at ETHS spends approximately eighteen hours of monthly professional development time, during some mornings and half-days, in the Mentor Program, an interdepartmental seminar attended by all teachers new to ETHS and facilitated by experienced ETHS teachers. These sessions include discussions about school resources, policies and procedures, special education and student support services, paperwork requirements, grading, and explanation of the teacher evaluation system. Participants said that these sessions emphasize classroom management and student discipline. For this seminar, new teachers are also required to observe experienced teachers both inside and outside their departments. One new teacher, who reported that the program offered "a lot of useful information as far as learning the ropes here," was grateful to get insight into the evaluation and tenuring processes, which loom large at ETHS, and to have a chance to reflect on his teaching methods. Another said she enjoyed the open forum for discussion and "venting."

In their second year, new ETHS teachers enroll in Studying Skillful Teaching, a course about pedagogy based on the work of teaching experts Saphier and Gower (1997) that is taught by respected veteran teachers and administrators. With administrators participating, this component of the program does not have the same protected, confidential atmosphere that new teachers' relationships with their mentors or staff developers do; it is not a "sanctuary," per se. Still, new teachers said they value it. One explained that it offers "a different way of thinking about teaching and it gives you a support group of persons who may be faced with the same situations." Another, who said her preservice preparation had been weak, credited the course for directly influencing what she does in the classroom—how she asks questions and how she introduces assignments.

This rich combination of resources and opportunities is sometimes more than new teachers can make good use of during their nontenured years. The intense pace and high demands of the school often are daunting. However, there is little doubt that a new teacher who seeks support can find it at ETHS.

Murphy Elementary School

Murphy Elementary School, which serves over nine hundred students, is located in an inner-city neighborhood of Boston. It is a bright, bustling, and impressive place. The student population is diverse: 44 percent African American, 26 percent white, 23 percent Asian, and 7 percent Hispanic. Nearly 80 percent of the students qualify for free or reduced price lunch. Parents jockey to get their children a place at Murphy School because, under the leadership of Principal Mary Russo, the school sets high expectations for students and then works nonstop to see that they are achieved.

Murphy School has long been something of a beacon among its peer schools, reputed to be a good school to attend and a good school in which to teach. However, when Russo arrived as principal in 1999, she was surprised to find disturbingly low standardized test scores.[2]

Today, however, the school is known for its rising test scores, its fine faculty, and its committed, tireless, and resourceful principal. It is designated as a "model school" within the district. Displays of students' work, mounted prominently throughout the school, are a testament to the focused, sustained, and collaborative efforts of everyone who works with the students. By employing nearly seventy teachers and creatively using substitutes, paraprofessionals, graduate student interns, and volunteers, Russo has managed to assign two adults to every classroom, thus ensuring close attention to individual needs and continuity in teaching when the regular classroom teacher cannot be there.

New Teacher Induction at Murphy School

Principal Russo leads a faculty and staff who are all well-versed in "the Murphy Way"—a schoolwide commitment to high student achievement, common instructional approaches, orderly and respectful behavior among students, continuous collaboration among staff, and ongoing professional growth. To that end, Russo began the fledgling induction program in 2003 as part of building what she calls her "farm team."

The induction program for the "farm team" has two main purposes. First, it is a way for Principal Russo and the experienced teachers in the school to rigorously train substitute teachers, paraprofessionals, and volunteers in pedagogy, curriculum, and classroom management. Thus, when permanent teachers need to leave their classes for professional development—a priority at the school—everyone can be assured that a team of individuals knowledgeable about "the Murphy Way" and the school's sophisticated ways of teaching were covering the classes. Second, the induction program for the farm team ensures a full roster of potential full-time teacher candidates, both well-trained and acclimated to their setting. In a district where hiring is often delayed by budget cuts, seniority-based teacher transfers, and temporary layoffs, many principals wait for vacancies to open before they begin to recruit new teachers. Russo's strategy is to anticipate openings and to prepare strong candidates to fill them when they do become official. Those wanting to teach at Murphy School often take jobs there as permanent substitutes or interns, recognizing that they will receive strong training and that these positions may be the route to eventual full-time jobs.

There is much for new staff to know about the way the Murphy School works. New and aspiring teachers told us that there is a shared sense of commitment to Murphy students that extends teachers' responsibilities beyond their own classrooms. One explained, "all the kids are everybody's kids . . . if something happens in the hallway, people come together." Expectations are high, but so is the level of support. There are a set of rules and procedures—some developed by the students, themselves—that are consistently followed, from the way students file through the hallways to the way paperwork for disciplinary cases is handled to the protocol for contacting parents. Teachers said they can see the benefits of this common approach. One explained, "Whether it's new or veteran teachers . . . everybody knows the rules . . . I feel like if one of my students was somewhere else in the building, they'd be sure to hear the same rules apply to them elsewhere."

New and aspiring teachers must be flexible about the roles they assume at Murphy School—particularly the substitutes who are frequently asked to fill in where they are needed—and they are expected to be open-minded and reflective about their practice. According to our interviews, new and aspiring teachers at Murphy School believe their colleagues are highly motivated and invested in the success of the school, and they find the school's expectations and challenges to be highly stimulating. Finally, new teachers must also be able to take initiative in seeking support, since many sources of assistance exist, though they are not yet all formalized in a systematic induction program.

The school has included both prospective and new teachers in professional development programs for several years. Unlike much professional development, which other teachers routinely dismiss as irrelevant to their teaching, programs sponsored by Murphy School are grounded in matters of day-to-day teaching: how to maintain an orderly classroom, how to teach the math curriculum *Investigations in Number, Data, and Space* (TERC, 1998), how to conduct reader's and writer's workshop. Taken together, the formal programs, personal supports, and informal affiliations converge to deliver a clear and consistent message about what Murphy School is all about and what teachers are expected to do.

Induction Starts Before Hiring. Where BHS and ETHS rely on hiring as the first step of induction, Russo's strategy for building the farm team starts even before the hiring process for teachers commences. She believes that teachers hired onto her faculty should be primed with information and understanding about the school, its mission, guiding philosophy, policies and procedures, norms for teachers' work, and expectations of students. Developing an internal cohort of acculturated, skilled prospects enables both the school and the aspiring teacher to know what each is really getting into. By the time it occurs, hiring from the farm team is largely a formality and newly appointed teachers move comfortably into their new assignments.

Teamwork. All new teachers at Murphy are assigned to grade-level teams, where they learn through regular meetings and formal and informal work together what is expected of them, what is expected of the students, and the specifics of school rules and procedures. As new teachers collaborate with their experienced colleagues on the details of instruction, they learn in a profound and sustained way about the importance of high expectations at Murphy School. They talk at length about the curriculum and its use and about individual students and their needs.

One of the most remarkable features of the school is the interdependent work of all staff. There are no sharp distinctions among full-time teachers, full-time substitutes, paraprofessionals, interns,

Exhibit 9.3. Key Components (Official and Unofficial) of Murphy Elementary School Induction Program—Boston, Massachusetts

Grade-level teams. Grade-level teams meet frequently at Murphy Elementary School. Through the teams, it is expected that new teachers will be made to feel welcomed at the school and valued. In the context of the grade-level teams, new teachers learn about the school's mission and how things work there. They learn about the curriculum they are to deliver; they receive the policy and programmatic information they need; they learn the expectations for student behavior; they are introduced to teachers' work norms; and they learn whom to go to for particular types of assistance. Each grade-level team has an experienced lead teacher who serves as the team leader.

ASPIRE. ASPIRE (Aspiring and Studying to become Powerful Instructors and Reflective Educators) is an eight session seminar, conducted during the second semester, that contains two sessions on literacy, two sessions on math, two sessions on behavior management, an introductory session at the beginning, and a wrap-up session at the end. Each session is 1.25 hours long and includes new teachers, substitute teachers, paraprofessionals, volunteers, and student teachers. For each topic, the first session is dedicated to a "wide angle view," that is, broad concepts and philosophical questions exploring the relationship of the topics to "the Murphy Way." The second session is dedicated to a "zoom view": concrete suggestions, plans, and strategies for implementing the more abstract ideas in each teacher's actual classroom teaching. The program was being assessed and revised for the 2003–2004 school year, with the expectation that it would begin in the fall.

Specialists and coaches. Murphy School has specialists and coaches provided by the district. These people work together with teachers, especially new teachers, to support them in their use of specialized literacy and math curricula and pedagogies.

Principal and teacher leadership. The principal and teacher leaders take a visible and deliberate role in new teacher induction. They take very seriously their responsibility to explain the school's expectations and rules and to establish the climate of support and encouragement that pervades the entire school.

Exhibit 9.3. Key Components (Official and Unofficial) of Murphy Elementary School Induction Program—Boston, Massachusetts, *continued*

Mentors. Mentors are assigned to new teachers at Murphy School through Boston's official mentoring program. Mentors are paid an additional 7 percent of their salary for mentoring a new teacher and 14 percent for mentoring two new teachers. At Murphy School, mentors' specific roles and activities with their mentees are informally and individually determined.

---

and volunteers. They all work together to accomplish a shared goal. One substitute teacher, who hopes to have a full-time position at the school, explained the professional and personal importance of her sixth grade team: "Upstairs, we *are* a team. If you need help, I'll cover for you . . . we work well together, and I really, really enjoy that. We take care of each other. That's a really good feeling." Similarly, a full-time teaching intern explained, "The teachers I have worked with are just amazing. The support here is unbelievable. . . . People will really go above and beyond if they know that you really need help. They'll make sure that you get the help that you need, whether it be with planning something, whether it be with a child. . . . I'm thinking of the . . . team that I work with . . . they're very, very tight-knit. We always talk about different kids and different ways we can better meet someone's needs."

The ASPIRE Seminar. The ASPIRE Program (Aspiring and Studying to become Powerful Instructors and Reflective Educators) was created after the winter break in 2003. Under Principal Russo's guidance, two graduate school interns, Beth Schiavino-Narvaez and Kenneth Kern, and several experienced Murphy teachers created ASPIRE, a set of seminars designed, as one of the founders explained, to help "new people that come into the Murphy" understand how the school works and what supports it provides.

ASPIRE was initially conceived to develop the farm team, but it served a critical induction function for newly hired teachers as well. Participation was voluntary—though strongly encouraged—and those who enrolled could earn professional development credit required by the state.

In 2003, ASPIRE consisted of eight sessions—two each dealing with behavior management, mathematics, and literacy, as well as an opening and a wrap-up session. According to Schiavino-Narvaez, each pair of sessions offered dual perspectives on the topic. First there was the "wide-angle lens," which explained the philosophy and the underlying rationale, connecting the topic to the Murphy Way. Then there was the "zoom lens," which was much more specific: "What does a [math] Investigations lesson look like? How do you set up your routines for reader's and writer's workshop? What are some strategies you can use in your classroom?"

Each pair of sessions was led by experienced Murphy teachers, several of whom had been designated lead teachers, coaches, or specialists by the district. They created a "user friendly" binder of materials for each participant, including sample homework formats or observation protocols for teachers to have "at their fingertips." One new teacher said that the program "did a nice job of providing some helpful materials that were practical. . . . I love to be able to take something away and make sense of it and put it to my own use."

Principal Russo regularly attended the sessions and enthusiastically affirmed their importance. One new teacher said it "was great" to hear Russo say, "We are here for you. We support you. We support your actions in the classroom and we're here to stand by you."

In many urban districts such as Boston, principals say that union contracts discourage teachers from spending extra time in professional development. But the ASPIRE seminars were popular and the union building representative, who presented the ASPIRE math sessions, explained that nothing in the contract prohibits teachers from attending things they choose. In addition, the seminar serves as a special bonus for substitute teachers who are not assured of professional development.

Mentors and Expert Teachers. New teachers and student teaching interns (though not other aspiring teachers) are assigned mentors at Murphy School. Mentoring appeared to be largely informal and dependent on the teacher's needs and level of experience. One teacher described how her frequent interaction with her mentor tapered off as the year went on: "Basically, she started out more giving me information, coming into my classroom, setting up my writer's workshop, modeling different things for me. She gave me opportunities to go observe her classroom. As things started getting going, I'd check in with her if I had some questions, she'd help with that or find some resources. At this point, it's more casual . . . we meet, but we don't always have a lot to sit down and go over, just kind of checking in." Lead teachers, specialists, and coaches also occasionally conduct classroom observations, but these, too, were said to be arranged as needed, rather than as part of a program. New teachers, substitutes, paraprofessionals, and interns observed other classes when they could, and said they found the experience valuable. This is not a school where teachers feel isolated or threatened; rather, teaching practice, with all of its challenges, is made public and supported intensely.

Lessons from the Three Exemplary Programs

Although the settings, driving philosophies, and particular components of these three schools' induction programs differ, they share important features. First, and in our view most important, these programs are *deliberately school-based*, that is, they meet the teachers where they are. They do not rely exclusively, or even primarily, on large district-sponsored meetings. Nor are they confined to one-to-one mentoring relationships. The programs are centered in the new teachers' schools and are created and implemented by experienced teachers with teaching expertise and knowledge about the particular school and how it operates. Not only are these programs school-based, but they also have as their central focus classroom teaching and student learning. They introduce new teachers to the mission and culture of the school, but also include explicit, guided opportunities to translate ideas into specific strategies and methods for classroom use.

Second, these programs are *integrated into the professional life and practice of the school.* They are not stand-alone programs, of the "hit-and-run" variety, nor are they at the margins of the work life of the school, as "add-ons" or "in-services." As a result, their boundaries are often blurred, and it is difficult in some cases to say precisely what the components of the induction program actually are. They are designed to simultaneously serve new teachers, experienced teachers, and the school. In these schools, where collective responsibility for students and colleagues was the norm, experienced teachers felt obliged to share what they knew and help bring new people into the fold. In describing the professional culture of Murphy School, one veteran teacher explained: "Whether you are new or veteran, the expectations are high. And as a veteran, again there is that feeling that you share the knowledge, you help your neighbors, you help your people to gain the experience that you've gained. And while they're gaining it, you give them your expertise. So the experiences are shared by everybody, and whether you are veteran or novice it is expected that you'll share and you will be part of a team. And that's how we do everything: by team."

By purposefully engaging new teachers and veterans in reciprocal observations, reflective discussions about practice, and collaborative teaching, leaders in these schools implicitly endorse an interdependent school organization, which defies the limits of an egg-crate structure. Experienced teachers reported that by participating in components of the induction program, they learned new approaches and acquired new techniques, such as how to assess students' learning needs or how to use technology in the classroom. They also were pleased to share their craft knowledge with new colleagues. Experienced teachers seemed to understand that the sooner new teachers could become full-fledged members of the school's faculty, the sooner they could share the responsibilities of improving the school.

Third, these programs are *constantly changing and being refined*, both because the schools' circumstances and needs are in constant flux and because the coordinators are intent on improving them. In addition, the programs need to be flexible because the needs of incoming teachers are also, in some ways, unpredictable. Those responsible for the programs regularly solicit feedback and suggestions, then adapt their program in response. Therefore, no matter how thoroughly we document the current programs, our descriptions will be dated within a year. For example, BHS and ETHS both have encountered dissatisfactions among teachers who are new to the school but come with years of experience elsewhere and, thus, find parts of the program repetitive or even condescending. The schools are considering different options for this group of experienced teachers who happen to be new to the school and who have somewhat different strengths and needs. Although ASPIRE's leaders at the Murphy School deliberately scheduled the seminar to commence in February, once teachers were settled in their classes, participants said that they wished the sessions had been earlier. And so the coordinators decided to begin the program in the fall.

Fourth, although those who developed these programs were inventive and had to be frugal in their budgeting, good induction is *dependent upon additional resources*. It cannot be done well on the cheap, both in terms of financial and time allotments. Each of these programs required the dedicated time of experienced professionals. BHS provided for Metzger and Davis to each be released from one course. ETHS did the same for their staff developers. Murphy School relied on coaches and specialists who had been freed by the district from full-time teaching. ETHS granted mentors an additional $250 to be used for professional development, and they also paid new teachers $25 per hour for their summer training. Given that time is the scarcest resource for most public school educators, ensuring that time will be committed to induction (with release time for observation or stipends for additional training) makes it more likely that the job can and will be done well. Moreover, reasonable compensation conveys a level of professional respect that schools so deeply need to promote. Many districts might be willing to provide more funding for induction if they realized the true costs of teacher turnover and repeated hiring—approximately 20 percent of the new teacher's salary (Benner, 2000).

Fifth, these programs succeed, in part, because they *develop and use professional capacity*. The strengths and commitment of experienced teachers run deep in these three schools, and that was evident in the expert assistance to which new teachers at these schools had access. Although particular individuals launched and now sustain the induction programs, they would never have succeeded without the active support of many other expert staff members. Schools that have capacity can build capacity. Regrettably, many start-up schools and schools in low-income areas lack the critical mass of professional experience needed to make this work. Such situations present enormous leadership challenges to capitalize on the experience and talent that does exist and to build capacity from the ground up, when necessary.

Ultimately, effective induction for new teachers is a system of supports, not simply a program. It is a long-term investment, not a short-term fix. Doing it well requires the sustained investment of expert teachers' time and talents, a sustained investment of budget dollars, the full advocacy of school and teacher leaders, and the willing participation of new teachers, themselves.

Chapter Ten

Sustaining New Teachers Through Professional Growth

Coauthor: Morgaen L. Donaldson

Hired in the late 1960s and early 1970s, today's retiring teachers constitute the first cohort to make teaching a lifelong career. But what does it mean to have a long-term career in a profession that offers only one role? Is a career simply the sum total of years spent in a classroom or students taught? Or is it something more? And how do today's new teachers, who differ in many ways from their retiring colleagues, conceive of their role in teaching over time?

Researchers have studied teachers' development over their careers and identified distinct stages in their experience as classroom teachers. Michael Huberman (1993), who studied teachers' "professional trajectories" (p. 2), focused exclusively on teachers' experiences within their classrooms. The broad questions he posed about career stages or satisfaction all focus on teachers' instructional roles with children. For example, he asks: "How does one perceive oneself as a classroom teacher at different moments of one's career? Is a teacher aware, over the years, of having changed her style of instruction, of interacting differently with pupils, of revising classroom organization, of shifting priorities or of attaining a greater or lesser mastery of her discipline?" (1993, p. 2). The questions Huberman raised in his study never open the possibility that a teacher's career might involve extended or redefined roles beyond the classroom. The stages he subsequently documented focus on teachers' attitudes and reflections on their pedagogy within the classroom.

In the mid-1980s, when school reformers seriously began to propose career ladders for teachers (Carnegie Forum on Education and the Economy, 1986; Holmes Group, 1986), Milbrey McLaughlin and Sylvia Mei Ling Yee (1988) set out to understand teachers' conceptions of a teaching career. The researchers laid out two conceptions of career: (1) "an *institutional* view that sees career in terms of organizational structures and rewards. . . . Career is conceived in largely external terms of vertical mobility;" and (2) a career conception that is "*individually* based, taking meaning from personal motivations and goals." McLaughlin and Yee note that, "in contrast to the first view, this subjective notion of career relies on an internally defined sense of advancement and satisfaction" (pp. 23–24). Based on interviews with eighty-five teachers from five diverse northern California school districts, they concluded that these teachers did not aspire to greater levels of responsibility, influence, and compensation. Rather, they found satisfaction and built their careers within the classroom, seeking to achieve depth rather than breadth of influence. McLaughlin and Yee concluded that, "Career, for the majority of these teachers, clearly was conceived in terms of classroom teaching and continued direct involvement with youngsters" (1988, p. 24).

There are two important points worth noting here. First, McLaughlin and Yee interviewed teachers who had chosen to remain in the profession and thus apparently had found satisfaction in the traditional teaching role available at the time. Second, the sample included a large proportion of veteran teachers. Only 5 percent of the sample was under age thirty (Yee, 1990). Although younger teachers constituted a small part of the teaching force at that time, they represent a much larger portion today.

With the changing demographics of the teaching force, it is important to ask whether entrants today hold the same conception of career as the teachers interviewed by McLaughlin and Yee in 1985 for their 1988 study. This means expanding Huberman's inquiry beyond the classroom walls to ask whether today's entrants also expect to spend many years refining their craft as classroom teachers or whether they have other things in mind. Behind these questions lies a related query: Did those in the retiring generation of teachers truly prefer a career confined to the classroom, or was it the only option available in a field that assigns a first-year teacher essentially the same job as a thirty-year veteran?

In today's job market, prospective teachers have access to many lines of work that offer them the chance to assume varied roles or specialize in particular fields over the course of a career. In other professions, it is possible to pursue a differentiated, "horizontal" career, developing expertise in various settings—the departments of a single company, for example—or to pursue a "vertical" career, advancing to greater levels of responsibility and influence. Our interviews show that many first-career entrants today have explored alternative careers in other fields. Also, although it is impossible to say how many other people have rejected teaching because of its limited career opportunities, presumably some have done so.

In an effort to understand how today's new teachers envision a career in teaching, we asked the fifty new Massachusetts teachers in our sample how long they planned to stay in teaching and what they expected to be doing during that time. If they anticipated short careers in teaching, we asked what might encourage them to stay longer. We inquired about additional roles that they were taking on, and asked whether they thought the teaching career should be restructured to create a career ladder, which would include new roles and higher pay for those who had acquired special levels of expertise or assumed more extensive responsibility.

As we reported in Chapter Two, a surprisingly large number of respondents do not plan to remain in teaching long-term. Fifteen of twenty-six first-career entrants and eleven of twenty-four midcareer entrants expect to remain in education, but only four first-career entrants and six midcareer entrants foresee teaching full-time for the duration of their careers. The rest of those who intended to work in education long-term hoped to hold positions such as curriculum developers, mentor coordinators, or staff developers, which are only beginning to emerge as roles in the public schools.

In their first few years, new teachers want to develop competence and confidence in the classroom in order to achieve success with their students. In this regard, their accounts echo those of veteran colleagues such as those interviewed by McLaughlin and Yee. How-ever, at the same time that the new teachers describe their com-mitment to mastering and refining instructional skills in these early years, they also speak about looking ahead to a future that will take many of them out of the classroom, at least part-time. Some plan to leave teaching entirely for work in other fields. Some intend to leave the classroom but remain in education as administrators or instructional specialists. Some foresee finding or fashioning new hybrid roles that combine classroom teaching with other responsi-bilities. For this group, the flat, undifferentiated teaching career does not offer the opportunities for professional growth that they seek. Without fundamental changes in the teaching career, public education risks losing these new entrants in alarming numbers.

The following discussion focuses first on the new teachers' ef-forts to master classroom teaching and then describes their interest in the possibility of new roles, which would provide greater variety and expanded influence in their work. In describing the emerging roles for teachers, we draw upon the accounts of the fifty new Mass-achusetts teachers as well as those of teachers and administrators at the three induction sites described in Chapter Nine: Brookline High School (BHS) in Massachusetts, Evanston Township High School (ETHS) in Illinois, and Murphy Elementary School in Bos-ton, Massachusetts. Finally, in an effort to see what it would take to institutionalize such roles, we consider the more elaborated and established efforts in Rochester, New York, and Toledo, Ohio.

Early Focus on Instructional Competence

The teachers within our sample voiced wide agreement that, as novices, they wanted most to develop instructional competence. As we saw in Chapters Five and Seven, some of them worked in schools where veterans or administrators provided extensive sup-port and feedback about their classroom teaching, whereas their counterparts in other schools received only periodic, summative evaluations. Amy, who took advantage of the opportunities for professional development provided by her urban school and district, was personally dedicated to a career in teaching, but even she envisioned taking on additional responsibilities as she gained instructional expertise.

Amy's Story

Committed at an early age to a career in teaching, Amy came to her urban, elementary position via a relatively traditional route: an undergraduate course of study in elementary education and psychology. Despite her extensive preservice preparation and a student teaching experience in the district where she was hired, Amy quickly realized that she still had much to learn: "[T]he preparation program was too short, and it didn't give enough information. . . . It was nothing I could use, almost. So, everything, [I] kind of wing it." This substantial gap between her university preparation and the demands of her second grade classroom led Amy to conclude she would have to learn on the job, and fast.

At the outset, Amy focused on expanding and honing her skills in the classroom. She acknowledged: "I feel lost in a lot of things. Like I don't know how to do things." In response, she systematically began to search for opportunities where she could fill the gaps in what she knew. She mined her student teaching experience for activities and lesson plans and listened intently at school-sponsored professional development sessions. She discovered that opportunities for professional development were more extensive and accessible than she had first realized, and she seized the chance to attend conferences and workshops outside the school. She recalled: "I went to the Curriculum Resource Center. . . I got cages, and newts, and fish, and ant things, and they just are willing to give you so much. It's just that no one takes advantage of it."

Although Amy's initiative in searching out such opportunities may not have been typical, her worries about instructional competence were common. During her first year, she also participated in a series of workshops on science teaching at the school district's resource center, and petitioned her principal for released time in which to visit other schools and classrooms to gather instructional techniques for teaching reading. In reflecting on her efforts to find professional development opportunities and gather resources for her classroom, Amy said, "I wish I had known all about this stuff because I would have started it in September. And they [the students] would have been way beyond what they are now."

Although Amy devoted considerable time to developing her teaching skills, she was careful to avoid taking on additional responsibilities at her school. She observed: "Not in my first year. I have too much on my plate as it is." In this regard, Amy's approach to professional growth is consistent with the traditional orientation of teachers documented earlier by McLaughlin and Yee (1988). In her first year, she focused on developing skills to be used within her classroom, not beyond its walls.

When we interviewed Amy at the end of her second year, however, she had already started to expand her influence beyond her classroom. She had accepted a new, unpaid role as a math coach for her grade level, and she served as informal mentor to a group of new teachers. She said that she was feeling far more confident about her teaching: "I feel knowledgeable." She felt complimented when the instructional coaches and her principal suggested to other teachers that they observe her teaching. As a designated math coach for the second-grade team, Amy saw herself in "a guidance role." She said, "I am excited about it. I really like it."

Informally, Amy's role also changed from her first year to her second. She explained, "a lot more people come to me for advice, which is interesting. There's a lot more first-year teachers. And it actually seems like I have a lot of free time because I know what I'm doing this year." In taking on this informal advising role, Amy, who had never been assigned a mentor of her own, realized how much assistance new teachers need. She recalled her own experience: "They threw me in there with the books and they didn't say anything. They didn't tell me what to do . . . I was just kind of thrown to the wolves and I got lucky. . . . [A]t least the teachers that come in now, I've been very supportive, you know what I mean? Kind of letting them know what we need to do." Determined to demystify the school and job for the new teachers, Amy volunteered to help them make sense of their new workplace.

As for Amy's future, a professor had encouraged her to consider administration, but she dismissed his suggestion out of hand— "definitely not." In her view, principals worked "too many hours, not enough money, not worth all the headaches." However, by her third year, she had begun to muse about other roles that she might combine with classroom teaching: "I could definitely see myself as being a lead teacher, eventually being a mentor, that kind of thing, as time goes by."

Indeed, she had already begun to fashion for herself a set of hybrid roles that would allow her to continue to work with children, refine her craft, and use her acquired expertise to influence teaching and learning beyond her classroom. By combining these roles and responsibilities, Amy believed she could build a career in teaching that would challenge, renew, and sustain her over time.

The Search for Competence and Confidence

Like Amy, the other new teachers we interviewed discovered early on that teaching was harder than they expected and thus would require their full attention for the time being. Four months into his first year, Bernie responded candidly to our question about how things were going: "Definitely feelings of 'Geez, this is doable,' mixed with 'Oh my God, what have I done?' . . .[I] just have a feeling as if I have lost control over certain classrooms. . . . And on the other hand, though, it's been exciting. No day has been mundane at all. And, you know, it's been definitely challenging—sometimes not in the way that I'd like it to be."

Although Bernie had entered teaching by an alternate route, few traditionally trained teachers reported feeling more competent. Derek, who had student taught for a semester before taking on a class of his own, confided that he was frustrated that he was "still a rookie teacher in that I don't have an expanded repertoire of things to draw upon . . . and I guess I'll feel like a rookie until I have a solid base, a chest of things I can just draw upon." Victoria, a traditionally prepared teacher who was more confident than most others, said that although she might want to become a coordinator "ten years down the line," for the time being, "my focus is to be in the classroom and to teach." Fred concurred: "[I]f there is ever a part [of my career] where I'm going to be able to master the ability to be a good classroom teacher, it's really early. . . ." Whether out of practical necessity or deliberate choice, the new teachers focused initially on gaining classroom competence.

Pursuit of Professional Development

Well aware of how much they needed to learn, the new teachers actively pursued classroom mastery in various ways. In addition to supervision and feedback (see Chapter Five), the new teachers welcomed professional development in various forms. Some preferred job-embedded learning, such as working in groups to develop curriculum or reflect on their own teaching experiences, and others wanted school-based professional development where they interacted with their colleagues in the process of learning new skills and content. Still others pursued more conventional forms of professional development such as workshops, seminars, and conferences held outside the school. In general, they welcomed a wide range of opportunities.

Carolyn found several forms of professional development through her urban elementary school. She recalled, "I participate in [a reflection group]. . . . It's just a few of us getting together talking about positive things going on in our classrooms, asking questions . . . it's sponsored by the school." Carolyn also joined reading and technology workshops and attended a district-sponsored, five-day training on Responsive Teaching, which she described as "a great experience."

Expanded Roles Beyond the Classroom

Focused though they were on classroom competency, the teachers we interviewed nonetheless continued to assess what a career in teaching could offer them over time. Many anticipated wanting new roles and responsibilities as they became more experienced. Keisha commented candidly, "If I do this for ten years, I will be bonkers . . . give me something different, either that or administration." Others also expected that as they perfected teaching techniques, they might become bored. With time, one teacher worried, "I'll have a pretty good idea of how to teach and it may lose its zest." Both midcareer and first-career teachers wondered whether teaching's traditional, flat career could sustain them. "When I was at IBM I was climbing that corporate ladder," a midcareer entrant explained, "so to feel that I would be here for twenty years and be stagnant, I hope not." Likewise, a first-career teacher observed, "I don't think it's healthy to be in the same position for more than ten years . . . I love this job but I think four or five years of it, I'd be bored. I wouldn't be challenged . . . you need variety or a new challenge."

Many of the teachers we interviewed began to venture beyond their classroom by their third or fourth year of teaching. Fred and Derek, for example, coached basketball and advised the student government, activities that added variety and enjoyment to their work but did not essentially change their role. Other opportunities, however, engaged new teachers in different kinds of relationships with their peers. Fred became the de facto department head of social studies in his small secondary school: "The principal has kind of put me in charge of making sure that the social studies curriculum is being covered." He also supervised two student teachers, which he especially enjoyed: "It worked great. I love it. Their ideas keep me fresh. And I think I lend a little bit of experience to them. And it's mutually enriching, you know."

In their charter schools, Mary, Derek, and Keisha participated in schoolwide governance committees that took charge of curriculum and hiring. Because these responsibilities were conceived as part of their teaching role, they did not move into new positions, although they worked with their peers in new ways and exercised broader influence on behalf of the school. They had to establish interdependent working relationships with their colleagues and expand their domain of responsibility. Although they were sometimes overwhelmed by all the work to be done, these teachers welcomed the chance to have a say in important matters. Indeed, one of the reasons Keisha moved to her second school was because it was "a school where you have voice."

Other teachers had access to governance groups or positions on schoolwide committees, but usually found these roles to be of little consequence. They sometimes expressed regret that the only place they exercised influence was in the classroom. Carolyn joined her school's leadership committee in order to work with colleagues and develop a consistent discipline system. She also tried to revive the Faculty Senate (a union-sponsored organization) by volunteering to serve as its vice president. Neither investment paid off. The proposals about discipline were never adopted and, in Carolyn's view, the Faculty Senate accomplished nothing. She explained: "So we volunteered to do this, but our principal had some real power control issues. . . . I'd spend all this time typing up notes, giving them to her, giving them back to the faculty and nothing changing. After four months of that we resigned. We said 'enough is enough'. . . . [F]or the rest of the year there was no Faculty Senate." Carolyn, who looked for ways to effect change in her school but was repeatedly discouraged, concluded from this experience that if she wanted to exercise influence, she might need to find a place where, in her words, "my talents are better met."

A Move into Administration

Historically, ambitious teachers who wanted to advance vertically in their careers while remaining in education had only one real option—a move into administration. Although Amy expressed no interest in such a move, others saw it as a possibility. Fred, who had completed several courses in administration, said "that's something on the back burner." Derek, however, became dean of students at his charter school after his third year of teaching. With the change, he could earn substantially more money and exercise broader influence on the school's policy and practice. He characterized his new position as "the best of both worlds," and explained his decision: "I've always wanted to branch out and do something different. I didn't think I'd be a teacher for more than three years, more than two actually . . . I didn't want to be a career teacher. I wanted to do something else socially responsible, social service oriented . . . but maybe a little more responsibility, more authority. And this position happened to open up this year at my school . . . and that's something I would love to do." Most others, however, saw little allure in the administrative option. Noting "there is one way you progress . . . from here to maybe a dean, or an assistant principal, to principal," one new teacher in our study concluded, "Unfortunately, sometimes, it will take great teachers out of teaching."

Differentiated Roles That Focus on the Classroom

Many of these teachers hoped eventually to take on a new role that would allow them to continue, at least part-time, as classroom teachers, while extending their experience and influence beyond their classroom. They believed that such a hybrid role might combat boredom and burnout while offering new challenges and rewards that would keep them engaged in teaching over the long term. Mary was enthusiastic about the possibility of a career ladder for teachers: "I think it's a great idea." She observed, "It's a rare person who can stay full-time teaching today for a really long period of time. . . . [T]his is an emotionally demanding job with little reward." She anticipated that, without new roles, many people would leave teaching: "You know, there's a lot of other things you could do with your skills, which pay better, and are less emotionally demanding, and that you can still make a difference. So, I think if you mix it a little bit. If you could say, 'OK, I'm going to spend half my day doing this really emotionally demanding work . . . and then a half a day supporting other people in working,' it to me is much healthier. . . . [Y]ou could sustain it because you wouldn't be burnt out."

Some new teachers liked the professional advancement inherent in a career ladder. A first-career entrant commented: "People want the chance to move up and to have different experiences and different opportunities. . . . I'm definitely looking to do different things. Maybe not necessarily a vertical rise, but I know that I will not be doing this for the next twenty years." Similarly, another teacher commented, "I would be frustrated in the long term if I couldn't be doing very intellectual work . . . if I stayed in teaching, I would need to do more in the curriculum development aspect."

Such positions might also provide professional development benefits to the school by offering a formal conduit through which experts could pass on teaching expertise to novices. As Mary explained, such roles would facilitate more exchange across experience levels among faculty members: "My sense is that there are a lot of people coming in, and then leaving with very little connection between the new people and the experienced people. Then you get experienced people . . . who want to share their experience, but don't really know how to. . . . There would be a value in passing along their experience and knowledge." Without such roles, Mary said, "I don't think people will stay."

Despite considerable interest in differentiated roles, with the exception of the well-established position of department head, few could point to examples of the kind of role they had in mind. One new teacher bemoaned this situation: "You're either a teacher or you're a coach or you're a principal, and I don't like that idea at all."

There was some evidence of hybrid roles, however, particularly in nontraditional settings such as charter schools and professional development schools. Fred's school had specialized roles for master teachers, who served as staff developers and worked with intern teachers. Like Mary, Fred observed that such positions were "enriching" both for the individuals holding them and for the people they assisted. Another teacher working in a professional development school noted: "Everyone is teaching, but they are doing something else as well, whether it is Project Zero or Project Evidence or working on the . . . grant in math." Similarly, a second-year teacher in a suburban charter school worked as an instructional coach for her colleagues. She explained, "You just take on different roles as a teacher. And I like it. I think it will keep me teaching." Examples such as this were rare, however, and the majority of the teachers we interviewed, particularly those working in conventional school settings, saw little promise of moving into new roles if they remained at their schools.

New Roles at the Induction Sites

As we expanded our research to look at schools where induction is deliberate and systematic, we found that schools with developed induction programs had engaged experienced teachers in differentiated roles. Thus, these induction programs benefited their schools in two important ways. As discussed in Chapter Nine, they supported large numbers of new teachers. In addition, these programs created roles for veterans that allowed them to exercise leadership and influence in the school at large while continuing to teach in the classroom.

Notably, each of these schools places a high value on adult learning and professional growth. There was an underlying assumption that students would benefit as teachers became more knowledgeable and skilled. Teachers' development was a purposeful, community endeavor, not the lone effort of a motivated, entrepreneurial individual. Administrators and teacher leaders encouraged learning and provided time and resources to make it happen. A new teacher at Evanston Township High School (ETHS) explained that he had accepted a job there because "becoming a good to great teacher is something that they want to [have] happen." A lead teacher and math specialist at Murphy Elementary School made it clear that successful teaching there required rapid learning: "They have to start immediately becoming professionally developed . . . I don't care what type of preservice training you've had or what type of school you've been in, it's the on-the-job training and the further reflection on what went wrong and what went right that improves their skills in the long run." Another experienced teacher at the Murphy School found such opportunities personally rewarding: "I learn something new every day. . .from new people, from veterans."

Differentiated Roles at Three Induction Sites

In developing their induction programs, all three schools had created differentiated roles for experienced teachers. At Brookline High School (BHS), many experienced teachers serve as mentors and two, Margaret Metzger and Gayle Davis, coordinate the induction program. The mentors assume their responsibilities on top of regular teaching assignments, whereas the coordinators are each released from teaching one course in exchange for their time and efforts. Mentors are paid a modest $400 stipend for their extra work, but the coordinators receive no additional pay beyond released time, even though their jobs require considerable expertise and additional administrative responsibility. They design the program, facilitate the seminars, and observe and provide feedback to all the new teachers. On the books, however, the coordinators remain classroom teachers.

Specialized roles at Murphy School are more formalized than those at BHS, in part because they are grounded in the reform initiatives of the district's teachers contract, first negotiated in the late 1980s. Through collective bargaining, the union and district negotiators established the position of lead teacher, which can add 7 to 20 percent beyond a teacher's base salary (Boston Teachers Union & Boston School Committee, 2000). Thus, the parties added a new rung beyond tenure to what had been only a very basic career

structure. Principal Russo makes good use of these positions by asking lead teachers to assume specialized roles within her school,
serving as mentors, content specialists, program planners, and staff
developers in the ASPIRE (Aspiring and Studying to become Powerful Instructors and Reflective Educators) induction program.
Drawing upon additional resources from the district and foundations, Russo has adroitly woven together districtwide and school-
based initiatives to offer an array of rich and challenging roles for
experienced teachers.

Teachers at Murphy School often take on more than one role.
For example, one full-time third grade lead teacher is a planner and
teacher leader in ASPIRE, as well as a mentor to a new colleague.
When she described what her mentoring involves, it became clear
how her job differs from that of a conventional classroom teacher:
"I spent a whole week helping [my new teacher] out, so I went in
and did all of her lessons of Writers' Workshop, gave her everything
she needed to include in kids' folders and stuff. . . . We talked about
the lessons and about some of the struggles she was having and [I
said] if she wanted to come down and watch a lesson in second
grade, that would be great. . . ." Murphy School is organized so that
this teacher could devote a week of time to mentoring the new
teacher because a substitute was prepared to teach lessons in her
classroom with little curricular interruption. As we saw in Chapter
Nine, Murphy Elementary School cultivates skilled "building substitutes," substitute teachers who work regularly in the Murphy
building, by including them in the ASPIRE program and offering
them numerous professional development opportunities.

Of the three sites we visited, ETHS has the most extensive set
of roles for teachers, many growing out of the induction program.
These include an induction coordinator, mentors, a mentor trainer,
a group of departmental staff developers, as well as course instructors for ETHS 101 and Studying Skillful Teaching. The position of
staff developer, for example, calls upon an experienced teacher to
advise new teachers about their work within a content area. Staff

developers observe often but never evaluate the new teachers. So that they have time to do their jobs, staff developers are released from one course and one duty. As with the induction coordinators at BHS, there is no change in pay.

One staff developer describes the position that he and his counterparts hold "not as some sort of pseudo-administrators" but as "colleagues with built-in time to help those new to ETHS." Staff developers teach model lessons, coach teachers on how to incorporate technology into instruction, advise departmental colleagues on the use of rubrics and projects, and facilitate the departments' relationships with external sources of support such as Northwestern University. One staff developer explained that the role fulfilled "some of my leadership desires without getting me into formal administration, which I'm not interested in, and keeping me in the classroom." He said, "I like the mix there." The role, in his view, was rich: "Aside from dealing with new teachers, there are always departmental issues, whether it's how we're implementing our standards or benchmark activities or looking at curriculum alignment or how we are supporting team teaching in general [or] how we hire people. Just because of my position [as staff developer], I make myself part of those discussions."

How Differentiated Roles Benefit Teachers and Schools

The veteran teachers at these schools value their new roles, which have brought them recognition for good work, improved their teaching practice, stimulated them intellectually, and warded off boredom and burnout. As one BHS mentor said: "I've gained as much as I've given." The teachers' satisfaction suggests that these three schools have discovered and devised the very kind of hybrid roles that many of the Massachusetts new teachers told us they hope to have in the future.

Notably, veteran teachers appreciated the opportunity to engage in deep, intellectual work with their experienced colleagues. An ETHS staff developer commented on the quality of discussions among the staff developers: "They are, without exception, remarkable people, highly motivated, creative, and intelligent. . . . The creativity, the organizational creativity, the sensitivity to the psychological realities of the job . . . of the people we are working with, it's just extraordinary. I have loved these conversations. It has been really wonderful."

In addition to enriching the work lives of veteran teachers, a career ladder or set of differentiated roles could benefit the school as a whole. A school where highly skilled teachers hold differentiated roles as instructional coaches, coordinators, or specialists can direct extra support to individuals or groups, such as a new social studies teacher who wants help in conducting a simulation or a grade-level team needing help with curriculum development. As a result, the school becomes more effective. Moreover, as educational researcher Andrew Hargreaves (2001) argues, a school with a focus on building-wide learning, for all adults and children, can stimulate more inspired teaching and better student outcomes.

A Differentiated Career System: Making It Work

Differentiated roles for teachers are not easy for schools to sustain. Often they depend on funding from short-term grants, and when the grant is gone, the roles disappear as well. At BHS, for example, funding for the induction program comes from an alumni foundation, which leaves the future of the program always somewhat uncertain. In many schools, hybrid roles are established informally rather than by contract, thus leaving them vulnerable to sudden changes in administrators' priorities. ETHS has the advantage of being a single-school district and, therefore, school leaders there are not obliged to comply with a different set of policies set by the district office. They *are* the district office. However, both BHS and Murphy Elementary School operate within school districts and thus are subject to the tugs, pulls, and directives from the central office, which may limit what they can do. A literacy coach at Murphy School said that since the arrival of Principal Russo, "leadership is booming. She just sees this little spark in you that you sometimes didn't even know was there and, boom, there it is." But, realistically, one must ask whether teacher leadership will continue to "boom" if the principal chooses to leave or is reassigned. Similarly, will the differentiated roles created by these schools weather district cuts or endure with the introduction of new reforms that use resources in a different way?

To date, career ladders and differentiated roles in most settings are more experiments than they are established practice. Some districts claim to have instituted career ladders by assigning labels to the early years of a teacher's career, for example, by designating a first-year teacher an "intern," a third-year teacher a "provisional" teacher, and a fourth-year teacher with tenure a "professional" teacher. The titles, however, are somewhat misleading, since they all refer to classroom teachers who hold the same position and carry a full course load. A few districts have created career ladders with substantive roles that are truly differentiated.

The Career in Teaching Plan in Rochester, New York

The Career in Teaching Plan, negotiated by the Rochester City School District and the Rochester Teachers Association in 1987, established a step beyond tenure for lead teachers, who could earn up to $70,000, a stunning salary at the time (Koppich, 1993). Lead teachers were to be selected through "an open competitive process for specific instructional and professional leadership roles," such as mentor or curriculum specialist, which require extra time, responsibility, knowledge, and skills (Rochester City School District & Rochester Teachers Association, 2000, p. 2). In Rochester, lead teachers serve primarily as supervisory mentors for new teachers and are chosen by a joint panel, consisting equally of teachers and administrators. It should be noted, however, that teachers' attainment of lead teacher status is not permanent; they must reapply for the role every two years and, since the process is competitive, their reappointment to the role is not guaranteed. Recently, an external review of the Career in Teaching Plan found evidence that it has contributed to the improvement and retention of teachers in the district (Koppich, Asher, & Kerchner, 2002).

The Toledo Plan

Toledo, Ohio, has also effectively institutionalized new roles for expert teachers in the city's schools. In 1981, the Toledo Public Schools and the Toledo Federation of Teachers collaborated to create the Toledo Plan, the nation's first Peer Assistance and Review Program. Expert Toledo teachers, selected by a joint panel of teachers and administrators (five from union and four from management), serve as consultants for ten to twelve teachers over the course of one year. This is a serious and sustained investment in teachers' development; each consultant spends approximately twenty hours per semester mentoring and evaluating each teacher. All new teachers participate in the program, as do veteran teachers judged by principals or peers to be in need of intervention. At the end of each year, consultants recommend to the governing panel whether a teacher should be reemployed or released (Toledo Federation of Teachers, & Toledo Public Schools, 2001).

There are several noteworthy features of this program. First, it involves experienced teachers in important decisions. Since the program began, the district annually has dismissed approximately 8 percent of its first-year teachers, a higher percentage than comparable districts that rely on administrators to evaluate new teachers (Cázaras & Harris, 2002). Notably, the consultants' recommendations can be overturned only by a two-thirds vote of the panel. Second, unlike ETHS, BHS, Murphy School, and many other induction programs, the roles of mentor and evaluator in Toledo are not divided between two people but are joined into the single role of the consultant. Therefore, there is no guarantee of confidentiality in any part of this consulting relationship. Third, because consulting teachers take on these roles for three years at a time and then return to their classrooms, this is not a career ladder that establishes steps for permanent vertical career advancement. Rather, the Toledo Plan creates a latticework of differentiated roles permitting teachers to move in and out of the classroom. Toledo's requirement that consultants must return to the classroom is intended to maintain the credibility of the consultants with other teachers. However, one effect it may have is to discourage teachers who seek to advance to a new and permanent change of role.

Finally, the costs for consultants' stipends constitute the greatest expense of the program, although a recent, external, cost-benefit analysis found the plan to be "cost-effective in both monetary and social terms" (Cazaras & Harris, 2002, p. 2). During the three years they serve as consultants, teachers earn an annual stipend of $5,165 beyond base pay; when they return to the classroom the stipend ends and they receive the same salary they would have if they had remained in the classroom during those three years. So although being selected as a consultant is viewed as a kind of informal promotion, it is accounted for as extra pay for extra work.

The Challenge of Selecting Expert Teachers for New Roles

If teachers, administrators, and the public are to invest in career ladders, they must be confident that the criteria for selecting lead or master teachers are appropriate and that the process for choosing them is even-handed. Unfortunately, there is no clear consensus among educators or the public about what excellent teaching is or how it can be assessed. Moreover, distrust between teachers and administrators often undermines confidence in the teachers who are selected, with teachers assuming that favoritism drives administrators' choices, and administrators dismissing teachers' choices as union-controlled. Some districts address this by appointing joint selection committees. Another option is to rely on the assessments of an external organization, such as the National Board for Professional Teaching Standards.

The National Board for Professional Teaching Standards

Over the past decade, the National Board for Professional Teaching Standards (NBPTS), a private organization with a sixty-three-member board, has developed a sophisticated process for certifying "accomplished teachers" in one of twenty-seven fields; for example, English language arts for adolescents and young adults. To date, the Board reports that it has awarded certification to 23,937 teachers (www.nbpts.org). The review process is rigorous and time-consuming for applicants. Candidates spend the good part of a school year documenting their practice. They videotape and analyze their classes, respond to written questions about their teaching, and take an exam covering both subject-matter content and pedagogy (Berg, 2003). The selection process is also impartial. Reviews are done anonymously, at a distance, thus reducing the possibility of political meddling. Many states and school districts grant substantial stipends to teachers who receive NBPTS certification. Mississippi currently awards NBPTS-certified teachers an annual bonus of $6 thousand for the ten-year life of their certificates, whereas Kentucky grants $2 thousand per year. Board-certified teachers in North Carolina earn an additional 12 percent on top of the state-funded portion of their salaries. Thus, despite the widely held belief that merit pay does not exist in public education, many states and districts reward teachers for being recognized as accomplished teachers by the NBPTS.

Educational experts continue to dispute the legitimacy of the NBPTS and the validity of these assessments (Ballou & Podgursky, 2000a; Kanstoroom & Finn, 2000). However, for districts that do endorse the NBPTS assessment process, NBPTS-certified teachers are logical candidates for leadership roles in a differentiated staffing system. Although NBPTS certifies teachers based on their work with students, not with adults, this recognition indicates attainment of a level of mastery that, through a leadership role, could be shared systematically with colleagues. As yet, however, few districts have seized this opportunity in any serious way, and many NBPTS-certified teachers have no other option but to return to their classrooms, to the benefit of their students but not to the betterment of the school as a whole.

Different Roles, Different Demands

As schools and districts experiment with new roles for teachers, it is important to remember that many of the emerging, hybrid roles are meant to involve teachers in work with colleagues, not with students. In some cases, as with the Toledo consultants, master teachers or coaches who are assumed to have superior skills or knowledge are asked to take on higher levels of responsibility than they would exercise in their classroom. The teachers who have hybrid roles, such as the staff developers at ETHS or the coaches at Murphy School, may seem to work side by side as equals with classroom teachers, but they are not truly peers. To do their jobs well, they must exercise greater authority than the teachers with whom they work. Yet often, as with NBPTS-certified teachers, individuals are selected primarily on the basis of their successful work with students, not adults. Those in Toledo have learned this over time and advise others who would adopt their model to select candidates who work effectively with adults, have the ability to write well, and can make the difficult decision to dismiss a teacher. Districts that reassign classroom teachers to take on roles that are essentially supervisory must arrange for training and ongoing support.

Constraints and Possibilities: What a School Can Do

New teachers benefit when their schools are organized to provide easy access to ongoing support from their expert colleagues. Moreover, these differentiated roles signal career possibilities to teachers in their early years as they look ahead to consider whether it is possible for them to build rewarding and viable long-term careers in education. Although becoming a principal or district administrator is potentially a rewarding move that could strengthen the school, many teachers we interviewed are not interested in these roles. They do not want to exit the classroom entirely, but they also do not want to be confined to that classroom. Rather, they seek hybrid roles that engage them regularly as teachers while allowing them to expand their learning and extend their influence. As the induction case studies show, the capacity of individual schools can be greatly enhanced when skilled, experienced teachers take on new roles and together become an additional level of support for new teachers. As we have seen, this increased capacity is especially important given that new recruits begin teaching today with widely varied levels of preparation and experience.

Despite the obvious value of creating a system of new roles for teachers, most conventional public schools are not free to establish their own staffing policies and practices. Rather, they must comply with state mandates and district regulations set by the school board, central office, or through collective bargaining. As a result of such district-based limitations, many of the schools' most creative strategies for establishing differentiated careers require school-based leaders to maneuver around the rules, roles, and pay scale established elsewhere. Sometimes they use creative compliance, sometimes creative insubordination, and sometimes they give up. Their staffing solution, which may serve the school well, is inevitably temporary and vulnerable.

One might expect to see more variation in teachers' roles within charter schools, since these schools presumably have more flexibility in staffing and are often smaller and less rigidly structured than their conventional counterparts. In fact, we saw some evidence of charter schools asking teachers to assume a variety of different roles. Yet even when the new teachers in our study stepped into such roles, the positions rarely were formalized through role-specific selection, training, and remuneration. Overall, we were struck by the incredible persistence of the traditional approach to staffing—one teacher, one classroom—that precludes establishing differentiated roles and career opportunities for classroom teachers. Serious change in those arrangements cannot be instituted solely by either the school or the district. Staffing options created by district officials must then be enacted by school-based leaders. This should not simply be a one-way process; the creative solutions devised in the schools must inform the framework that the district adopts.

Long-standing districtwide models such as those in Rochester and Toledo suggest the importance of having an established framework for titles, roles, and pay that is explicitly supported by all the parties. However, those essential structures will not improve the capacity of the schools until school leaders make the most of what the district structures provide. The induction cases described in Chapter Nine reveal how much school leaders—both teachers and administrators—can do when they have the flexibility and resources they need.

Chapter Eleven

Finders *and* Keepers

The context of teaching has changed dramatically over the past three decades, but the schools where teachers work have not kept pace with this transformation. As Esther Crane and her counterparts in the next generation of teachers join the profession, far too many find themselves in schools that are ill-prepared to assist them in their work. Notably, the schools that are least organized to hire and support new teachers are often located in low-income communities, where there are the greatest concentrations of new teachers. When these schools are unable to support new teachers, they also fail the students who most depend on public education for their future.

Early in the 1900s, Maggie Haley, a teacher unionist in Chicago who campaigned on behalf of social justice and better working conditions for teachers, contended that what is good for teachers is good for students (Reid, 1982). There are certainly times when this principle does not hold and the self-interest of teachers is at odds with the best interests of students. However, Haley's comments ring true as we consider what it will take to recruit, support, and retain a new generation of teachers over the next decade. The current period of turnover in the teaching force marks a choice point for public education, one that presents both a challenge and an opportunity. Stated simply, the challenge is to make all schools places where teachers find the support they need to succeed with their students. The opportunity is to attract and retain a strong, effective cohort of teachers to replace the retiring generation, thus ensuring that all students will receive the superior education they deserve.

The Retiring Generation and the Context They Entered

The retiring generation of teachers, who have taught school as a life-long career, have made a remarkable contribution to public education and society. Well-educated and committed to public service, many of this cohort have been sustained by the intrinsic rewards of teaching, even though their paycheck compared poorly with what they might have earned in another profession. These teachers have persisted in the classroom despite the fact that society has never granted their work the recognition it deserves. The schools these teachers entered some thirty years ago were virtually all of the egg-crate variety: one teacher, one classroom. From the start, the teachers were expected to work in parallel fashion with their peers, as independent and self-sufficient workers.

Theirs was also the first cohort of teachers to unionize after many states passed public sector collective bargaining laws in the 1960s and 1970s. During the past thirty to forty years, teachers unions have become a mighty political force in education, but individual teachers have remained largely subordinate in their schools, receiving little sincere encouragement to exercise influence beyond their classrooms or to be deeply involved in schoolwide decision making. During the 1980s, reformers proposed that schools be restructured as inter-dependent organizations and that teachers exercise expanded influence (Carnegie Forum on Education and the Economy, 1986; Holmes Group, 1986). These proposals widely met with quiet but determined resistance from large numbers of teachers, who made it clear that they preferred to work on their own in their classrooms (Evans, 1996). Generally, the retiring generation of teachers have valued and protected their privacy—a privacy that has allowed some to refine and deepen a personal teaching style and craft, and others to conceal their failure to become the teachers they had hoped to be.

The flat, segmented structure of schools and the one-role career of teaching have reinforced generational norms of privacy and self-sufficiency, which persist in schools today. Given the implicit terms of these teachers' employment—that they were generic workers expected to educate their students on their own—it should be no surprise that many of them have, in fact, chosen to focus on their students and invest in their classroom rather than committing time and energy to school improvement efforts. Despite a recent emphasis on collaboration within schools, the teacher celebrated in fiction and film is still always a solo performer, not a team player. These teachers understood early on that in the world of their work, excellence in teaching was to be developed alone and performed only before a small audience of students.

As this generation of teachers retires, taking with them the knowledge and expertise that they have developed, the structures and cultures of the schools they leave are, on the whole, remarkably unchanged. These schools preserve the isolation and sanctity of the classroom over interdependent work among teachers, which would better support successful teaching. Given that the environment of education is increasingly complex and dynamic, one might expect schools to have responded by becoming more differentiated, responsive, and flexible organizations. Although a small number have, most have retained simple and relatively primitive structures, particularly compared with how other organizations in society have evolved during this period. One of the clearest findings of our study is that traditional, egg-crate schools will not satisfy the next generation of teachers, who enter schools in a different context, with different career options, and different expectations about how they will do their work and build their futures.

The Rising Generation and the Context They Enter

The rising generation of teachers is not simply a younger version of the retiring generation; it is a different generation altogether. These new teachers consider the prospects of teaching from the perspective of a transformed labor market and bring to public schools a new set of hopes, expectations, and concerns.

Shared Attitudes Across the Cohort

Teachers within this new generation share certain attitudes. For example, they are less accepting of top-down hierarchy and fixed channels of communication, less respectful of conventional organizations, and generally more entrepreneurial than their predecessors. Most new entrants to teaching, it turns out, do not expect or want to work alone, which may come as a surprise to people who are convinced that teachers, as an occupational group, prefer isolation (American Federation of Teachers, 2002; Public Agenda, 2003). In fact, many entrants—particularly midcareer entrants who have worked extensively on teams in prior employment settings—assume that taking a job in an organization (as opposed to being a private vendor) means working with, not simply next to, other people. New teachers report that they seek, rather than avoid, frequent feedback about their performance. The prospect of being isolated in a classroom is, for most new entrants, troubling rather than reassuring.

Also, although these new teachers do expect to be treated fairly, they do not seek uniform treatment. The women, who constitute nearly 80 percent of the new generation of teachers, are far less intimidated than their predecessors by social prohibitions against distinguishing themselves or taking charge. Overall, this generation seeks opportunities to excel and to be recognized for their accomplishments. They are attracted by opportunities to develop new skills, and they see themselves eventually exercising influence beyond the domain of their classroom. They believe that schools should encourage and reward them as they grow and improve their practice. Rather than rejecting differentiated pay, they expect their salaries to reflect, in some fair way, their growth and success as teachers. Over time, they hope for opportunities to advance in their work and to exercise greater influence in their schools and profession.

Differences Within the Cohort

Despite such consistent themes in this cohort's accounts, there are important differences within the group as well. As we have seen, they enter teaching at different stages in their careers, which means that they come to their schools with very different experiences and strengths. Many midcareer entrants bring from their prior workplace knowledge about how a particular subject is used in practice. For example, a former software developer can explain to students how technology is used in medicine or a former lawyer can describe how an individual's Constitutional rights are protected in a jury trial. Many first-career entrants start their teaching with up-to-date information gleaned from college courses, expertise using the latest technology, and recent memories of what it was like to be a student. As a result, their teaching is current and well-informed, enhanced by multimedia, and responsive to their students' interests.

Teachers in this cohort also have had various kinds of teacher preparation, and thus they come to teaching with different needs. Within our sample of fifty teachers, there are individuals, like Fred, who had completed an extensive undergraduate and graduate pre-service program, including a full-year internship co-teaching in a professional development school. There were others, like Bernie, who began teaching full-time after only a seven-week summer training program, and still others who began their work in charter schools with no formal training at all.

Finally, there are differences within the cohort in the intentions they have for their teaching career. Unlike the prior generation, who entered teaching for the long-term, this cohort also includes individuals who have made a short-term commitment to teaching. They will spend several years in the classroom before moving on to another line of work. In addition to these "contributors," there is a more tentative subgroup of "explorers," who are considering teaching as one of several career possibilities. If teaching turns out to be satisfying, the "explorers" may stay. Although a substantial portion of this new generation intends to remain in education long-term, they do not all plan to remain in the classroom full-time, but rather, expect that at least part of their work will be outside the classroom. Therefore, very few will closely follow the paths of their predecessors—entering teaching as a first-career and remaining full-time in the classroom until retirement.

These differences are important in two ways. First, if schools are to adequately support teachers with such varied experiences and expectations, they must deliberately and innovatively address their individual needs and interests. Carefully designed induction programs can engage expert teachers in identifying and providing the particular supports that new teachers need. For example, a midcareer entrant who completed student teaching in the relative calm of summer school may need extra advice about classroom management when confronted with the activity and tumult of a regular school year. A first-career entrant who is reluctant to exercise the authority needed to maintain an orderly classroom may need to observe and be observed by experienced teachers who can coach and encourage him.

Second, schools can increase their capacity by drawing upon the varied talents and experiences of the entering cohort. A midcareer entrant with experience in a large corporation can help the school develop a more interactive and informative hiring process. A first-career entrant with skills in technology can help expert teachers become even more effective in their classrooms. But increasing the school's capacity in this way means starting with the assumption that all teachers are different and that their differences matter and can enrich the school. Teachers and administrators dare not hold fast to past practice and wait for the "real" teachers—those traditionally prepared, first-career entrants who expect to teach for a lifetime—to show up. For if new teachers do not find that schools are responsive to their talents and needs, they are far more likely than their predecessors to leave their schools and the profession without looking back. Therefore, school officials and experienced teachers must acknowledge and respond to the diversity within this new cohort—their work experience in other settings, their varied preparation, and their sometimes tentative or short-term commitment to classroom teaching—while also taking seriously the new set of priorities that this generation brings.

Schools That Find and Keep Teachers

Schools that support teachers over time succeed not only in hiring new teachers, but also in retaining and developing them. These schools are finders *and* keepers. They leave little to chance and do not assume that good teaching inevitably flows from innate talent, best nurtured in privacy and isolation. Rather, they purposefully engage new teachers in the culture and practices of the school, beginning with their first encounter. In such schools, hiring is the first step of the induction process, a time when both prospective teachers and their future colleagues can exchange rich information about what each has to offer and expects from the other. Induction does not end with a signed contract or one day of orientation at the opening of school. Rather, it encompasses a deliberately crafted set of supports for new teachers extending through the first year of teaching and beyond.

New teachers report that when schools focus on a compelling mission, organize to achieve clear purposes, maintain a focus on student learning, and make efficient use of time and other resources, they become engaged in a joint professional enterprise that affirms their contributions and sustains them. When they encounter curricular and collegial support in their schools, they are better able to succeed with their students from the start and refine their teaching skills over time. When they work in schools where faculty members acknowledge and support each other in the challenges of teaching across boundaries of race, ethnicity, and language, teachers are likely to experience greater success with their students. If they are well supervised and see opportunities for professional growth beyond their classroom, they are more likely to consider the possibility of a long-term career in teaching that is varied and responsive to their interests, abilities, and development.

Efforts to address the teacher shortage must take note of these findings and pay careful attention to the school conditions that new teachers find upon entry.

Some new teachers in our study said that they had good curricula, sufficient supplies, and supportive colleagues who could provide them with sound advice and constructive feedback, but many more did not. Some respondents could count on schoolwide systems to guide and support them, as they managed student discipline or responded to students with special needs. But many others were left to figure things out and fend for themselves. Some could rely on a knowledgeable mentor who observed their teaching, but many more reported that their mentors were seldom available or had little to offer. Overall, the experiences of new teachers fell far short of what they had hoped and what might have been. As a result, two-thirds of the teachers we studied transferred to other schools or left teaching altogether within their first four years.

Some teachers' accounts captured examples of satisfying teaching experiences, profound connections with students, and inspiring leadership. Although these stories reveal the promise that might await the next generation of teachers at their schools, not all novice teachers can count on such positive experiences. However, our respondents' accounts of both rewarding and disappointing experiences suggest many specific things that principals and teachers can do to increase the prospects of success.

The Opportunity to Act

One question that often emerges as we consider how best to staff the schools in the years ahead is whether policies and practices should be gauged to meet the interests and needs of those who traditionally have chosen teaching or those who might choose teaching, if only schools and the career of teaching were different. It seems clear to us that this is not a real choice, for even those who appear to be "traditional" entrants—new graduates of a teacher education program—have different experiences, expectations and career plans than their predecessors did. To be certain that students will have the teachers they need and deserve, policies must be designed with a wide range of potential teachers in mind. Rather than waiting for the next generation of teachers to resemble the retiring generation—a futile expectation—policymakers and practitioners should recognize and embrace this new, more complicated reality, with all its challenges and opportunities.

What District Leaders Can Do

District-level officials, including administrators, school board members, and union leaders, can create the districtwide conditions that make teaching an attractive profession and make their schools places where teachers want to be. They can ensure basic support and expect high student performance across all schools, while also allowing schools to innovate. For example, recognizing that school-based induction programs are needed so that new teachers can get off to a good start in their first few years, district officials can fund positions for experienced teachers within the schools to devise and implement such programs, without specifying just how they should operate. Thus, the new teachers' induction experience would be grounded in the culture and practices of their new school, where they will need to build contacts and support. In designing and presenting the program, their experienced colleagues could model ways of interacting professionally that might carry throughout the school year. New teachers would come to understand the mission of the school, as well as what teachers do each day to achieve that mission. By situating the induction process within the schools rather than at the district office, administrators signal to the principal and teacher leaders that the district will invest in their capacity to become stronger and more self-sufficient.

If schools that operate within districts want to create differentiated roles or experiment with a differentiated pay plan, they cannot do it alone, for this is the province of labor and management. Therefore, school and union officials have the opportunity to exercise leadership by introducing, nurturing, and refining creative alternatives to the single-role career and the standardized salary scale. Our interviews show that new teachers are looking for a new approach to rewards and opportunities in their work; district and union leaders are in the position to jointly initiate such ventures.

By establishing school-based hiring practices, administrators at the district level can acknowledge that the hiring process is successful if it achieves good matches between candidates and schools. For if centralized hiring and assignment leads to poor matches, schools will pay the price of instability and turnover. Making it possible for school-based hiring teams and prospective teachers to exchange rich information during the hiring process will increase the chances that good choices will be made, and the school will be strengthened as a result. However, in most districts, schools cannot handle the entire process on their own, for they still must rely on the district for accurate information about candidates and authorized job openings in their schools. Human resource administrators can support effective hiring by providing that information in an efficient way. Also, because school-based administrators and teachers will have little opportunity to actively recruit candidates outside the district, they must count on district officials to search for prospective teachers on their behalf. Therefore, human resource administrators who delegate hiring to the schools still have a vital job to do in recruiting widely to find a strong, diverse pool of candidates.

Achieving school-based hiring may require that unions give back some of the protections that have been won in past negotiations, yet they might also gain a greater role in the hiring process for experienced teachers within their schools. Administrators and union leaders also can work together to ensure that principals and human resource administrators have the authority they need to recruit and hire teachers in a timely way. These administrators can be empowered to exercise discretion in salary placement for new recruits by granting credit for experience teaching in other districts or working at nonteaching jobs in other fields. Having this flexibility is especially important when schools must staff shortage areas such as special education, math, or science. District and union officials also can agree, as they did in Boston and Seattle, to minimize the role of seniority in staffing decisions and to settle transfer requests early so that hiring can proceed quickly and efficiently. This approach is particularly important in large urban districts, for these districts often compete unsuccessfully for candidates with wealthier suburban districts, which typically can recruit and hire candidates earlier than urban districts can.

What School-Based Administrators and Experienced Teachers Can Do

Because what happens at the school site is so important in retaining new teachers, principals and experienced teachers who work there have the greatest opportunity and responsibility to create conditions that will support and retain a strong cohort of colleagues. Where those in the schools have the authority to hire new staff (and where the district authorizes hiring in a timely way), principals, teachers, and parents can take full advantage of the process, thus providing for a rich exchange of information between the school and candidates. Prospective teachers should know what the school stands for and expects of teachers. They should understand what their job will entail and what support they can count on from the school or the district. Those in the school should realize that they are choosing a future colleague and, therefore, use an expansive hiring process to learn through formal interviews, informal conversations, and teaching demonstrations what the candidates have to offer and what they would expect on the job. When a good hiring process is over, there should be no surprises.

The greatest responsibility for the induction of new teachers also rests with the school, and it takes resources, planning, expertise, and goodwill to do it right. Although the principal is crucial in making this happen, it should not be up to the principal alone to make it work. Given the demands on the principal's time and the importance of developing strong collegial bonds between new and experienced teachers, it is far better that expert teachers take on this responsibility, in exchange for either a substantial stipend or a reduced teaching load.

Schools that attend to the development of new teachers initially provide them some shelter—a less demanding assignment or slightly reduced load, additional help, staged expectations—so that they can gradually gain instructional competence and professional confidence. In many schools, this support comes in the form of an assigned mentor. However, given what we have learned about the hazards and limits of one-to-one mentoring, scarce money might be better spent on schoolwide coordinators for whom planning induction is a central, not a marginal, responsibility. When there are sufficient additional funds and enough skilled veteran teachers to provide one-on-one mentoring, every effort should be made to ensure that this is more than a buddy system by providing mentors with training and ongoing consultation in how to observe new teachers and give useful feedback. When there are not enough skilled teachers who want to be mentors, new teachers can work in groups along with a single, well-compensated mentor and thus benefit from learning alongside peers under the guidance of an expert teacher.

Those responsible for assigning teachers to classes, such as principals and high school department heads, need to recognize how important new teachers' initial assignments are. An unfair or undoable assignment can drive new teachers out of public education (as with Brenda) or to another school (as with Keisha). Schools have long allowed senior teachers to claim the best classes and schedules, with the implicit understanding that plum assignments are to be earned over time. However, if novices today are assigned the most demanding courses, students, and schedules, they may well leave before the year is over. Because the most difficult assignments often involve teaching the students with greatest needs, balanced teaching assignments also will ensure that all students are more fairly served.

Another way to attend to the development of new teachers is to provide them with adequate curricular supports. Giving new teachers difficult teaching assignments is bad enough; giving them difficult assignments with little or no curriculum is irresponsible. As we saw in Chapter Six, most of the new teachers in our study encountered a curriculum void, and they struggled to plan and teach their classes with little curricular guidance. Together, schools and districts can greatly enhance new teachers' experience by providing them with detailed curriculum materials that are aligned with the state frameworks and that can be adapted to the needs of their particular students. Schools can also provide regular opportunities for new teachers to work with their experienced colleagues on learning how to implement the curriculum in their classrooms.

Experienced teachers have a vital role to play in the induction and support of their new peers, for novices look to them for their expertise in the classroom and their understanding of the students and community. First, experienced teachers can be welcoming and generous in their offers of support. By opening their classrooms to new teachers who want to observe and by taking the time to visit the new teachers' classrooms and offer feedback if asked, experienced teachers can greatly enhance the new teachers' experience. Our studies of exemplary induction programs also reveal how much veteran teachers have to gain in the process, both in discovering new techniques for their own teaching and in creating a professional legacy by contributing to a new teacher's career.

Successful, information-rich hiring, the provisions of sheltered experiences for new teachers, and the creation of school-based induction programs call for considerable school-level capacity. They require time, money, and expertise that is more readily available at some schools than at others. However, schools can start small, recognizing the importance of fit and support in developing new teachers into the kind of faculty members who will eventually share leadership for the life of the school.

What New Teachers Can Do

New teachers entering schools today take on challenging work in a context where resources and support are always in short supply. However, there are many things that new teachers can do to ensure that the school where they first teach is right for them. And wherever they are, they can solicit support for their work. The first step toward having a good first year is to conduct an active job search. This involves starting early, before jobs have been posted and when school is still in session. Finding a teaching job—particularly in places where budget cuts and layoffs have made the market tight—requires the same kind of initiative as hunting for an apartment or house. The most sought-after positions are claimed or informally offered before they are posted. It is important for teaching candidates to make their interest and talents known to the principals of schools they like, to see those schools at work, and to judge whether they would be good places to teach. This is particularly critical for teachers who want jobs in urban districts, since the school may be empty and teachers gone for summer break when positions finally are posted.

During the hiring process, new teachers should insist on meeting some of their prospective colleagues and ask what kind of support will be there for them if they take the job. Often new teachers are so anxious about landing a job, any job, that they accept the first offer, only later to discover its many problems—no classroom, a teaching assignment made of leftovers, a faculty that distrusts the principal, or a principal who is aloof and excludes teachers from making important decisions about the school. A prospective teacher should be concerned about a principal who seems unnecessarily hurried to make a decision or who pressures a candidate to sign a contract quickly. If the school has serious deficits and will require the new teacher to be engaged in major reforms, she is far better off knowing this from the start and taking the job with an understanding of what it will involve. Because both the principal and the teacher are often impatient to finish the process fast, they frequently collude in skipping important steps of the hiring process, such as meeting with prospective colleagues or teaching a demonstration lesson. This is a mistake and may well lead to serious dissatisfactions for the principal, new teacher, others on the faculty, and students. By asking questions of many people at the school during the hiring process, the new teacher can be assured that a job offer and a signed contract represent an informed decision on both sides.

New teachers also should recognize that, because of increasing demands and new programs—for example, the introduction of standards-based accountability and high-stakes tests—schools are currently in a period of tremendous change. Most, therefore, are unprepared for the new teachers' arrival. That does not mean, however, that teachers and administrators will be unresponsive to new teachers' requests and questions, but that entrants should not be reticent to ask their more experienced peers for help. New teachers who would benefit from professional development opportunities outside the school should seek them out and request permission and funding to attend. Amy's school, for instance, was not well organized for her induction, but the principal made training possibilities known and arranged for teachers to attend them. Amy, for her part, was confident and resourceful in tracking down such opportunities. New teachers who need resources for their classrooms can explore whether there are partner businesses that might supply them, or they can learn which faculty members successfully wrote grants to equip their classrooms and then ask for advice in preparing a proposal. New teachers can ask students who their best teachers are and then observe them at work.

As retirements increase and the number of experienced teachers declines, there will be many opportunities for novice teachers to move into positions of leadership in their schools. Although our interviews suggest that novice teachers should not be expected to do too much too soon, it seems unlikely that they will have to wait long for the chance to exercise real influence beyond their classrooms. New teachers who have expectations, questions, and initiative should feel confident seeking out and acting on the possibilities that exist.

What Policymakers Can Do

Finding a willing recruit to cover every classroom may not be the impossible task it seemed to be four years ago. In a period of financial downturn when budget cuts reduce the number of teaching positions, the requirements for earning a teaching license are relaxed, and laid-off workers from other fields seek a new career, policymakers may turn away from the challenge of staffing schools. This would be a mistake, for although there may not be a shortage of employable people, there is surely a shortage of well-qualified, promising, and dedicated teachers. The teachers that students deserve are not those who will be hired simply because they have nowhere else to go. Rather, they are highly competent individuals with many talents and, therefore, many options.

Public education will never attract these individuals in sufficient numbers until the work of teachers commands higher salaries, greater respect, and more extensive career opportunities. New teachers today have chosen to forego higher-paying work outside of education because they want to make a difference in the lives of students. However, the costs of teaching (opportunity and out-of-pocket, short-term and long-term) have increased substantially over the past thirty years, as have the demands that society makes of teachers. Policymakers must recognize that staffing schools with outstanding entrants will continue to be a difficult and crucial challenge requiring their ongoing attention and financial support.

Probably more important, recruitment is only a first step in addressing this problem. Retaining excellent teachers will call for greater and more sustained investment in public education over the next decade. Budget cuts that threaten support services for students, eliminate school-based professional development, further reduce resources, or abbreviate induction programs for new teachers will certainly accelerate teacher attrition, especially when such cuts are accompanied by higher expectations for student achievement and tougher school accountability measures. Therefore, policymakers at the local, state, and national levels cannot be satisfied to maintain current levels of public funding for educational salaries and services; they must increase them.

In addition to ensuring sufficient, continued funding, local school board members and state policymakers can explore the possibility of promoting a differentiated career structure that provides varied roles for teachers who want to expand their responsibility and skills while remaining close to the classroom—roles such as mentor coordinator, peer reviewer, curriculum coordinator, instructional coach, or staff developer. Also, they might fund more local experiments with differentiated pay for teachers, which allow teachers to have more options for higher income than the standard salary scale permits. Although some school districts have developed certain components that might be used in differentiated career and pay systems, there is, as yet, no well-developed model that could be adopted by many districts. However, with encouragement and funding, local districts could tailor plans for their local needs, incorporating elements of programs that have worked in other settings and that, in combination, respond to what we know to be the priorities and interests of new teachers today.

Preparation and Licensing

One of the most controversial issues that state policymakers face today is to define standards for teacher preparation and licensing that will ensure that there are sufficient numbers of new entrants and that they are well qualified for their work. For several years, policy analysts have fiercely debated whether new teachers need extensive preservice coursework before being given their own classroom. Proponents of traditional teacher education programs make the case that teaching is complex work that requires considerable preparation (Darling-Hammond, Wise, & Klein, 1999; National Commission on Teaching for America's Future, 1996). Meanwhile, opponents contend that one can learn to teach on the job and that prospective teachers need only demonstrate subject-matter knowledge in order to deserve their own classroom. They propose that many routes to teaching be opened so that university-based teacher education programs are not the only path to the classroom for prospective teachers (Ballou & Podgursky, 2000a, 2000b; Kanstoroom & Finn, 2000).

Our research suggests that although each of these arguments has its strengths, neither proposal is sufficient to meet the demand for large numbers of high-quality teachers across all subject areas and in all schools. The first approach discourages candidates who decide to teach late, are uncertain about whether teaching will be right for them, want to teach for only part of their career, or would like to make a career change from another line of work. The second approach underestimates the importance of pedagogical skills and discounts the value of knowledge that teachers should have before entering the classroom. Neither position, however, directly considers the potential of on-the-job training or identifies what essential school-based supports all teachers should have, whatever their preparation. On the basis of our small, purposive sample, we cannot offer any clear answer about the necessity of pedagogical coursework or the wisdom of a particular preservice program. However, we can make several observations about job-embedded learning.

Of the teachers we interviewed, those who reported being most confident about their teaching from the start—Fred and Victoria, for example—had spent an entire year as an intern, co-teaching with an expert teacher. Such an internship provides a new teacher with a sustained, staged, and sheltered entry to teaching. Notably, serving as an intern differs from doing student teaching, in that the intern is a co-teacher for the full academic year, not a substitute teacher during two or three months. By working collaboratively with an expert colleague, these novices get to experience being a regular teacher from the first school day to the last, within a context that allows them to make mistakes because it is both sheltered and educative. Working in the classroom, they closely observe an expert at work and they receive ongoing feedback about their own teaching. Although many educators would agree that this is an ideal arrangement, it is not always possible.

Also, it is extremely difficult to fully prepare a new teacher in advance for all that it takes to do a good job in the classroom. Many teachers in our sample had completed traditional preparation programs but still found their early years very trying. Since schools vary so much in the students and communities they serve, the program they offer, and the curriculum they teach, no preparation program can prepackage sufficient preparation to succeed in every site. Therefore, schools must be prepared to support all the teachers they hire, realizing that most of them will have had relatively brief experiences in practice teaching.

There are many ways that schools might provide such support. School-based, on-the-job training could be provided in a new teacher's classroom by staff developers, instructional coaches, mentors, or peer reviewers. Alternatively, new teachers might participate in a regular seminar with colleagues from their grade level or department, discussing classes they have observed, relevant readings, or curricula they are teaching. Indeed, many of the teachers we interviewed at the three induction sites described in Chapters Nine and Ten—Murphy Elementary School, Brookline High School, and Evanston Township High School—were engaged in such activities. Each site also provided a regular seminar for new teachers, and the participants reported finding those sessions very valuable. When such seminars address current challenges and are moderated by expert teachers who are skilled in their own classroom and effective in their work with peers, they can ensure that new teachers have the resources and feedback they need during the first year or two.

A good induction program is, essentially, job-embedded training, and individual experiences and needs should inform the content of that program. A recent college graduate who has majored in both math and math education may have done student teaching with a cooperating teacher who used algorithms and repetitive practice to teach math. Having taken a job in a middle school that uses an inquiry-based curriculum, this new teacher will need customized support in learning how to teach the new curriculum. Similarly, a research scientist who becomes a chemistry teacher may have solid mastery of the subject and extensive experience training lab assistants, both of which will enhance his teaching. However, knowing how best to organize a lab experiment for twenty-five tenth grade students is a new skill that must to be learned through activities such as observing the class of an expert teacher and discussing it afterward. Schools must be funded and staffed so that they can accommodate and respond to the wide range of preparation and experience that new teachers bring today.

Although the No Child Left Behind Act of 2001 is designed to reduce the number of teachers hired on emergency credentials, it will not guarantee that teachers are well prepared. Many schools and districts—particularly in low-income communities—will continue to hire teachers with minimal formal training because they have no choice but to fill positions. Therefore, entrants will continue to need tailored, sustained assistance if they are to teach well. We must increase their knowledge and facility as classroom teachers in little time, efficiently, and on-site.

Further, the next generation of teachers will include both those who envision long-term careers as well as short-term stays in teaching. Given the enormous staffing changes that schools will undergo during the current decade, it is essential to have a cadre of dedicated, accomplished teachers who can provide continuity within schools, offer the support that new teachers need, and maintain standards in the profession. Over time, members of this group can take on roles as mentors, peer reviewers, professional developers, team leaders, and curriculum writers. They can oversee the effective induction of novices, both those who plan to teach long-term and those who enter teaching as one of several careers. This model would reward and financially compensate long-term teachers for the knowledge and skills they acquire in both preservice training and subsequent professional development, such as certification by the National Board for Professional Teaching Standards. It would provide differentiated roles for them as they master their craft, take on varied assignments, and assume broader responsibilities in their schools.

Simultaneously, there should be well-defined alternative pathways by which prospective entrants can reach the classroom and then find sustained feedback and support as they establish themselves. Critics may contend that those who are unwilling to invest in formal, multiyear preparation are not sufficiently serious about a career in teaching. Our study would suggest that these short-term novices are not fly-by-night teachers, but rather, individuals with a genuine interest in, and serious commitment to, their students and their school. By endorsing a model that provides alternative access to teaching, we are by no means suggesting that schools should abandon high standards for teachers' performance. Rather, we are proposing that more of the effort to prepare and assess the quality of new teachers be moved to the schools.

The Challenge of Achieving Equity

Finally, an issue of great concern to policymakers, practitioners, and the public is the challenge of ensuring that all students, whoever they are and wherever they live, have good teachers. If schools fail to attract and retain a strong, committed cohort of new teachers in the coming years, students will be severely penalized, and those in low-income communities will be likely to pay the greatest price. However, if policymakers and practitioners make teaching a rewarding career that sustains teachers over time, the schools, themselves, will inevitably change for the better to the benefit of both students and the public.

Building greater capacity and stability in low-performing schools that serve high-poverty students should be the highest priority for policymakers and practitioners, for there is persuasive evidence that these schools perpetually have the weakest teachers—those least capable and prepared by any measure—as well as the least experienced (Haycock, 1998). Moreover, they endure the drain and additional demands of constant turnover.

The teachers in our study who moved to different schools all transferred to sites serving students with somewhat higher family incomes. Our interviews revealed, however, that these teachers moved primarily in response to a dysfunctional or problematic school, rather than because of the social class or race of its students. Often teachers who had been committed to teaching in high-need schools left in frustration when they did not find the support—curricular, administrative, or collegial—that they needed to do their work. Elizabeth Useem (2003), who followed sixty new teachers in seven high-poverty middle schools in Philadelphia, found that after three years, only one-third remained in their original schools. Notably, one school lost all twelve new teachers, who were "unhappy with the school's climate and administrative practices" (p. 18).

To take these problems seriously often requires bringing in a first-rate, collaborative principal and a diverse group of experienced and novice teachers who begin together to recreate the school and reinvigorate its culture. The prospects for developing strong schools in high-poverty communities are dim if the school administration dismisses teachers' views or discounts their experience. To reform such schools requires drawing on everyone's talents and ideas. If the school is to truly serve all students, then a faculty of new and experienced teachers must work together with the school principal. There is no question that this is an enormous undertaking, and those who begin it must be ready to build on small accomplishments, increasing their capacity to do more over time.

Some reformers advocate that teachers should be given financial incentives to encourage them to teach in low-achieving, high-poverty schools. This approach is consistent with the need to empower new teachers to have a say in determining their salary. However, our work suggests that this approach will meet with little success unless it is combined with sensible strategies and substantial funding for strengthening the school as a place that supports effective teaching and learning. The fact that eight of the thirteen recipients of the Massachusetts Signing Bonus left the state's public schools before receiving their full bonus suggests that extra money, in itself, will never attract and retain effective teachers in the most challenging teaching assignments.

The task of recruiting and retaining strong teachers for all schools within this decade is indeed daunting, but to ignore it is to leave students in jeopardy and the future of public education in doubt. Schools of 2010 can be well-staffed and effective only if today's policymakers, school officials, and teachers recognize and respond to the challenge in a comprehensive, coordinated, and sustained way. No single player can solve the problem; no single strategy will work. The fact that this effort will require attention, funding, and dedicated response from so many people on so many fronts means that it is an imposing challenge. But it also means that everyone's contribution is important, from the legislator who votes on the education budget to the veteran teacher who reaches out to the novice next door. Only if we embrace this challenge can we take seriously our nation's commitment to the future of all children.

Epilogue

Our latest contact with the new teachers who participated in the study of Massachusetts new teachers was in spring and summer 2003, nearly four years after the start of our longitudinal study.

Where Are the Ten Featured Teachers Now?

Derek Lewis is an administrator at the urban charter high school where he taught for two years. He plans to teach one class this coming year.

Fred Chambers still teaches social studies courses at the urban professional development school where he first student taught five years ago. He recently completed a master's degree in school leadership. Fred's school achieved its goal of having all students accepted to college with its first graduating class, the class of 2003.

Victoria Tran taught third grade for three years at her suburban elementary school before moving out of state and securing a job at another suburban public school. She is still a classroom teacher and also serves as a mentor for new teachers.

Amy Day is on maternity leave, but will return to teach second grade at the same urban elementary school where she began four years ago. She serves on the school's math leadership team and as a mentor for new teachers.

Carolyn Harrington left teaching after four years at the same urban elementary school. She will attend graduate school full time in pursuit of a master's degree in public policy, with a concentration in education policy.

Esther Crane continues to teach math at a suburban high school while completing her master's degree in education, but she still dreams of working on the space program. Her father has become very supportive of her work as a teacher.

Bernie Fallon continues to teach history at the urban high school where he began his teaching career four years ago. He maintains a small legal practice on the side.

Keisha Williams took time off for a leave, but is teaching again as a second grade reading specialist at her urban charter school. She mentors new teachers.

Mary Donahue is still teaching history at a suburban middle school. She is concerned that she may be laid off due to budget cuts.

Brenda Keppler left teaching after two years and now works at a nonprofit organization. She had been working in the research and education division, but is transferring to the fundraising office.

Where Are the Fifty New Massachusetts Teachers?

Thirty-three of the fifty teachers in the study are still teaching in public schools. Seventeen of these work in the schools where they started; sixteen have moved to different schools.

Seventeen of the fifty are no longer teaching in public schools. Two of these individuals are still involved in public education, one as a math specialist and another as a school administrator. Four are teaching in private schools. The other eleven left teaching altogether.

Notes

Chapter One

1. The respondents in the study of Massachusetts new teachers were assured confidentiality and, therefore, are identified with pseudonyms through this book.
2. The immediate demand for teachers is affected by the current financial condition of states and local districts. Given that over 80 percent of school budgets are allocated for personnel, substantial cuts in funding for public education inevitably lead to teacher layoffs. Many districts in California, which declared a large teacher shortage in 2001, had virtually no job openings in the spring of 2003 following budget cuts imposed by the state. Oregon and Massachusetts reported similarly dramatic reductions in many districts. These changes are likely to lead to reduced educational services for students—consolidated classes, fewer schools—that call for fewer, not more, teachers. Those reading such headlines may well conclude that the predicted teacher shortage was, in fact, mistaken or fabricated. However, over time it may well be that these are short-term adjustments to funding crises rather than long-term solutions to staffing needs. As states and districts adjust their budgets, veteran teachers retire, and the public demands good services for students, a shortage of well-qualified teachers may well reappear and persist.

Chapter Two

1. We began our study before an economic downturn, and there were no midcareer entrants in our sample who had been laid off from previous employment.
2. Notably, however, the requirements for a license have been loosened so that charter school teachers are not required to attend traditional preparation programs.
3. Twelve of the thirty-six traditionally prepared entrants completed undergraduate programs in teaching, whereas twenty-four attended graduate school, earning master's degrees.
4. This assumes that the teacher is qualified and competent; attrition of unqualified teachers is another issue.

Chapter Three

1. Three of the teachers in our sample were teaching approximately half time. Their salaries are converted to their full-time equivalents for the purposes of reporting.
2. Average undergraduate tuition and fees at public four-year institutions rose 79 percent from 1976–1977 to 1996–1997 from $1,670 to $2,987 (constant 1996 dollars). Average tuition and fees at private four-year institutions rose 88 percent from $6,859 to $12,881. At the same time, according to the US Census Bureau, median household income has stayed flat (from $34,244 to $36,446 in 1998 dollars).

Chapter Five

1. Johnson and Landman (2000) examine this issue closely in a set of case studies about teachers' work in state-sponsored and within-district charter schools.

Chapter Eight

1. Research in organizational behavior and management studies has found links between person-organization or person-job fit and work outcomes such as job satisfaction and intentions to

quit (Cable & Judge, 1996; Kristof, 1996; Rynes, Bretz, & Gerhart, 1991). Very few of these studies, however, have examined person-organization fit between teachers and schools.

2. A recent report from the New Teacher Project (2003) provides some new data on the discouraging effects of late hiring. The authors found that in four urban school districts "anywhere from 31 percent to almost 60 percent of applicants withdrew from the hiring process" out of frustration with the time line (p. 5).

3. These provisions remain in the latest Seattle teacher's contract (2001–2004), which is available at http://www.wa.nea.org/Info/Orgnztn/SEAHomepage/Contract/01CCBA_Index.html.

4. One possible problem with involving many individuals in the hiring process is that doing so may introduce more noise than clarity. If individuals within a school differ greatly in what they look for in a candidate, involving them in the hiring process might be problematic. The solution to this, however, is not to restrict hiring to the principal or top school administrators, but rather to use the hiring process as a way of building (or reinforcing, if it already exists) a shared sense of what the school is about.

Chapter Nine

1. Unlike in other chapters, where pseudonyms are used for confidentiality purposes, real names are used in these descriptions of exemplary induction programs.

2. In 1999, one in every three students (35 percent) failed the English language arts test at grade four; one in every two students (56 percent) failed the math test at grade four. In Spring 2003, the failure rate in grade four was reduced to 9 percent in English language arts and 12 percent in math.

Appendix A: Background and Methods

The following section describes the background and methods for three major studies that inform this book: a longitudinal study of fifty Massachusetts teachers, a four-state survey study of first-year and second-year teachers, and a three-site study of exemplary school-based induction programs.

Longitudinal Study of Fifty Massachusetts Teachers

Planning for the Longitudinal Study of Fifty Massachusetts Teachers began in mid-1999. After reviewing the literature on new teachers, we decided on four related lines of inquiry and designed an initial study to explore new teachers' (1) conceptions of a career in teaching, (2) views on the incentives and rewards that teaching offered, (3) experiences with the professional culture of their schools, and (4) experiences with curriculum. These topics reflected the individual research interests of team members, as well as important topics that required further research, particularly in the context of a predicted teacher shortage and the entry of a new generation of teachers. Collectively, we designed an interview protocol that could address all four topics within a ninety-minute interview. The protocol was revised multiple times and piloted with several new teachers.

Sample

Our original sample included fifty first-year and second-year teachers who worked in a wide range of Massachusetts public schools: urban and suburban; elementary, middle, and high; large and small;

conventional and charter. In selecting our sample of fifty, we sought to maximize diversity on a wide range of measures and thus identified four sources of potential respondents, which together would enable us to learn about the experiences of a wide range of teachers. These sources included private college and university teacher education programs; public university teacher education programs; charter schools (both state-sponsored and within-district); and the 1999 list of recipients of the $20,000 Massachusetts Signing Bonus, participants in a state-sponsored alternative certification program.

In each case, we sought variety within the source groups as well, including, for example, teacher education programs focusing on both undergraduate and graduate preparation, charter schools offering different kinds of instructional programs, and Massachusetts Signing Bonus recipients who came from various professional backgrounds. We selected both first-career and mid-career entrants to teaching. We contacted charter schools directly, either through the heads of these schools or through individual teachers working there. We contacted recipients of the Signing Bonus Program directly, using a list of names and schools provided by the Massachusetts Department of Education. In total, only two teachers we contacted chose not to participate in the study.

We built this sample gradually and purposively, seeking to attain variation in the gender, race, ethnicity, and age of the individuals and the types of schools in which they worked. The respondents, who were assured confidentiality and anonymity in any written reports, are identified by pseudonyms throughout this discussion.

Data Collection

The first round of data collection involved one tape-recorded, face-to-face interview (one and one-half to two and one-half hours) with each respondent; the interview protocol is included in Appendix B. The five team members at that time each interviewed ten new teachers.

During the summer of 2001, we conducted follow-up interviews with forty-seven of the original fifty respondents. These interviews

Table A.1. A Summary of Sample Composition Illustrating Total Number and Percentages of New Teachers by Gender, Race-Ethnicity, Age, Career Stage, and Experience Level (N = 50)

Gender		Race, Ethnicity		Age		Career Stage		Experience Level	
Female	33 66%	White	35 70%	22–29	30 60%	First–career	26 52%	First year	36 72%
Male	17 34%	Person of color	15 30%	30–39	14 28%	Midcareer	24 48%	Second year	14 28%
				40–49	4 8%				
				50–54	2 4%				
Total	50 100%		50 100%		50 100%		50 100%		50 100%

Table A.2. Summary of Sample Composition Illustrating
Total Number and Percentages of New Teachers
by School Characteristic (N = 50)

Level			Setting			School Type		
Elementary	22	44%	Urban	30	60%	Traditional public	37	74%
Middle	15	30%	Suburban	20	40%	Charter	13	26%
High	13	26%						
Total	50	100%		50	100%		50	100%

lasted twenty to forty minutes and were completed by telephone or in person. (One respondent who had left the United States replied by e-mail.) Two members of the original sample did provide updates on where they were working, but did not respond to our subsequent request for an interview. One additional participant could not be located, having left the state to pursue another line of work. Interview questions for this second round, which are included in Appendix B, focused on the respondents' career decisions. Have they stayed at the same school, moved to another school, or left teaching altogether? How do they explain their choices?

In the spring of each subsequent year, we have sent the study participants brief questionnaires asking them to update us on the career decisions they made that year and their plans for the following year. We also asked them about what additional roles they have taken on at their schools.

Data Analysis

In analyzing our transcribed interview data, we engaged in a method of multistaged coding. Immediately following each interview, we composed a narrative summary for each respondent, highlighting emphasized topics, unveiling emergent themes, and capturing prominent responses in each of our four areas of inquiry. We analyzed these summaries holistically in an effort to understand the broad themes emerging from new teachers' descriptions of their experiences. We then engaged in a rigorous analysis of the transcript data, coding them first according to our four major areas of inquiry and then again according to a series of sub-area codes based on our analysis of the narrative summaries, a thorough review of the literature, and preliminary data analysis. We also created analytic matrices to summarize the data and facilitate cross-case comparisons. In refining emerging concepts, we relied on an iterative testing process, moving back and forth from the concepts to the details of the interview data and the thematic summaries.

After the second wave of data collection, we sorted the respondents according to their career decisions and levels of satisfaction, attaching descriptive labels such as "Leaver," "Mover," or "Stayer" to different subgroups—these descriptors were borrowed from Richard Ingersoll (2001). We again engaged in a rigorous analysis of the transcript data, verifying and testing the coding categories and seeking detailed explanations for the respondents' decisions. We reviewed the respondents' initial interviews for further insight into their decisions.

The purposive sample of teachers we interviewed precludes us from generalizing to all new teachers in all settings, or even to all new teachers in similar settings. However, the respondents' accounts and appraisals are nonetheless informative, provocative, and cautionary. They can assist policymakers and practitioners as they contemplate the needs of the next generation of teachers and assess competing strategies for recruiting them and supporting the early years of their work. The accounts can also guide the way for further research.

Four-State Survey of New Teachers' Experiences of Hiring and Professional Culture

The four-state survey grew directly out of the first set of findings from the Longitudinal Study of Fifty Massachusetts Teachers. With the guidance of Susan Moore Johnson, Susan Kardos and Ed Liu worked together on this study. They designed it to further explore new teachers' experiences of hiring and professional culture, seeking to test hypotheses that had grown out of the earlier qualitative study and to generate broader, more generalizable findings (Kardos, 2003; Liu, 2003). The study was first piloted in one state, New Jersey, before being conducted in four others.

Kardos and Liu administered a mail-out survey in California, Florida, Massachusetts, and Michigan. These states were chosen because they share some key policy features and because they are diverse in terms of size, population, and geographic location. All four states are experiencing some degree of teacher shortage; all have alternative routes to certification; all have charter school legislation; all have adopted standards in core subjects; all use criterion-referenced assessments aligned to standards; and all are collective bargaining states.

The sample comprises 486 randomly selected first-year and second-year, K–12 public school teachers (excluding arts and physical education). We used two-stage stratified cluster sampling to draw the sample. In stage 1 of our sampling process, we stratified the sample by state, school level (elementary, middle, high), and school type (charter, conventional). We drew a total of 258 schools; 72 percent of these schools agreed to participate.

We contacted principals in each of the schools and asked for names of all first-year and second-year academic teachers. All new teachers in each randomly selected school were included in the sample. We were given the names of 751 first-year and second-year teachers, and achieved a response rate of 65 percent (486 teachers). Sampling weights were used in analyses to correct for the over- and undersampling.

Study of Exemplary School-Based Induction Programs

In an effort to understand what a comprehensive induction program offers and how it works, we studied three schools—two high schools and one elementary school—each of which was reporting early success in the induction and retention of its new teachers. These three schools differed in size, the racial and socioeconomic composition of the student body, and the resources available to them. Each faced, or anticipated facing, substantial turnover among retiring teachers and the hiring of many new teachers. We conducted site visits at these schools in the spring of 2003: Brookline High School (Brookline, Massachusetts), Evanston Township High School (Evanston, Illinois), and Murphy Elementary School (Boston, Massachusetts). At each school, we first met with the administrators or teachers responsible for coordinating the induction programs. We interviewed them regarding the history, goals, and design of the program. We then conducted a series of interviews with new teachers, experienced teachers, and administrators involved in the induction programs.

At Brookline High School, we interviewed nine new teachers, six mentors, and the two induction coordinators. At Evanston Township High School, we interviewed thirty-one teachers, including new teachers, mentors, mentor coordinators, staff developers, seminar leaders, and department chairs. We also met with the schoolwide team responsible for coordinating the induction program as a whole. At Murphy Elementary School, we interviewed the principal, two graduate school interns who had played major roles in designing an implementing the induction program, and a total of eight teachers (new and experienced) and aides. We also attended and observed the final ASPIRE seminar session. All of the interviews were designed to fit within a class period and each lasted thirty to fifty minutes.

Immediately following each interview, we composed a narrative summary for each respondent, highlighting emphasized topics, unveiling emergent themes, and capturing prominent responses. We analyzed these summaries holistically in an effort to understand the broad themes emerging from new teachers' descriptions of their experiences. We also created analytic matrices to summarize the data and facilitate cross-case comparisons.

Appendix B: Interview Protocols

Initial Interviews for the Fifty Massachusetts Teachers (December 1999)

1. Before I get into the specific questions, I would like to get a general sense of your experience. How's it going?

2. Has teaching been what you expected? Why? Why not? What did you expect before you entered?

3. How would you describe your school—the people and programs—to someone who doesn't know it? How many teachers teach here?

4. What is it like to teach here?

5. I understand that your assignment is to teach X. Beyond that, what other responsibilities do you have?

6. How did you decide to teach?

   If First-Career:

   What other career options did you consider?

   Did your parents influence you? What do/did your parents do?

   Why did you decide to reject those other careers?

   If Mid-Career:

   What did you do before you decided to teach? Why did you decide to make the career change?

7. People come to teaching by different pathways. What type of teacher preparation have you had?

Are you certified by the state?

How did you come to teach at this school?

8. Can you describe the type of support you've received as a new teacher, either within the school or the district?

Did you have a mentor?

Is the support you received what you needed?

9. I am interested in the contact that you have on a regular basis with other teachers, both formal and informal.

Can you tell me how often you talk with other teachers, in what kinds of situations, and what you talk about?

Do you watch other teachers teach?

10. Is what you just described typical of other teachers in this school?

How would you characterize the way they work together?

11. Is there a common sense among teachers of what teachers in this school should do in their work? Are there certain norms and expectations?

If Yes:

Could you describe these norms and expectations?

Where do these norms and expectations come from?

How do you know/how did you learn what is expected of you?

Do you share these norms and expectations?

If No:

Why do you think this is the case?

Are there groups within the faculty that have certain norms and expectations?

12. How does it feel to be a member of this faculty?

13. Principals take on different roles in different schools. I am interested in understanding how you see your principal. What role would you say he or she plays?

Is this what you think a principal should do?

14. Do you have a curriculum that you are expected to follow?

If Yes:

What kinds of things does it specify? (General goals, specific topics, specific lessons, how to use time?)

In your view, is it a good curriculum? Why? (depth, structure, support, ideas, resources, creativity, results, consistency). Do you like using it? Does it work well for your students?

Does anyone check to see that you're following the curriculum?

Some people think that their curriculum provides too little freedom and some think that their curriculum provides too little structure. What do you think?

If No:

How do you decide what to teach and how to teach?

In your view, does this process of deciding what to teach and how to teach it work well for you? Do you think this works well for your students?

Does anyone monitor what you're teaching?

Some people think that their curriculum provides too little freedom and some think that their curriculum provides too little structure. What do you think?

15. Are there tests you are required to give to your students?

How closely are they tied to what you teach?

How are the results used?

Do the tests affect what and how you teach?

Does the Massachusetts Comprehensive Assessment
System (MCAS) affect what you teach and how you
teach it?

16. Do you feel sufficiently prepared to teach in the way you're
expected to teach here?

Where do you go for information or advice about what
and how to teach?

17. We are interested in incentives and rewards for teachers.
What is your salary and how is it set?

What benefits do you get? Are there any other perks?

Was there any way to negotiate your salary when you
started?

How are your raises determined?

Can you take on additional responsibilities for extra pay?
Do you?

Do you supplement your pay with additional work outside
the school?

Can you cover your living expenses on what you make?

Midcareer: How does your salary compare with what you
made in the past?

First-Career: How does your salary compare to what you'd
be making if you pursued your second choice career?

18. What do you think of the idea of salary being based on
performance?

19. Do you know anything about national board certification?

If No: It's a national process of identifying master teachers
and paying them more. What do you think about this?

If Yes: What do you think about this?

20. What do you think about the Massachusetts Signing Bonus
Program?

Recipient: What would you have done if you had not
received the bonus?

21. There have been some efforts to create a structure, sometimes called a "career ladder," where a teacher would take on different responsibilities and earn more pay. Is that of interest to you?

22. Does teaching offer you a "good fit" as a career?

23. How long do you plan to stay in teaching?

    Will family influence your plans?

    If Respondent Plans to Leave Teaching:

    What would it take to keep you in teaching longer?

    If a career ladder were in place, would that affect your decision to remain in teaching?

24. These are the four topics we are researching: teacher careers, professional culture, curriculum and assessment, and incentives and rewards. Given these topics, is there anything else that you would like to add?

Follow-up Interviews of the Fifty Massachusetts Teachers (Summer 2001)

Stayers Protocol

Note: Throughout the interview, probe for comparisons between (1) expectations and actual experience, (2) this and prior year(s), and (3) current and prior school(s).

1. Did you have any doubts that you would be back at the same school this year?

    - Did you think about changing schools?
    Yes: What would you have been looking for? Why did you decide to stay at this school?

    - Did you think about changing to another job other than teaching?
    Yes: What would you be looking for? Why did you decide to continue teaching?

2. What do you like about teaching there? Are there things you dislike?

> *Probes Related to Professional Culture (Use if Respondent Raises Topic)*

- Is the way you interact with other teachers helpful to you as a new teacher?
- What *group* of teachers do you work with most? Novices? Veterans? Or a mix?
- About how many first- and second-year teachers were in your school?
- How does this year compare to last year?

> *Probes Related to Curriculum (Use if Respondent Raises Topic)*

> Are your curriculum guidelines and materials helpful to you as a new teacher?

- Do you have the guidance and materials you need for the curriculum you are expected to teach?
  What do you have that you find useful? Where do you get it?
  What do you most need that you do not have?
- Do you feel that your curriculum offers you the right balance between structure and autonomy in deciding what to teach and how to teach it?
- Do you spend more or less time preparing for teaching this year compared to last? Why?
  Does the MCAS affect your work? If so, how?

3. Now that you are a ____-year teacher, is your role in the faculty or the expectations others have of you any different? How?

- Role and opportunities outside of the classroom
- Expectations for work inside the classroom.
- Do you have a mentor? Are you a mentor?
- What do you think of this?

- Do you feel that you were treated as a new teacher this year? [Be careful if you ask this question. Respondents might interpret "being treated as a new teacher" as a bad thing.]
4. What was your salary this past year?
5. What are your plans for the future?

  - Short-term: What are your plans for next year?
  - Long-term: How long do you expect to stay in teaching?
  - Is teaching a good fit for you as a career? Why or why not?
  - [Probe for distinctions between classroom teaching and other educational roles.]

Movers Protocol

Note: Throughout the interview, probe for comparisons between (1) expectations and actual experience, (2) this and prior year(s), and (3) current and prior school(s).

1. What prompted the move to a different school this year?

   Voluntary Movers:

   - Tell me more about your decision to change schools.
   - What were you looking for in a new school?
   - Did you ever think about changing to another job other than teaching?
   - At what point in the year did you decide to change schools?

   Involuntary Movers:

   - Tell me more about why you had to move.
   - What were you looking for in a new school? [Only if they chose the new school.]
   - At what point in the year did you find out that you had to change schools?

   Movers Who Changed Districts:

   - Was there something in particular about this district that appealed to you? What?

- How does your salary here compare to what you would have made in your old district? Was that a factor in your decision?

2. How did you end up in your present school?

   - What was the hiring [or transfer] process like?
   - Did you consider other schools?
   - Did anybody interview you at your new school? If so, who? What sorts of things did you discuss?
   - Did you get an accurate sense of the school and what it would be like to work there before you took the job?

3. Are you more satisfied at your new school? Why or why not?

   - Are there things at the new school that are better?
   - Are there things from your other school that you miss?

   Probes Related to Professional Culture (Use if Respondent Raises Topic)

   Is the way you interact with other teachers helpful to you as a new teacher?

   - What *group* of teachers do you work with most? Novices? Veterans? Or a mix?
   - About how many first- and second-year teachers were in your school?
   - How does this year compare to last year?

   Probes Related to Curriculum (Use if Respondent Raises Topic)

   Are your curriculum guidelines and materials helpful to you as a new teacher?

   - Do you have the guidance and materials you need for the curriculum you are expected to teach?

   What do you have that you find useful? Where do you get it?

   What do you most need that you do not have?

- Did you feel that your curriculum offers you the right balance between structure and autonomy in deciding what to teach and how to teach it?
- Do you spend more or less time preparing for teaching this year compared to last? Why?
  Does the MCAS affect your work? If so, how?

4. Now that you are a ___-year teacher, is your role in the faculty or the expectations others have of you any different? How?

- Role and opportunities outside of the classroom
- Expectations for work inside the classroom.
- Do you have a mentor? Are you a mentor?
- What do you think of this?
- Do you feel that you were treated as a new teacher this year? [Be careful if you ask this question. Respondents might interpret "being treated as a new teacher" as a bad thing.]
- [Distinguish between differences based on experience level and differences between the two schools.]

5. What was your salary this past year?

6. What are your plans for the future?

- Short-term: What are your plans for next year?
- Long-term: How long do you expect to stay in teaching?
- Is teaching a good fit for you as a career? Why or why not?
- [Probe for distinctions between classroom teaching and other educational roles.]

Leavers Protocol

Note: Throughout the interview, probe for comparisons between expectations and actual experience.

1. Could you tell me why (and how) you decided not to teach this year?

- Tell me more about your decision.
- When did you decide not to return?

- Would anything have kept you in teaching longer?
- Did you consider changing positions, schools, or districts instead?

  Probes Related to Professional Culture (Use if Respondent Raises Topic)

  Was the way you interacted with other teachers helpful to you as a new teacher?

- What *group* of teachers did you work with most? Novices? Veterans? Or a mix?
- About how many first- and second-year teachers were in your school?

  Probes Related to Curriculum (Use if Respondent Raises Topic)

  Were your curriculum guidelines and materials helpful to you as a new teacher?

- Did you have the guidance and materials you needed for the curriculum you are expected to teach?

  What did you have that you found useful? Where did you get it?

  What did you most need that you did not have?

- Did you feel that your curriculum offered you the right balance between structure and autonomy in deciding what to teach and how to teach it?
- Did you spend more or less time preparing for teaching this year compared to last? Why?

  Did the MCAS affect your work? If so, how?

2. What are you doing now?

3. How do you like what you're doing now? How does it compare with teaching for you?

   - What were you looking for in a new line of work? Did you find it?

4. What was your salary this past year?

5. What are your plans for the future?
   - Short-term
   - Long-term
   - Do you think you will return to teaching one day?
   - Is there anything in particular that would bring you back to teaching?

References

Adelman, N. E. (1991). *Preservice training and continuing professional development of teachers*. Washington, D.C.: Policy Studies Associates.

American Council on Education Division of Government and Public Affairs. (1997). *ACE policy brief: New information on student borrowing*. American Council on Education. Available: http://www.acenet.edu/washington/policyanalysis/student_borrowing_1997.html [2000, March 20].

American Federation of Teachers. (2000). *Survey and analysis of teacher salary trends 2000*. Washington, D.C.: American Federation of Teachers.

American Federation of Teachers. (2002). *Taking action against the quiet crisis in recruitment and retention*. Washington, D.C.: American Federation of Teachers.

Ball, D. L., & Cohen, D. K. (1996). Reform by the book: What is—or might be—the role of curriculum materials in teacher learning and instructional reform? *Educational Researcher, 25*(9), 6–8, 14.

Ballou, D., & Podgursky, M. (1997). *Teacher pay and teacher quality*. Kalamazoo, MI: W. E. Upjohn Institute for Employment Research.

Ballou, D., & Podgursky, M. (2000a). Gaining control of profession licensing and advancement. In T. Loveless (Ed.), *Conflicting missions: Teachers unions and educational reform*. Washington, D.C.: Brookings.

Ballou, D., & Podgursky, M. (2000b). Reforming teacher preparation and licensing: What is the evidence? *Teachers College Record, 102*(1), 5–27.

Benner, A. D. (2000). *The cost of teacher turnover*. Austin, TX: Texas Center for Educational Research.

Berg, J. H. (2003). *Improving the quality of teaching through national board certification*. Norwood, MA: Christopher-Gordon.

Blair, J. (2000, August 2). Districts wooing teachers with bonuses, incentives. *Education Week, 19*, 1,17.

Bohrnstedt, G., & Stecher, B. (Eds.). (2002). *What we have learned about class size reduction in California, Capstone Report*. Sacramento, CA: California Department of Education, CSR Research Consortium.

Boston Municipal Research Bureau. (2002). *Implementing the Boston Teachers'*

Contract: Process is generally successful but key opportunities missed. Boston: Boston Municipal Research Bureau.

Boston Teachers Union, & Boston School Committee. (2000). *Collective bargaining agreement between the Boston Teachers Union and the Boston School Committee.* Boston, MA.

Boyd, D., Lankford, H., Loeb, S., & Wyckoff, J. (2002). *Initial matches, transfers, and quits: Career decisions and the disparities in average teacher qualifications across schools.* Unpublished manuscript.

Bradley, A. (2000, January 13). The gatekeeping challenge. *Education Week/ Quality Counts 2000,* pp. 20–26.

Breaux, A. L., & Wong, H. K. (2003). *New teacher induction: How to train, support, and retain new teachers.* Mountain View, CA: Harry K. Wong Publications, Inc.

Brewer, D. J. (1996). Career paths and quit decisions: Evidence from teaching. *Journal of Labor Economics, 14*(2), 313–339.

Bryk, A., Camburn, E., & Louis, K. S. (1999). Professional community in Chicago elementary schools: Facilitating factors and organizational consequences. *Educational Administration Quarterly, 35,* 751–781.

Bryk, A. S., & Schneider, B. (2002). *Trust in schools: A core resource for improvement.* New York: Russell Sage Foundation.

Cable, D. M., & Judge, T. A. (1996). Person-organization fit, job choice decisions, and organizational entry. *Organizational Behavior and Human Decision Processes, 67,* 294–311.

Carnegie Forum on Education and the Economy. (1986). *A nation prepared: Teachers for the 21st century.* New York: Carnegie Forum on Education and the Economy.

Cázaras, L., & Harris, A. (2002). *Professionalism through collaboration: A social cost-benefit analysis of the Toledo Plan.* Unpublished manuscript.

Cohen, D. K. (1988). Teaching practice: Plus que ça change . . . In P. W. Jackson (Ed.), *Contributing to educational change* (pp. 27–84). Berkeley, CA: McCutchan.

Darling-Hammond, L. (1999). *Solving the dilemmas of teacher supply, demand, and standards: How we can ensure a competent, caring, and qualified teacher for every child.* Washington, D.C.: National Commission on Teaching and America's Future.

Darling-Hammond, L. (2001). The challenge of staffing our schools. *Educational Leadership, 58*(8), pp. 12–17.

Darling-Hammond, L., Wise, A. E., & Klein, S., P. (1999). *A license to teach.* San Francisco: Jossey-Bass.

Datnow, A., & Castellano, M. (2000). Teachers' responses to Success for All: How beliefs, experiences, and adaptations shape implementation. *American Educational Research Journal, 37*(3), 775–799.

Delpit, L. (1988). The silenced dialogue: Power and pedagogy in educating other people's children. *Harvard Educational Review, 58*(3), 280–298.

Dilworth, M. E., & Brown, C. E. (2001). Consider the difference: Teaching and learning in culturally rich schools. In V. Richardson (Ed.), *The handbook of research on teaching* (4th ed.). Washington, D.C.: American Education Research Association.

Editors. (2000, January 29). The future of work: Career evolution. *The Economist,* 89–90.

Elmore, R. F., Peterson, P. L., & McCarthey, S. J. (1996). *Restructuring in the classroom: Teaching, learning, and school organization.* San Francisco: Jossey-Bass.

Evans, R. (1996). *The human side of school change: Reform, resistance, and the real-life problems of innovation.* San Francisco: Jossey-Bass.

Feiman-Nemser, S. (1983). Learning to teach. In L. S. Shulman & G. Sykes (Eds.), *Handbook of teaching and policy* (pp. 150–170). New York: Longman.

Feiman-Nemser, S., & Floden, R. E. (1986). The cultures of teaching. In M. C. Witrock (Ed.), *Handbook of research on teaching* (3rd ed., pp. 505–526). New York: Macmillan.

Feistritzer, C. E., & Chester, D. T. (2003). *Executive summary: Alternative teacher certification: A state-by-state analysis 2003.* Washington, D.C.: National Center for Education Information. Available: http://www.ncei.com/2003/executive_summary.htm [2003, October 17].

Ferdinand, P. (1998, July 9). Massachusetts weighs giving signing bonuses to teachers. *Washington Post,* pp. A08.

Ferris, J., & Winkler, D. (1986). Teacher compensation and the supply of teachers. *The Elementary School Journal, 86*(4), 389–403.

Fideler, E. F., Foster, E., & Schwartz, S. (2000). *The urban teacher challenge: Teacher demand and supply in the great city schools.* Belmont, MA: Recruiting New Teachers, Inc.; Council of the Great City Schools; Council of the Great City Colleges of Education.

Finn, C. E. (2003, April 17). *Recommended Reading: USDOE suggests that states create test-based routes to full teacher certification; The gadfly: A weekly bulletin of news and analysis,* Volume 3, Number 13, [WWW]. Thomas B. Fordham Foundation. Available: http://www.edexcellence.net/gadfly/v03/gadfly13.html [2003, April 17].

Fowler, R. C. (2001). *An analysis of the recruitment, preparation, attrition, and placement of the Massachusetts Signing Bonus teachers.* Unpublished manuscript.

Fowler, R. C. (2003, April 22). *The Massachusetts Signing Bonus Program for New Teachers: A model of teacher preparation worth copying?* Education Policy Analysis Archives, 11(13). Available: http://epaa.asu.edu/epaa/v11n13/ [2003, July 15].

Fullan, M. G. (1991). *The new meaning of educational change.* New York: Teachers College Press.

Gold, Y. (1996). Beginning teacher support: Attrition, mentoring, and induction. In J. Sikula, T. J. Buttery & E. Guyton (Eds.), *Handbook of research on teacher education* (2nd ed., pp. 548–594). New York: Simon & Schuster Macmillan.

Goldhaber, D. D. (2002). The mystery of good teaching. *Education Next: A Journal of Opinion and Research. Spring*(1), 50–55.

Grant, G., & Murray, C. (1999). *Teaching in America: The slow revolution*. Cambridge, MA: Harvard University Press.

Hanushek, E. A., Kain, J. F., & Rivkin, S. G. (2001). *Why public schools lose teachers* (Working Paper 8599). Cambridge, MA: National Bureau of Economic Research.

Hargreaves, A. (2003). *Teaching in the knowledge society: Education in the age of insecurity*. New York: Teachers College Press.

Hargreaves, A., Earl, L., Moore, S., & Manning, S. (2001). *Learning to change: Teaching beyond subjects and standards*. San Francisco: Jossey-Bass.

Haycock, K. (1998). Good teaching matters: How well-qualified teachers can close the gap. *Thinking K-16, 3*(2), 3–14.

Haycock, K. (2000). No more settling for less. *Thinking K–16, 4*(1), 3–12.

Henke, R., Choy, S. P., Geis, S., & Broughman, S. P. (1996). *Schools and staffing in the United States: A statistical profile, 1993–94*. Washington, D.C.: National Center for Educational Statistics, U.S. Department of Education.

Henke, R. R., Chen, X., & Geis, S. (2000). *Progress through the teacher pipeline: 1992–93 college graduates and elementary/secondary school teaching as of 1997*. Washington, D.C.: National Center for Educational Statistics, U.S. Department of Education.

Holmes Group. (1986). *Tomorrow's teachers*. East Lansing, MI: The Holmes Group.

Holmes Group. (1990). *Tomorrow's schools: Principles for the design of professional development schools*. East Lansing, MI: The Holmes Group.

Huberman, M. (1989). On teachers' careers: Once over lightly, with a broad brush. *International Journal of Educational Research, 13*(4), 347–361.

Huberman, M. (1993). *The lives of teachers*. New York: Teachers College Press.

Hussar, W. J. (1999). *Predicting the need for newly hired teachers in the United States to 2008–09*. Washington, D.C.: National Center for Education Statistics, U.S. Department of Education.

Ingersoll, R. (2002). The teacher shortage: A case of wrong diagnosis and wrong prescription. *NASSP Bulletin, 86*, 16–31.

Ingersoll, R., & Smith, T. (2003). The wrong solution to the teacher shortage. *Educational Leadership, 60*(8), 30–33.

Ingersoll, R. M. (2001). *A different approach to solving the teacher shortage problem* (Teaching Quality Policy Brief Number 3). Seattle, WA: Center for the Study of Teaching and Policy, University of Washington.

Irvine, J. J. (1990). *Black Students and School Failure*. Westport, Connecticut: Greenwood Press.

Johnson, S. M. (1990). *Teachers at work: Achieving success in our schools*. New York: Basic Books.

Johnson, S. M., & Landman, J. (2000). "Sometimes bureaucracy has its charms": The working conditions of teachers in deregulated schools. *Teachers College Record, 102*(1), 85–124.

Johnson, S. M., Nelson, N.C.W., & Potter, J. (1985). *Teacher unions, school staffing, and reform*. Cambridge: Harvard University Graduate School of Education.

Johnston, R. C. (2002, November 6). Voters widely support educational measures. *Education Week*. Available: http://www.edweek.com/ew/ewstory.cfm?slug=10ballot_web.h22 [2003, October 17].

Kanstoroom, M., & Finn, C. E., Jr. (2000). *Better teachers, better schools*. Washington, D.C.: Thomas B. Fordham Publications.

Kantrowitz, B., & Wingert, P. (2000, October 2). Teachers wanted. *Newsweek*, 37–42.

Kardos, S. M. (2001). *New teachers in New Jersey schools and the professional cultures they experience: A pilot study*. Unpublished Special Qualifying Paper, Harvard University Graduate School of Education, Cambridge.

Kardos, S. M. (2003). *Integrated professional culture: Exploring new teachers' experiences in four states*. Paper presented at the American Educational Research Association, Chicago, IL.

Kardos, S. M., Johnson, S. M., Peske, H. G., Kauffman, D., & Liu, E. (2001). Counting on colleagues: New teachers encounter the professional cultures of their schools. *Educational Administration Quarterly, 37*(2), 250–290.

Kauffman, D. (2002). *A search for support: Beginning elementary teachers' use of mathematics curriculum materials*. Unpublished Special Qualifying Paper, Harvard University Graduate School of Education, Cambridge, MA.

Kauffman, D. (2004). *Second-year teachers' experiences with curriculum materials: A three-state survey*. Cambridge, MA: Harvard University Graduate School of Education.

Kauffman, D., Johnson, S. M., Kardos, S. M., Liu, E., & Peske, H. G. (2002). "Lost at sea": New teachers' experiences with curriculum and assessment. *Teachers College Record, 104*(2), 273–300.

Kegan, R. (1983). *The evolving self*. Cambridge: Harvard University Press.

Kegan, R. (1994). *In over our heads: The mental demands of modern life*. Cambridge, MA: Harvard University Press.

Koppich, J. E. (1993). Rochester: The rocky road to reform. In C. T. Kerchner & J. E. Koppich (Eds.), *A union of professionals*. New York: Teachers College Press.

Koppich, J. E., Asher, C., & Kerchner, C. T. (2002). *Developing careers, building a profession: The Rochester Career in Teaching Plan*. New York: National Commission on Teaching and America's Future.

Kristof, A. L. (1996). Person-organization fit: An integrative review of its conceptualizations, measurement, and implications. *Personnel Psychology, 49,* 1–49.

Ladson-Billings, G. (1994). *The dreamkeepers: Successful teachers of African American children.* San Francisco: Jossey-Bass.

Lankford, H., Loeb, S., & Wyckoff, J. (2002). Teacher sorting and the plight of urban schools: A descriptive analysis. *Educational Evaluation and Policy Analysis, 24*(1), 37–62.

Levin, J., & Quinn, M. (2003). *Missed opportunities: How we keep high-quality teachers out of urban classrooms.* New York: New Teacher Project.

Little, J. W. (1982). Norms of collegiality and experimentation: Workplace conditions of school success. *American Educational Research Journal, 19*(3), 325–340.

Little, J. W. (1990a). The mentor phenomenon and the social organization of teaching. In C. Cazden (Ed.), *Review of Research in Education* (Vol. 16, pp. 297–351). Washington, D.C.: American Educational Research Association.

Little, J. W. (1990b). The persistence of privacy: Autonomy and initiative in teachers' professional relations. *Teachers College Record, 91*(4), 509–536.

Liu, E. (2001). *New teachers' experiences of hiring.* Unpublished Special Qualifying Paper, Harvard University Graduate School of Education, Cambridge, MA.

Liu, E. (2003). *New teachers' experiences of hiring: Preliminary findings from a four-state study.* Paper presented at the American Educational Research Association, Chicago, IL.

Lortie, D. C. (1975). *Schoolteacher: A sociological study.* Chicago: University of Chicago Press.

Louis, K. S., & Marks, H. (1998). Does professional community affect the classroom? Teachers' work and student experience in restructured schools. *American Journal of Education, 106*(4), 532–575.

Mapp, K. L. (1999). *Making the connection between families and schools: Why and how parents are involved in their children's education.* Unpublished Doctoral Dissertation, Harvard University, Cambridge, MA.

Massachusetts Department of Education. (1997). *History and social science curriculum framework.* Malden, MA: Massachusetts Department of Education.

Massachusetts State Legislature. (1998). *Chapter 260, Section 4 of the Acts of 1998.* Available: http://www.state.ma.us/legis/laws/seslaw98/s1980260. htm [2003, August 1].

McDonald, F. J. (1980). *The problems of beginning teachers: A crisis in training.* Vol. I. *Study of induction programs for beginning teachers.* Princeton, NJ: Educational Testing Service.

McDonald, F. J., & Elias, P. (1983). *The transition into teaching: The problems of beginning teachers and programs to solve them. Summary report.* Princeton, NJ: Educational Testing Services.

McLaughlin, M. W. (1993). What matters most in teachers' workplace context? In J. W. Little & M. W. McLaughlin (Eds.), *Teachers' work: Individuals, colleagues, and contexts*. New York: Teachers College Press.

McLaughlin, M. W., & Yee, S. M.-L. (1988). School as a place to have a career. In A. Lieberman (Ed.), *Building a professional culture in schools* (pp. 23–44). New York: Teachers College Press.

Merrow, J. (1999, October 6). The teacher shortage: Wrong diagnosis, phony cures. *Education Week*, pp. 38, 64.

Murnane, R., & Levy, F. (1996). *Teaching the new basic skills: Principles for educating children to thrive in a changing economy*. New York: Free Press.

Murnane, R., Singer, J. D., Willett, J. B., Kemple, J., & Olsen, R. (1991). *Who will teach?: Policies that matter*. Cambridge, MA: Harvard University Press.

Murphy, J. (Ed.). (2002). *The educational leadership challenge: Redefining leadership for the 21st century*. Chicago, IL: University of Chicago Press.

National Commission on Teaching and America's Future. (1996). *What matters most: Teaching for America's future*. New York: National Commission on Teaching and America's Future.

Nelson, N. F., & Drown, R. (2003). *Survey and analysis of salary trends 2002*. Washington, D.C.: American Federation of Teachers, AFL-CIO.

Newmann, F., & Associates. (1996). *Authentic achievement: Restructuring schools for intellectual quality*. San Francisco: Jossey-Bass.

Olson, L. (2000, January 13). Finding and keeping competent teachers. *Education Week/Quality Counts 2000*, 12–18.

Olson, L. (2003, January 9). The great divide. *Education Week/Quality Counts 2000, 22*, 9–18.

Peske, H. G., Liu, E., Johnson, S. M., Kauffman, D., & Kardos, S. M. (2001). The next generation of teachers: Changing conceptions of a career in teaching. *Phi Delta Kappan, 83*(4), 304–311.

Podgursky, M. (2003). Fringe benefits: There is more to compensation than a teacher's salary. *Education Next: A Journal of Opinion and Research*. Summer, 71–76.

Public Agenda. (2000). *A sense of calling: Who teaches and why*. New York: Public Agenda.

Public Agenda. (2003). *Stand by me: What teachers really think about unions, merit pay, and other professional matters*. New York: Public Agenda.

Quality Education Data. (2002). *QED's school market trends: Teacher buying behavior & attitudes 2001–2002 [Press version]*. Denver, CO: Quality Education Data, Inc.

Reid, R. L. (Ed.). (1982). *Battleground: The autobiography of Margaret A. Haley*. Urbana, IL: University of Illinois Press.

Rochester City School District, & Rochester Teachers Association. (2000). *Career in teaching: Highlights*. Rochester, NY.

Rosenholtz, S. J. (1985). Effective schools: Interpreting the evidence. *American Journal of Education, 93*(3), 352–388.

Rosenholtz, S. J. (1989). *Teachers' workplace: The social organization of schools*. New York: Longman.

Rury, J. L. (1989). Who became teachers?: The social characteristics of teachers in American history. In D. Warren (Ed.), *American teachers: Histories of a profession at work* (pp. 7–48). New York: Macmillan.

Russell, S. J. (1997). The role of curriculum in teacher development. In S. N. Friel & G. W. Bright (Eds.), *Reflecting on our work: NSF teacher enhancement in K-6 mathematics* (pp. 247–254). Lanham, MD: University Press of America, Inc.

Rust, F. O. (1994). The first year of teaching: It's not what they expected. *Teaching & Teacher Education, 10*(2), 205–217.

Rutter, M., Maughan, B., Mortimore, P., & Ouston, J. (1979). *Fifteen thousand hours: Secondary schools and their effects on children*. Cambridge, MA: Harvard University Press.

Rynes, S. L., Bretz, R. D., & Gerhart, B. (1991). The importance of recruitment in job choice: A different way of looking. *Personnel Psychology, 44*, 487–521.

Sanders, W., & Rivers, J. C. (1998). *Cumulative and residual effects of teachers on future students' academic achievement*. Knoxville, TN: University of Tennessee Value Added Research and Assessment Center.

Saphier, J., & Gower, R. R. (1997). *The skillful teacher: Building your teaching skills*. Carlisle, MA: Research for Better Teaching.

Shen, J. (1997). Has the alternative certification policy materialized its promise? A comparison between traditionally and alternatively certified teachers in public schools. *Educational Evaluation and Policy Analysis, 19*(3), 276–283.

Shivers, J. A. (1989). *Hiring shortage-area and nonshortage-area teachers at the secondary school level*. Unpublished Doctoral Dissertation, Harvard University, Cambridge, MA.

Smith, M. M., & O'Day, J. (1991). Systemic school reform. In S. H. Fuhrman & B. Malen (Eds.), *The politics of curriculum and testing: 1990 yearbook of the Politics of Education Association* (pp. 233–267). London: Falmer Press.

Smith, T., & Ingersoll, R. (2003, April). *Reducing teacher turnover: What are the components of effective induction?* Paper presented at the American Educational Research Association, Chicago, IL.

Snyder, T., & Hoffman, C. (2003). *Digest of Educational Statistics 2002* (NCES 2003–060). Washington, D.C.: National Center for Educational Statistics, U.S. Department of Education.

Spencer, D. A. (2001). Teachers' work in historical and social context. In V. Richardson (Ed.), *Handbook of research on teaching* (4th ed., pp. 803–825). Washington, D.C.: American Educational Research Association.

Stecher, B., Bohrnstedt, G., Kirst, M., McRobbie, J., & Williams, T. (2001). Class-size reduction in California: A story of hope, promise, and unintended consequences. *Phi Delta Kappan, 82*(9), 670–674.

Steinberg, L. (1996). *Beyond the classroom: Why school reform has failed and what parents need to do.* New York: Simon and Schuster.

Stutz, T. (2001, March 8). Texas' teacher crisis worsening. *The Dallas Morning News.*

Teitel, L. (2003). *The professional development schools handbook: Starting, sustaining, and assessing partnerships that improve student learning.* Thousand Oaks: Corwin Press.

TERC. (1998). *Investigations in number, data, and space.* Menlo Park, CA: Dale Seymour Publications.

Termin, P. (2003). Low pay, low quality. *Education Next: A Journal of Opinion and Research.* Summer, 8–13.

Toledo Federation of Teachers, & Toledo Public Schools. (2001). *Agreement between the Toledo Board of Education and the Toledo Federation of Teaches.* Toledo, OH: Toledo Federation of Teachers.

Troen, V., & Boles, K. C. (2003). *Who's teaching your children? Why the teacher crisis is worse than you think and what can be done about it.* New Haven, CT: Yale University Press.

Tyack, D. B. (1974). *One best system: A history of American urban education.* Cambridge, MA: Harvard University Press.

Useem, E. (2003, March 1). *The retention and qualifications of new teachers in Philadelphia's high-poverty middle schools: A three-year cohort study.* Paper presented at the Annual Conference of the Eastern Sociological Society, Philadelphia, PA.

Vedder, R. (2003). Comparable worth. *Education Next: A Journal of Opinion and Research.* Summer, 14–19.

Waller, W. (1932). *The sociology of teaching.* New York: Wiley.

Wideen, M., Mayer-Smith, J., & Moon, B. (1998). A critical analysis of the research on learning to teach: Making the case for an ecological perspective on inquiry. *Review of Educational Research, 68*(2), 130–178.

Wilson, C. L. (2000). The salary gap. *Education Week/Quality Counts 2000, 19*(18), 36.

Wirt, J. (2000). *The Condition of Education, 1999; Indicator of the month: Salaries of teachers* (NCES 2000–011). Washington, D.C.: National Center for Educational Statistics, U.S. Department of Education.

Wise, A. E., Darling-Hammond, L., & Berry, B. (1987). *Effective teacher selection: From recruitment to selection.* Santa Monica: The RAND Corporation.

Yee, S. M. (1990). Careers in the classroom: When teaching is more than a job. New York: Teachers College Press.

Young, B. (2003). *Public school student, staff, and graduate counts by state, school year 2001–02* (NCES 2003–358). Washington D.C.: National Center for Educational Statistics, U.S. Department of Education.

Zernike, K. (1998, July 9). Senate chief sees an elite teacher force; Says only top hopefuls would be eligible for $20,000 signing bonus. *Boston Globe,* pp. A1.

Index